An Author A Month

(for Dimes)

An Author A Month

(for Dimes)

Sharron L. McElmeel
Illustrated by Deborah L. McElmeel

1993
TEACHER IDEAS PRESS
A Division of
Libraries Unlimited, Inc.
Englewood, Colorado

TEACHER IDEAS PRESS
A Division of Libraries Unlimited, Inc.
P.O. Box 6633
Englewood, CO 80155-6633
1-800-237-6124

Library of Congress Cataloging-in-Publication Data

McElmeel, Sharron L.
    An author a month (for dimes) / Sharron L. McElmeel ; illustrated by
Deborah L. McElmeel.
    xiv, 185 p. 22x28 cm.
    Includes bibliographical references and index.
    ISBN 0-87287-952-6
    1. Libraries, Children's--Activity programs. 2. Literature--Study
and teaching (Elementary) 3. School libraries--Activity programs.
4. Children--Books and reading. I. Title.
Z718.1.M368   1992
027.62'5--dc20   92-21381
                                                 CIP

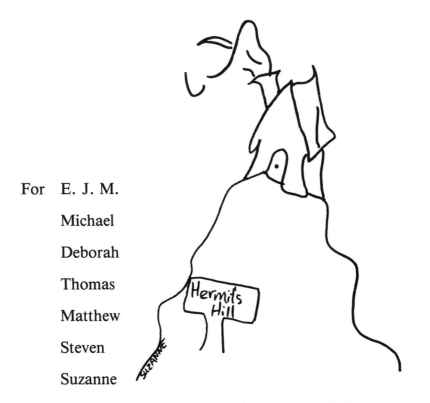

For   E. J. M.

Michael

Deborah

Thomas

Matthew

Steven

Suzanne

— seven who are the sun, the moon, and the stars.

Contents

Acknowledgments

This book, like the eight that preceded it, could not have been written without the support, encouragement, and cooperation of the many people in my life. I am deeply indebted to my family for their patience and help, and for the energy they infuse into our household. But most of all I thank Jack, who does more than his share of everything. He provides structure and the resource that contributes most to my writing—time. I am grateful to my friends and colleagues in the Cedar Rapids Community Schools (Iowa) and elsewhere who graciously encourage and support my efforts. My constant association with these colleagues has continued to inspire me and to spark more ideas for sharing books and their creators with those who will use the information to motivate children to read.

Many professionals in the book-publishing industry provided assistance by putting me in contact with authors and illustrators and by providing the general information on which to build the author/illustrator units. The details came from additional research, correspondence, and interviews.

The help of several publishers and the people in their publicity departments has been invaluable. To those people I extend a special thank you: Martha Dunn, Simon & Schuster Children's Books; Louise Bates, Putnam & Grossett Group; Sarah Shealy, Harcourt Brace Jovanovich; Kate H. Briggs, Holiday House; Peg McColl, Penguin Books Australia; Mary Jo Rhodes and Kathy Ward, Dial Books for Young Readers; Emily Widmann, Scholastic; Julia MacRae, Julia MacRae Books/Random Century Children's Books; Heather Zousmer, Random House; M. Adams, Harry N. Abrams; and Alison Wood, Clarion Books. I appreciate very much the encouragement and cooperation these people gave me and the very gracious assistance of many of the authors/illustrators featured in this book—assistance that helped bring the book from idea to reality.

With special gratitude for their patient and professional help I wish to acknowledge the efforts of the personnel in the reference department and the children's department of the Cedar Rapids (Iowa) Public Library. And thanks once more to an avid bibliophile, Nancy Jennings of the Bookhouse at O. G. Waffle's in Marion, Iowa, who shares wonderful new books with me. Thank you all.

Introduction

It has now been almost thirty-five years since Mauree Applegate wrote *Easy in English: An Imaginative Approach to the Teaching of Language Arts*. In her book Applegate said, "A language arts program today must, of necessity, be based upon the four skills of communication: speaking, listening, reading, and writing. If the language arts program stopped there, curriculum planning would be comparatively easy. But it doesn't. What about thinking—a skill that must precede and accompany speaking, listening, reading, and writing? ... School is no longer merely a place where a child learns to read but where attitudes toward reading are as important as the reading itself."[1]

Applegate's statements from the early 1960s are as true today as they were then, and as they were in 1988 when the first *An Author a Month* book was published. In the late 1980s the term *whole language* began to emerge as the "new" term for a methodology many educators embraced. Now, in the early 1990s, additional terms are being used—in a effort, I believe, to clarify or refine the whole language concept: integrated curriculum, whole group teaching, thematic units, and a host of other terms. Those of us who have been in the field of education for a number of years will recognize these terms as having been around for a long time. Some who wish to feel that they have always been on the cutting edge will be quick to say: "I've always taught thematically" or "I always have taught using whole group teaching." But that is not the premise upon which the whole language movement has been built. The "old" thematic units are not the same as today's. In early times teachers, and sometimes curriculum directors or committees of teachers, developed full-blown thematic units on a particular topic. Those units were *taught* to children from start to finish, regardless of the needs or interests of the children and regardless of all the other options that existed for reaching established goals. The units had a set beginning, middle, and end. Those types of thematic units are now recognized as one more way to "can" the curriculum. They have little or nothing to do with the *whole language* philosophy.

The thematic units used within the whole language approach provide strategies similar to previous units, but they grow out of the children's interest, prior knowledge, questions, and needs. Units, with their thematic focus, provide many options to pique the interest of children. But the crucial point is that the units actually develop as the children's interests develop. For example, educators who teach classification based on two attributes might begin with a study of rocks. However, when students read a book about koalas and begin to be interested in other animals from the same region, the teacher might shift the classification unit to one dealing with types of animals: those with pouches, those without, those that lay eggs, those that bear their young alive, those that live in the United States, and those that do not. Not only will literature sources be invaluable but so will teacher resource books. In addition to the standard books in the school or public library dealing with animals, resources such as this book strive to help integrate the original goal with basic language arts activities.

---

[1]Mauree Applegate, *Easy in English: An Imaginative Approach to the Teaching of the Language Arts* (New York: Harper & Row, 1960), pp. 6, 15.

For example, the material about Caroline Arnold presented in this book could be incorporated into the study of animals; suggestions for reading nonfiction and fiction titles about animals are provided. Those who read fiction books are encouraged to identify facts about the animal that the author used in the fictionalized story. The importance of research in writing is emphasized. Responses incorporating the expressive arts are also suggested. Teachers need to be creative and resourceful and be able to draw upon a number of resources to develop with their students the path they take together to reach a specified goal. Along the way teachers must be aware of other general goals that could be accomplished by integrating literature/content area objectives with the target goal.

The selection of the author/illustrator to be featured during a time period can be motivated by the content of a specific unit the class is studying; or the author/illustrator may be selected simply because of the group's interest in that person's work. Sometimes teachers must arouse students' interest through introductory activities. As far as possible students should be allowed to select the author/illustrator to be featured. For example, one focus unit on Patricia Polacco was motivated by reading *The Keeping Quilt*. During the course of that reading, information was shared about Polacco's own life and how it tied into the story told in the book. On a world map the class located Russia, Michigan, and Oakland, California. The students suggested the story was like those written by Cynthia Rylant, who also told stories about growing up. Because of their prior experience with and excitement about the Rylant titles, the children asked to know more about Polacco. They created an author bulletin board and set out to focus on books by Polacco. The focus on Polacco's stories quickly evolved into a emphasis on personal family stories. Children interviewed their parents and grandparents and recorded in writing some of the family stories they heard. They learned about other events that were going on during the time their own stories had taken place. Knowing who was president of the United States, whether electricity had been invented, and whether indoor plumbing existed at the time helped put the stories in perspective. Some students who were familiar with the Laura Ingalls Wilder stories compared the time setting of their stories to that of Laura's growing-up years. They were finding the connections to other literature and to other curriculum areas. The role of the teacher was to learn with the students and to project and plan ahead. Ways to integrate activities had to be found. Sometimes the integration was within one of the language arts, sometimes between the language arts, and sometimes across the curriculum. But in all cases the goals were kept firmly in mind.

A focus on an author is just one way of structuring literature experiences and just one more way of providing a literature experience within the context of curriculum goals. The focus on any author/illustrator is not limited to that author's books. The goal of a focus is to promote literature and to provide opportunities for integration and activities within the whole language concept.

A focus on a book creator is an exciting way to achieve some of your curriculum objectives. The road taken to the culmination of the focus is sure to be an interesting one if students are allowed to lead the way with their imaginations. Once an author focus has been decided upon, set up an author's corner. Photocopy the author poster pages (picture page and large print information page) in this book. Please note that this suggestion does not constitute permission to reproduce these materials for further distribution; only the original purchaser is entitled to make a copy. Mount the photocopies to the inside of a file folder. Add some color in the form of an edging or small, colored illustrations gleaned from a periodical or publisher's catalog. Laminate the folder. Later, after the folder is used for the author center, you will be able to store it in a standard file cabinet and add companion material as it becomes available. When you want to use the file folder, open it up and place it on a bulletin board; or if bulletin board space is at a premium, the folder can stand in a chalk tray or on a small author's table. If you anticipate using it as a standing display, it might be a good idea to decorate the outside of the folder with drawings of the book characters or with the book jacket from one of the author's books. Other material for the author's board or corner can be created by enlarging book characters onto manila/white oak tag, using an opaque projector or an overhead projector. Add color and laminate. Once the author board is in place, gather your resources (or make arrangements to have them available in the school's library) and start sharing, reading, and enjoying.

When this volume of *An Author a Month* was being planned, several people requested that I include Martha Alexander. Byrd Baylor, whose writing reflects a reverence for nature and animals, also emerged as a favorite. Readers wanted to know about the writer and the person. Other colleagues identified some emerging artists and authors who were capturing their students' interest. As the children with whom my colleagues and I worked became more interested in books and reading, they discovered the joys of "new" authors and illustrators. Together we discovered Caroline Arnold's photo-filled information titles about animals. We became intrigued with the visual feasts in the books illustrated by Australian Graeme Base. Favorite folktales illuminated with Jan Brett's inspired illustrations brought a fresh perspective to those old tales. On the hundredth day of school, we read Keiko Kasza's *The Wolf's Chicken Stew*, and we all wanted to read more of her books and to know more about her. We read *Uncle Vova's Tree* and *Just Plain Fancy* and then realized that Patricia Polacco had written both of them. We chuckled over the art created by Janet Stevens for *The Three Billy Goats Gruff*. We wanted to know about the leather jacket on the Big Billy Goat Gruff.

And so those authors/illustrators joined book creators Eric A. Kimmel, Anthony Browne, Joanna Cole, and Demi to become part of *An Author a Month (for Dimes)*. I wanted to bring information about some of these "new" favorites to those who are interested in developing a literature-rich environment in their classroom/library.

Consider focusing on Martha Alexander when the class is discussing pets, sibling rivalry, or imaginary friends. Caroline Arnold's books will be enjoyable reading during a study of fossils and dinosaurs, or when animals of all types are part of the interest/curriculum topic. Graeme Base's books can provide many hours of intriguing thinking activities. Students can identify the animals in his books and locate their homelands. Base's native Australia can also be a topic of discussion. Eric A. Kimmel's stories of Hanukkah can bring about a cultural awareness that some children may not have. A close look at the illustrations of Jan Brett's *The Owl and the Pussycat* can lead to an interest in the Caribbean islands and the cultures of that area. Settings depicted by Brett and other illustrators can motivate interest in other regions and cultures. Ideas for integration possibilities can be gleaned by reading the biographical sections included for each author/illustrator. When Demi's interest in Chinese culture is highlighted, possibilities arise for focusing on China's heritage and culture. Joanna Cole's many books dealing with science-oriented topics lead naturally into science studies. And any study of nature and animals could incorporate many of Byrd Baylor's writings. In many cases these options will be missed if teachers are not aware of the possibilities and do not bring them to their students' attention.

The information in this book should help teachers know the options and possibilities and to move forward with sharing books. The response and activity suggestions are intended to provide basic ideas for activities or responses, but actual implementation must be adapted to both the children's abilities and background and the targeted goal. For example, when a suggestion is made that a particular title be read, the teacher can either read the book aloud to the group or ask students to read the book for themselves. If a writing activity is suggested, the teacher might use the overhead projector to model the actual writing process while taking dictation from a group of students. The act of making a draft copy, revising and editing it, and producing a finished piece of writing would be demonstrated for the group. Also, the writing activity could be suggested to specific individuals who might enjoy responding in such a manner and who have been involved in preliminary activities that would allow them to succeed in a writing activity. Expressive activities might involve small groups or the entire class. The amount of teacher direction and involvement in the process will be determined by the students' level of ability and their prior experience with similar activities. The actual implementation of any of the suggestions given in the Idea Cupboard sections must be refined and adapted to meet individual and group needs.

Using literature in the classroom and motivating responses to literature have two basic goals: to make literature more enjoyable and to encourage more reading. Response activities must always be purposeful in the eyes of the reader. The activities must provide a pleasurable experience with reading, and although reading itself must always take priority over other response activities, well-motivated activities that help integrate content area material with literature can accomplish objectives in many curriculum areas. Activities encourage interaction between children, provide a breathing space between books, and allow readers to reflect upon a book and its meaning. Activities can help children ask relevant questions and can give confidence to reluctant students to participate in the classroom. Care must be taken that students are given a choice among activities. Sometimes a specific objective will require a specific activity, but most often there are several objectives, and these can be met by a variety of activities.

At a meeting during the 1991 International Reading Association's convention in Las Vegas, Joanna Cole said, "After reading a book, have the Great Discussion, NOT the Great Inquisition." It is good advice, I think. The activities in this book are intended to allow readers to enjoy books and to respond in the manner that is most meaningful to them. Never underestimate the power of choice. Using literature and information about authors and illustrators is just one way to help children make connections with literature and with other curriculum areas. The focus on an author or an illustrator encourages a respect for the body of work of that writer or illustrator. The connections between individual books become apparent as they are read in conjunction with one another. The ability to recognize universal themes and topics is strengthened. Response activities help readers make connections and bring reading into their everyday lives—a connection with reading that will help develop lifelong readers.

Read, share, and enjoy!

Martha Alexander

Nobody Asked *Me*
If I Wanted a Baby Sister

STORY AND PICTURES BY
Martha Alexander

From *An Author a Month (for Dimes)* by Sharron L. McElmeel (Libraries Unlimited, 1992)

Martha Alexander

Martha Alexander has been an artist most of her life, but she was forty-five before she began to illustrate books. She was born in Augusta, Georgia, on May 25, 1920, but later moved to Cincinnati, Ohio, where she grew up and attended art school. In 1943 she married a soldier and later they moved to Honolulu, Hawaii, with their daughter, Kim. Their son, Allen, was born in Hawaii three years later. While the children were growing up, Martha Alexander created mosaics, murals, and collages for offices and waiting rooms for children in doctors' offices. In 1959 she and her two teenage children moved to New York City, where she began to use her art to create illustrations for magazines. In 1965 she illustrated six books that had been written by other authors but then began creating her own books.

Out! Out! Out! was the first book in which Martha Alexander illustrated her own story idea. When one of her grandchildren tried to give away her baby sister, she wrote a story about it, *Nobody Asked Me If I Wanted a Baby Sister*. While Martha Alexander's grandchildren (Lisa, Christina, Leslie, Mia, and Scott) were growing up, they provided ideas for many stories. After living in New York City for almost twenty years, Martha Alexander moved to Oregon, where she met the moose featured in *Even That Moose Won't Listen to Me*. She now lives in Olympia, Washington.

1

Martha Alexander

ABOUT THE AUTHOR/ILLUSTRATOR

Martha Alexander was born in Augusta, Georgia, on May 25, 1920. She spent her first nine years in Georgia, where she remembers visiting a ninety-three-year-old former slave who told her stories of Martha's grandfather as a boy. She also remembers seeing chain gangs working on the roads. In 1929 she moved to Cincinnati, Ohio, with her parents and four sisters. A teacher in her new school encouraged her drawing. Later, in high school, a history teacher encouraged her further when he let her draw historical pictures for extra credit. After high school she studied for four years at the Cincinnati Academy of Arts earning scholarships each year. During those years she became acquainted with the whimsy and magic of Paul Klee's drawings, Leonardo da Vinci's portrait of Mona Lisa, and painter Marc Chagall's work. These artists helped her to understand that she needed to use her art to evoke strong responses from those who view it. She discovered how complete stories can be told through pictures. Even then she thought about creating children's books.

In 1943 she married a serious painter who seemed to feel that the only real art was "fine art." Soon after their marriage, her husband, then a member of the U.S. military, was sent overseas. When he returned after World War II, the two of them, along with daughter Kim, settled in Honolulu, Hawaii. Three years later their son, Allen, was born. During the next sixteen years Martha Alexander spent her time giving silk screening lessons and creating murals and paintings for children. Many of her murals were commissioned for pediatricians' offices and children's waiting rooms.

After she and her husband divorced in 1959, Alexander decided to act on her previous desire to try illustrating. She sent some photographs and samples of her work to a friend in New York, who persuaded her to come to New York and to work in the illustrating field. She struggled for the first five years in New York to support her children as she illustrated stories in teen and women's magazines. In 1965 she decided to submit some samples of her work to a children's book publisher. The editor at Harper & Row liked her work and offered her a book to illustrate—then five more. By 1968 she had authored and published her first book, *Out! Out! Out!* It was a wordless book that tells of a small boy's success in luring an uninvited pigeon out of the house. Her first book with words, *Maybe a Monster*, was published that same year.

Alexander creates her books in dummy form. She folds about thirty pages into the form of a book and then sketches on those pages pictures and words as they come to her. Ofter her books will contain many pages without words. The story is told through her pictures. Books like *Blackboard Bear* sometimes contain as many as fifteen pages with no text.

Many of Alexander's stories come to her in such a way that she does not really know how they get on paper. Ideas for books come from everywhere, but most often they involve a child around

her. *Blackboard Bear* came from meeting one of her young relatives. The four-year-old had an extremely vivid imagination and told of being rescued by his brave father; he later handed his aunt twelve baby kangaroos to hold for him. After visiting the child's family for three days, Alexander returned home, folded paper into a dummy form, and the story began to come. That was the beginning of the *Blackboard Bear* books.

Nobody Asked Me If I Wanted a Baby Sister is an example of a book that deals with feelings. Alexander's two-year-old granddaughter suggested that her baby sister, Leslie, go live with Grandma. Alexander used the incident to talk about sibling rivalry. The first part of the story came rather easy, with Oliver attempting to "give away" his baby sister. He gave the baby to various people who gave the baby back for various reasons. One family was going to keep Oliver's baby sister but eventually returned the baby when they, and Oliver, realized that Oliver's baby sister needed him. Only Oliver could manage to stop his sister from crying. Oliver decided to take her home. And he did.

Alexander has written many beginnings, middles, and ends of stories that do not go with any of the other parts. So she has a lot of unpublished work. She has spent most of her illustrating career, since 1960, in New York. In 1988 she moved from Sag Harbor, New York, to Oregon, where she met the moose in *Even That Moose Won't Listen to Me*. She now lives in Olympia, Washington. Her grandchildren (Lisa, Christina, Leslie, Mia, and Scott) are now grown, but Alexander continues to search her own childhood and the childhood of her family and friends for more story ideas.

SETTING THE STAGE

Cover a large bulletin board with background material or paper and then place a large sheet of black construction paper or oak tag on the board left of center. Frame the paper with a narrow brown frame. Add a long yellow strip, across the top, with the alphabet in black. You will have created a mock blackboard. Using another sheet of black paper the same size, draw a figure of the Blackboard Bear with chalk. Make the outline of the bear with wide strokes. Using the outside of the chalk outline as a cutting guide, cut out the bear and superimpose it on the mock blackboard. Use another piece of black paper to back the author poster page and the large-print author information sheet. Title the bulletin board "Meet Martha Alexander and Blackboard Bear." If there is room, add some cutouts of other Alexander book characters. Display as many of Alexander's books as are available to your students. Include some of the collaborative titles suggested in this chapter.

Spoken Arts has a set of four filmstrips with cassettes of the Blackboard Bear books: *Blackboard Bear*; *And My Mean Old Mother Will Be Sorry, Blackboard Bear*; *I Sure Am Glad to See You, Blackboard Bear*; and *We're in Big Trouble, Blackboard Bear*. Put these filmstrips and cassettes in a listening/viewing center. Blackboard Bear's adventures can lead to a discussion of issues: jealousy, responsibility, anger, sharing, parental love, stealing, and kindness.

Alexander uses pencil and delicate tempera paints to create many of her illustrations. Much of all her stories is told in the gestures and actions of the figures she draws. Discuss the medium Alexander uses in her illustrations. In the classroom's illustration and writing corner, place thick soft-lead pencils, drawing paper, and pastel-colored chalk. Before inviting children to use the center independently, give them some instruction and practice in creating pencil drawings and chalk coloring. When illustrations are completed, the chalk can be kept from smearing by "fixing" it with a commercial chalk fixative or by using inexpensive hair spray (the cheaper the better).

In introducing Martha Alexander, share some of the author information about her. Invite children to bring their own special bears or stuffed friends. Each animal should be tagged with the student's name. As the animals arrive at school, incorporate them into the display. During the unit set aside special times when the students can read aloud to their animals. Have them tape the stories to put in a listening center for others to enjoy. Invite children to share and enjoy all of Alexander's stories during a "Read with Martha Alexander" session.

IDEA CUPBOARD

Alexander, Martha. *And My Mean Old Mother Will Be Sorry, Blackboard Bear*. Dial, 1972.

While feeding his teddy bear, Anthony manages to leave sticky honey all over the kitchen floor. And boy is mother mad! She yells and tells Anthony that he had better be in bed. That prompts Anthony to throw his bear out the window and vow to run away. "And my mean old mother will be sorry." Anthony again takes Blackboard Bear from his chalkboard and together they crawl out the window and eat berries and a wiggling fish, sleep in a cave (without a pillow and a blanket), and arise in the morning to face eating berries again for breakfast (no orange juice, cereal, or milk). Anthony decides he should return home and is carried there by Blackboard Bear. Anthony retrieves his teddy bear from under the window and climbs inside the house hugging his teddy bear and saying, "I love you too, Teddy."

1. It seems sometimes as if Anthony doesn't really want his teddy. In Ginnie Hofmann's *Who Wants an Old Teddy Bear, Anyway?* (Random, 1978), Andy doesn't want his teddy bear either. But his adventure is quite different from Anthony's. Compare and contrast the story grammar in Alexander's Blackboard Bear story with Hofmann's title.

2. Extend the friendship of the reader with Anthony and his protector, Blackboard Bear, by reading other stories by Martha Alexander about the two characters:

Blackboard Bear. Dial, 1969.

I Sure Am Glad to See You, Blackboard Bear. Dial, 1976.

We're in Big Trouble, Blackboard Bear. Dial, 1980.

3. Discuss the personalities of Anthony and the Blackboard Bear. Make a list of other situations in which Anthony might need Blackboard Bear. Use the list to help develop another episode featuring the two characters.

Alexander, Martha. *Blackboard Bear*. Dial, 1969.

A little boy asks to play with four bigger boys who are playing cops and robbers. The older boys tell the younger one that he's "too little" and that he should go "play with your teddy bear." Disappointed, the little boy uses a big piece of chalk to draw a big bear, which comes alive and is led off the board and outside to play. Now it is Anthony's turn to tell the other boys that they can't play with his bear. Eventually, Anthony returns the bear to his house where he draws four playmates (which look very similar to the boys who would not let him play) and a jar of honey. The bear promptly eats all but the hats on the board. (Since many schools now use a "chalkboard" and the board is generally green in color, one might have to explain the use of the term *blackboard* and its relationship to today's chalkboard.)

1. Have students discuss what was really happening in the book. Did the bear really come alive?

2. Help build the readers' understanding of imagination versus reality by reading and discussing some of the following books that might extend the theme of drawings and imagination:

    Browne, Anthony. *Bear Hunt*. Atheneum, 1979.

    Demi. *Liang and the Magic Paint Brush*. Holt, 1980.

    Johnson, Crockett. *Harold and the Purple Crayon*. Harper, 1955.

    McPhail, David M. *The Magical Drawings of Moony B. Finch*. Doubleday, 1978.

3. Near the end of *Blackboard Bear*, the little boy is seen at his window being asked by six other boys, "Can you and your bear come fishing?" The boy responds, "I'll ask him when he finishes his lunch." What do you think the bear's answer will be? If it is yes, what will happen when the two of them go fishing with the other boys? If the answer is no, what will be the next thing that the two of them do together?

4. Give each child a piece of black construction paper and a piece of white chalk. Ask each one to draw an animal they would like to have for a friend. Encourage them to write about their animal. Follow with a discussion of reality versus imagination.

Alexander, Martha. *Bobo's Dream*. Dial, 1970.

In this wordless story a young boy rescues his dog's bone from a larger dog. So when the grateful pet naps, he dreams of protecting the boy. In his dream the pet is a large, fierce dog. His dream makes him so confident that when he awakens he actually does frighten away a larger dog.

1. Alexander's illustrations make clear the difference between the dog's dream and the real confrontations. Help readers to differentiate between reality and imagination.

2. Discuss the concept of confidence and the ability to do something once a person gains confidence, in relation to the confidence shown by the dog.

3. Another book that will help readers understand the concept of confidence is Anthony Browne's *Willy the Wimp* (Knopf, 1984). Read that book and compare the stories and main character in terms of the confidence shown by the dog and the confidence shown by Willy.

Alexander, Martha. *Even That Moose Won't Listen to Me*. Dial, 1988; Pied Piper, 1991.

Rebecca's mother and brother do not believe that a great big moose is munching away in the garden. Rebecca's father is too busy to even listen. So Rebecca takes matters into her own hands. Armed with a drum, a dog, and a hairy monster suit, she sets out to convince the moose to go away. The title is a clue to Rebecca's frustration. In the end the moose goes away, and when her family comes outside they cannot figure out "what happened to the garden." In a turn of events, Rebecca is far too busy to tell them until she has finished her rocket ship.

1. Compare Alexander's story with *The Judge* by Harve Zemach, illustrated by Margot Zemach (Farrar, 1969). Both authors use the element of others not believing as a major theme in their story. The pattern of disbelief results in predictable consequences. In *The Judge* the prisoners tell the tale the judge will not believe. The judge feels that the horrible thing about to devour them cannot possibly exist, and orders them to jail. Only when the horrible thing does show up does the judge believe. But by then it is too late for him.

2. Another tale of disbelief is John Burningham's *John Patrick Norman McHennessy: The Boy Who Was Always Late* (Crown, 1987). Every day John Patrick Norman McHennessy "sets off along the road to learn." Every day he arrives at school late and with some other outrageous story to explain his tardiness. The headmaster never believes his story. As with *The Judge*, the consequences for the nonbeliever are not pleasant. Compare Burningham's books to Alexander's in much the same way as you did with Zemach's story.

3. Use any of the three stories (Alexander's, Burningham's, or Zemach's) as the basis for creating additional episodes to fit between the beginning and the end of the story. In each story there is a pattern to the episodes of disbelief. Create new episodes and read them as part of the story, between the author's first few episodes and the author's concluding twist on the story's pattern. For example, after reading the first three problems encountered by the young student in Burningham's *John Patrick Norman McHennessy: The Boy Who Was Always Late*, insert episodes telling of the event that made the boy late to school, repeat the headmaster's standard phrases, and add the punishment imposed on the boy. Continue reading the innovations created and then conclude by reading the end of the story—a conclusion that has the headmaster hanging from the ceiling trying to convince the boy that a hairy gorilla is trying to get him. The innovations on the story pattern could be written by individuals, partners, or the class during a group writing session.

Alexander, Martha. *Four Bears in a Box*. Dial, 1981.

This boxed miniature set includes Alexander's four Blackboard Bear titles: *Blackboard Bear*; *And My Mean Old Mother Will Be Sorry, Blackboard Bear*; *I Sure Am Glad to See You, Blackboard Bear*; and *We're in Big Trouble, Blackboard Bear*.

1. See entries in this section for the individual titles.

2. Give each child or pair of students four other books that have a common idea, character, or theme. Ask students to identify the common element that connects the four titles and to use that element to suggest a name for the boxed set of books if the books were to be packaged. For example, Arnold Lobel's Frog and Toad books might be packaged as "Frogs and Toads in a Box." Books by Else Minarik, Ezra Jack Keats, Mercer Mayer, Margot Zemach, and Marcia Brown will be likely choices to use for this activity focusing on common themes. Older students might find common themes in the books by Scott Corbett or Beverly Cleary or the information titles by Caroline Arnold or Gail Gibbons.

3. To provide student interaction and discussion about the common themes within each group of books, suggest that each group of books be displayed in a box decorated to represent the theme or other common element. Display the boxed sets and encourage others to read the books.

Alexander, Martha. *How My Library Grew by Dinah*. Wilson, 1983.

Dinah and her teddy bear get dressed and go outside so they can watch the bulldozers work to build a new library. While Dinah watches, Father plants a garden. After standing on a box to watch, Dinah goes into the house to get her old high chair—the perfect place to sit and watch the library being built. Each day Dinah goes outside to watch. One day she must put on her sweater. And another day the snow comes and she "can hardly even see the library." Finally, the library is almost built. Father tells her it will be just another month. But Dinah has a problem; she is making a surprise for the library and to finish it she must see how they build the inside. Father takes her to see the foreman. Inside she gets to see the electrician, the wall plasterer, and the carpenters who will build the bookshelves. Finally, the library is ready and so is Dinah's surprise for the library. The surprise is a book called "How My Library Grew." The librarian puts her book on the library's bulletin board and Dinah finds some books she wants to borrow. But she does not have her own library card — she has to learn to write her name. She practices all day and finally shows Bruce, the library clerk, that she can write her own name. And one of the first books she checks out on her own card is a special book about a teddy bear.

1. Help readers develop their schematic background about libraries and their use by reading other fiction and information books on the topic.

   Baker, Donna. *I Want to Be a Librarian*. Illustrated by Richard Wahl. Children's, 1978.

   Bartlett, Susan. *A Book to Begin on Libraries*. Illustrated by Gioia Fiammenghi. Holt, 1964.

   Daly, Maureen. *Patrick Visits the Library*. Illustrated by Paul Lantz. Dodd, 1961.

   Gibbons, Gail. *Check It Out! The Book about Libraries*. Harcourt, 1985.

   Little, Mary E. *ABC for the Library*. Illustrated by Mary E. Little. Atheneum, 1975.

   Rockwell, Anne F. *I Like the Library*. Illustrated by Anne Rockwell. Dutton, 1977.

   After reading the available titles from the list above, have students discuss what they learned about libraries. Make a list, "Things I Know about the Library."

2. Dinah wrote and illustrated a book about something that was happening around her. She watched (and researched) all year. Discuss the steps necessary for research: identify a problem or question, suggest ways the problem can be solved or the question answered, conduct experiments or observations, record findings, and report conclusions. Read Tom Parker's *In One Day: The Things Americans Do in a Day* (Houghton, 1984) and suggest that students research and create "In One Day: The Things Students at _____ School Do in a Day."

   a. Make a list of possible activities that could be researched and formulate questions about those activities. For example, one activity that goes on in every school is the sharpening of pencils. Formulate a question about that activity: How many trips to the pencil sharpener are made each day? How many ounces or cups of pencil shavings are created each day?

   b. After the specific question is decided upon, discuss how the question could be answered. If the question being asked is how many trips to the pencil sharpener are made each day, it might be decided that someone should observe, tally, and total those trips in one classroom on one day. If the statistic sought is for that one classroom the tabulation would be complete. If, however, the research should determine the number of trips taken throughout the school, the statistics for the one classroom would be multiplied by the number of classrooms in the school to yield an approximate total number of trips. Or, observers could be stationed in each classroom throughout the day to gather the statistics.

c. Have students report orally or compile in a book (following the format of Parker's book) questions they developed for the research and the statistical results they obtained. If the book is to be published, the class will have to plan its production: the writing or typing of the actual pages, the procedure for making copies (unless one class copy is sufficient), and the method for binding the pages together.

Alexander, Martha. *I'll Be the Horse If You'll Play with Me*. Dial, 1975.

Oliver, the older brother who tried to give away his baby sister, Bonnie, in *Nobody Asked Me If I Wanted a Baby Sister*, now takes advantage of his sister, no longer a baby, by playing with her only when there is an advantage for him. He "agrees" to let her play with him if she will be the horse and pull him in the little red wagon, or if he can use her new crayons. And he plays "fifty-two pickup" — a game where he throws a deck of cards in the air and she has to pick them up. Toward the end of the story Bonnie observes Billy, their baby brother, pulling the little red wagon. The final scene is of Billy being the horse and pulling Bonnie in the wagon.

1. To help students think about the manner in which they relate to their own siblings or peers, discuss suggestions that students might give Oliver about how he should treat his little sister, Bonnie.

2. Some students may not have experience with decks of cards and thus not understand the reason why the game is called "fifty-two pickup." Observe that a regular deck of cards has fifty-two cards in it and discuss the term *fifty-two pickup*. To further build the children's background and information regarding cards, count the cards and categorize the sets that can be found in the deck; for example, there are four sets of thirteen cards each (spades, hearts, clubs, and diamonds), thirteen sets of four with the same value, etc. This schematic building activity could also be incorporated into mathematical lessons focusing on categorization, and on sorting by various attributes.

Alexander, Martha. *I'll Protect You from the Jungle Beasts*. Dial, 1973.

A little boy bravely protects his teddy bear from the strange noises he hears in his dreams. He protects the bear, that is, until the noises get too loud. Then the boy decides that a bear must have something special that only bears have. He decides that bears have a special kind of stuffing. That special stuffing helps the bear become strong enough to protect the little boy and to take him home.

1. Discuss the point where the little boy's imagination really takes over. What part of the book could have been real? What part of the book has to be imaginative? How can the reader tell the real parts from the imaginative parts? What did the author or illustrator do to help the reader know?

2. After enjoying Alexander's book, use that enjoyment to motivate students to read stories about other bears and their travels. Dorothy Butler's *My Brown Bear Barney*, illustrated by Elizabeth Fuller (Greenwillow, 1989), and Michael Rosen's *We're Going on a Bear Hunt*, illustrated by Helen Oxenbury (McElderry, 1989), are naturals for participatory reading sessions. A participatory reading session involves the teacher reading the book aloud while inviting the listeners to chime in during the repeated refrains. After the books have been shared in read-aloud or participatory reading sessions, children will enjoy reading the books independently or in partner reading sessions.

Alexander, Martha. *I Sure Am Glad to See You, Blackboard Bear*. Dial, 1976.

Blackboard Bear and his little boy playmate, Anthony, go on another adventure. This time Anthony is really happy to have the magical bear as his friend. This is a companion title to *Blackboard Bear*; *And My Mean Old Mother Will Be Sorry, Blackboard Bear*; and *We're in Big Trouble, Blackboard Bear*.

1. Anthony and his bear are similar in some respects to Harold and his purple crayon. Read books about Harold by Crockett Johnson: *Harold and the Purple Crayon* (Harper, 1955); *Harold at the North Pole* (Harper, 1955); *Harold's ABC: Another Purple Crayon Adventure* (Harper, 1963); *Harold's Circus* (Harper, 1959); *Harold's Fairy Tales: Further Adventures with the Purple Crayon* (Harper, 1956); and *A Picture for Harold's Room* (Harper, 1960). Discuss how Anthony and Harold are alike and how they are different.

2. Read this book and correlate it with the activities suggested for the other books about Anthony and his friend Blackboard Bear.

Alexander, Martha. *Maybe a Monster*. Dial, 1968.

A young boy builds a trap, a brush-covered hole. He thinks he might catch a monster, so he goes home to build a cage—a cage for a monster with wings and two heads, a monster who shoots fire out of its nose. When the cage, a monster-sized structure, is finished, the boy decides that he must be protected in case the monster is mean. He goes home to get his football helmet, a rope, etc., and then returns to the trap. The brush has fallen in so he figures he must have trapped something. He has. The next page reveals a trapped rabbit. Undaunted the boy takes the rabbit home and puts him in the "rabbit cage" he had built.

1. Introduce *Maybe a Monster* by setting the stage for a hunt. Going on a hunt is the theme of an old camp-and-story-hour activity commonly referred to as "going on a bear hunt." This game is portrayed nicely in Michael Rosen's picture book *We're Going on a Bear Hunt*, illustrated by Helen Oxenbury (McElderry, 1989). A British version of the bear hunt game is presented in Maurice Jones's *I'm Going on a Dragon Hunt*, illustrated by Charlotte Firmin (Four Winds, 1987).

   a. Encourage children to participate as these books are read aloud. Reading them several times will help children become comfortable enough to participate in the verses.

   b. Discuss what might be needed if one really did go on a hunt—for example, a cage in which to put the captured animal, a leash to restrain the animal, or whatever children can justify.

   c. Rosen's book portrays a family going on a bear hunt. Oxenbury's illustrations in this book help to create a situation where listeners will want to actively participate in the bear hunt. Read the story and encourage listeners to act out the story's actions as it is being read aloud.

2. In *Maybe a Monster* a boy builds a monster-sized cage where he will put the monster that he captures in his trap. If this story is a new one for children, read *Maybe a Monster* to the page where the boy returns to the trap to find out what he has caught. Ask listeners to draw a picture of what each of them thinks the boy might have caught in his trap. Ask each individual, pair, or group to write a description of the animal (or thing) caught in the trap. After the illustrations and descriptions have been created, reread the story, this time to its conclusion.

3. On a bulletin board titled "Maybe a Monster," display the drawings and descriptions created in activity 2.

4. Extend the hunt idea even further by introducing one of the following:

   deRegniers, Beatrice Schenk. *Catch a Little Fox: Variations on a Folk Rhyme*. Illustrated by Brinton Turkle. Seabury, 1970.

Langstaff, John. *Oh, A-Hunting We Will Go.* Illustrated by Nancy Winslow Parker. Atheneum, 1974.

In deRegniers's book children catch a fox and put him in a box, a frog and put him in a log, and a dragon and put him in a wagon. The Langstaff book is more humorous as they "catch a bear/and put him in underwear." Either of these books could be used as a model to create new verses about the hunting trip. Begin each verse as Langstaff or deRegniers does, and then insert students' innovations in the blanks (see examples). The first set of sentences gives the shell for the verse as used in deRegniers's book. The second set provides the shell from the Langstaff book. If several children create innovative verses, those verses might be combined to create an original student version of "A-Hunting We Will Go." Create a cover and a title page, number the pages, and bind all the pages together to create a class book.

Oh a-hunting we will go.
A-hunting we will go.
We'll catch a little_____,
And put him in a _____
And never let him go.

Oh a-hunting we will go.
A-hunting we will go.
We'll catch a _____,
And put him in_____,
And then we'll let him go.

Alexander, Martha. *No Ducks in Our Bathtub.* Dial, 1973.

According to David, his mother is a "mean old crab." She has decreed that their apartment have no bugs, no pigeons, and no ducks. What should a boy do? David thinks he has found the answer when he finds fish eggs in the pond—everyone has fish in their apartments. So he brings them home. He has 103 fish eggs. In preparation for the fish he is sure will hatch, he prepares to go dig worms. But again, Mother declares that there will be no worms in this apartment. He goes to buy fish food instead. When he returns he prepares the old baby bathtub for the fish eggs; in fact, one hatches almost immediately. All of his friends come to look and think David has a "nice mom." While the family is on vacation, Mr. Garfunkel agrees to feed the fish. When David gets home he is eager to know about his fish. He is told that he'll have a nice surprise. The surprise is in the bathtub—103 frogs. "That's all right. I'd rather have frogs anyway."

1. Read the book to the part where Mr. Garfunkel tells David that he has a surprise in the bathtub. Discuss and predict the surprise. Finish reading the story.

2. Steven Kellogg's *The Mysterious Tadpole* (Dial, 1977) has a similar theme as Alexander's title. In Kellogg's book a tadpole is expected to hatch into a frog; instead, the tadpole develops into a huge, strange-looking (but lovable) monster. After reading both stories, compare and contrast the elements of the stories. Focus on the story grammar in each. How are the stories alike and how are they different?

3. Focus on the end of *The Mysterious Tadpole*. The final picture is a natural beginning for another story, a story begging to be told. Together tell the story of what hatches out of the egg and what happens during the next year.

4. Research and read information about tadpoles and how they develop and hatch. The catalog in your school or public library will help you find books with this information. One source for pictures of a frog and toad and the development of a tadpole is the March 1986 issue of *Your Big Backyard* (published by the National Wildlife Federation).

Alexander, Martha. *Nobody Asked Me If I Wanted a Baby Sister*. Dial, 1971.

Oliver is indignant that his baby sister, Bonnie, is getting all the attention, so he puts her in his little red wagon and sets out to give her away. He first approaches triplet girls, whose mother would take the baby if she were a boy. The next man wants someone who can balance a ball in his circus act. Nobody seems to want her. Finally he comes to a newsboy who says his mother "loves babies," but the baby won't stop crying for the mother or for Jane, who tries to hold her. It is Jane who discovers that the baby wants only Oliver. Oliver decides that Bonnie is "a lot smarter than I thought." The final picture is that of Oliver pulling Bonnie back home in his little red wagon. He is saying, "When you get big enough maybe we could play horse and wagon." And the image in his head is of an older Bonnie pulling him in the wagon. This image is a perfect lead into the book's sequel, *I'll Be the Horse If You'll Play with Me*. Illustrations are typical Alexander.

1. After reading this book, read the book's sequel, *I'll Be the Horse If You'll Play with Me*. Correlate response activities with those suggested for the sequel (see entry for that title in this chapter).

2. Discuss the term *sibling rivalry* and what it means to each of the students and how it is portrayed in Alexander's book. Then read some of the following books and discuss how the books portray the relationships between the siblings:

Greenfield, Eloise. *She Come Bringing Me That Little Baby Girl*. Illustrated by John Steptoe. Lippincott, 1974.
    Kevin dislikes all the attention being given to his baby sister until his uncle tells him about caring for his own baby sister, Kevin's mother.

Keats, Ezra Jack. *Peter's Chair*. Harper, 1967.
    Peter decides to run away when all of his favorite possessions are painted pink.

Lasky, Kathryn, and Maxwell B. Knight. *A Baby for Max*. Illustrated by Christopher G. Knight. Scribner, 1984; Aladdin, 1987.

Max learns what it means to be an older brother. (This book is also useful as an introduction to photographer Christopher Knight and author Kathryn Lasky. Knight and Lasky are husband and wife, who, along with their son Max are preparing for the arrival of a second child.)

Scott, Ann. *On Mother's Lap*. Illustrated by Glo Coalson. McGraw, 1972.

An Eskimo child learns to share parental love.

Steptoe, John. *Stevie*. Harper, 1969.

A boy is jealous of a child his mother is caring for in a foster situation.

Alexander, Martha. *Out! Out! Out!* Dial, 1968.

In this wordless story a pigeon flies into the kitchen window of a young family's apartment. Several adults attempt to get the pigeon to fly back out of the window. It is the little boy who thinks to string cornflakes from the pigeon to the window sill. The pigeon follows the trail and is brushed back outside of the window. The last scene is a warm one showing Mother hugging her son.

1. Use this wordless book to motivate students to write a sequential story line. Share the pictures and, as a group, tell the story orally. Then tell the story once again and write the text to accompany the group's interpretation of the story.

2. Help children develop problem-solving skills by discussing the following question: What if the trail of cornflakes had not worked? What else would you have tried to get the pigeon out of the apartment?

3. As an activity that will help students develop a sequential story line, ask them to make a wordless story that each will share with a partner.

   a. Fold a piece of 8"-×-11" paper in four equal squares.

   b. Open the paper and number each section, one through four, in the lower right-hand corner.

   c. Think of a story about something you did yesterday. Show what happened by drawing four pictures. The pictures should be in logical order. Words may not be used unless they are part of the picture, such as a store sign.

   d. After drawing the four pictures, put the story's title in the first section (with the first illustration).

   e. Exchange story pictures with a partner. Tell your partner's story based on his or her pictures, and ask your partner to tell *your* story.

   f. Share the stories with classmates.

Alexander, Martha. *Sabrina*. Dial, 1971; 1991.

Sabrina is embarrassed by her unusual name. When she starts nursery school she decides she wants to change her name to Lisa or Susan. Only when she discovers that her name is a "princess" name does she change her mind.

1. Help each student build a sense of pride in one aspect of her or his life. Obtain several books about names from your public or school library—the kind often used by new parents to select a name for their child—and read the meaning of each child's name. Celebrate the uniqueness of each child's name by having students make bookmarks, plaques, or miniature name books giving the meanings of the children's names.

2. Have each child draw an illustration depicting the meaning of his or her name. Post the illustrations along with a picture of the child whose name is represented.

3. A child often has two "given" names. If the child could choose an additional "given" name what would it be? Why?

4. Share stories that focus on names and the origin of names. The following titles will help develop a basis for a discussion of names and how one feels about the name one was given.

Galbraith, Kathryn O. *Laura Charlotte*. Illustrated by Floyd Cooper. Philomel, 1989.

Henkes, Kevin. *Chrysanthemum*. Greenwillow, 1991.

Lester, Helen. *A Porcupine Named Fluffy*. Illustrated by Lynn Munsinger. Houghton, 1986.

Alexander, Martha. *The Story Grandmother Told*. Dial, 1969.
Lisa begs her grandmother to tell her a story. When Grandma asks what story Lisa wants to hear, Lisa tells of the day she and her cat, Ivan, bought a big green cat-shaped balloon. It was a fine balloon and everyone they met admired it until Ivan jumped on the balloon and broke it into tiny bits. But that was all right because they still had each other. After telling the story to Grandma, Lisa says, "And that's the story I want you to tell, Gramma." And that is the story Grandma told.

1. Write the story you would want your own grandmother to tell. Record the story on a cassette and give it to your grandmother or an older friend as a present.

2. As a long-range project, create a book of family stories. Many stories can be gathered during holiday get-togethers. Solicit stories from grandparents, aunts, uncles, and other relatives. If possible, tape-record the stories and listen to them. After you are familiar with the stories, retell them in your own words. Illustrate the stories if you wish. The book created could include one or many stories. After writing the stories you wish to include, create a book cover and title page, and number the pages. If the book includes more than one story, create a table of contents. The pages may be spiral-bound, but the pages could also be three-hole punched and put in a clear-cover plastic binder. Give the book to someone special in your family. Family stories told in junior novels or picture book format may provide some inspiration.

Carrick, Carol. *Lost in the Storm*. Illustrated by Donald Carrick. Clarion, 1974.

Levinson, Riki. *Watch the Stars Come Out*. Illustrated by Diane Goode. Dutton, 1985.

Rylant, Cynthia. *When I Was Young in the Mountains*. Illustrated by Diane Goode. Dutton, 1983. (1984 Caldecott honor medal)

Say, Allen. *Tree of Cranes*. Illustrated by Allen Say. Houghton, 1991.

Shecter, Ben. *Grandma Remembers*. Illustrated by Ben Shecter. Harper, 1989.

Taylor, Mildred. *The Gold Cadillac*. Illustrated by Michael Hays. Dial, 1987.

Taylor, Mildred. *Songs of the Trees*. Illustrated by Jerry Pinkney. Dial, 1975.

Alexander, Martha. *We're in Big Trouble, Blackboard Bear*. Dial, 1980.
    In this Blackboard Bear book it is Anthony's turn to help his friend and protector, Blackboard Bear. The big trouble is not so big when Anthony is there. This is a companion title to *And My Mean Old Mother Will Be Sorry, Blackboard Bear*; *Blackboard Bear*; and *I Sure Am Glad to See You, Blackboard Bear*.

1. Use this title in conjunction with the companion titles cited above. See entries in this chapter for those titles.

2. Use the enjoyment of this book to motivate students to read more books about imaginary friends. Compare and contrast the types of imaginary friends that are portrayed in the following books.

    Dauer, Rosamond. *My Friend, Jasper Jones*. Illustrated by Jerry Joyner. Parents, 1977.

    Dillon, Barbara. *The Beast in the Bed*. Illustrated by Chris Conover. Morrow, 1981.

    Hazen, Barbara Shook. *The Gorilla Did It!* Illustrated by Ray Cruz. Atheneum, 1974.

    Hazen, Barbara Shook. *Gorilla Wants to Be the Baby*. Illustrated by Jacqueline Bardner Smith. Atheneum, 1978.

    Hoff, Syd. *The Horse in Harry's Room*. Illustrated by Syd Hoff. Harper, 1970.

    Krensky, Stephen. *The Lion Upstairs*. Illustrated by Leigh Grant. Atheneum, 1983.

    Morris, Terry Nell. *Good Night, Dear Monster!* Illustrated by Terry Nell Morris. Knopf, 1980.

    Pinkwater, Daniel Manus. *Pickle Creature*. Illustrated by Daniel Manus Pinkwater. Four Winds, 1979.

    St. George, Judith. *The Halloween Pumpkin Smasher*. Illustrated by Margot Tomes. Putnam, 1978.

Caroline Arnold

Caroline S. Arnold

From *An Author a Month (for Dimes)* by Sharron L. McElmeel (Libraries Unlimited, 1992)

Caroline Arnold

Caroline Scheaffer Arnold was born May 16, 1944. She grew up in Minneapolis, Minnesota, but she spent summers at a Wisconsin camp where she was able to watch deer and porcupines in the outdoors. She enjoyed learning about animals and was very curious.

Caroline Arnold still enjoys learning about animals and is still curious. She has written about fossils, dinosaurs, electric fish, the Golden Gate Bridge, and many kinds of animals. She traveled to Australia to research information about koalas and kangaroos. She found that koalas smell like eucalyptus leaves and that their claws are needle sharp. When she and her husband traveled to east Africa she was chased by an angry elephant, and during that same trip she watched a mother cheetah play with her cubs. In North America she has observed peregrine falcons and tule elk.

Caroline Arnold and her family live in Los Angeles, California. She spends her mornings writing and her afternoons answering letters, talking with editors, collecting information for her books, or going to schools to talk about her books. When she is not working on a book, she enjoys playing tennis, cooking, watching movies, and working in her garden.

Chapter

2

Caroline Arnold

ABOUT THE AUTHOR

Caroline Scheaffer Arnold was born in Pittsburgh on May 16, 1944, to Lester L. Scheaffer and Catherine Young Scheaffer. She spent the first ten years of her life in a settlement house in Minneapolis, where her parents were social workers. She spent her summers in northern Wisconsin at a small summer camp. The camp's original name was Camp Hodag. It had been named for the Hodag, a monster with the head of an ox, the feet of a bear, the back of a dinosaur, and the tail of an alligator. During each camp session the campers would sit around the first campfire and tell the story of the Hodag. Arnold enjoyed that story and also the chance to let her curiosity about animals grow. At camp she could watch deer leaping through the underbrush and porcupines scurrying up trees. She enjoyed learning all she could about the animals she saw. She especially enjoyed learning those facts that might be considered "amazing." She loved to read and remembers especially liking books by Minnesota authors Maude Hart Lovelace and Carol Ryie Brink, and books by Laura Ingalls Wilder.

After graduating from high school and earning a B.A. degree from Grinnell College in Iowa, Caroline Scheaffer went on to earn a master's degree in art from the University of Iowa. In 1967 she married Arthur Arnold and for ten years worked with young people as an art teacher. When her own two children were young, she illustrated books for them and soon came to realize that she had to write the stories to go with her illustrations. Before long her work was being published. One of her first books, *Electric Fish* (Morrow, 1980), was selected an Outstanding Science Trade Book by the Children's Book Council and the National Science Teachers' Association.

When the family moved to Los Angeles, Caroline Arnold became interested in the La Brea tar pits. Later, when she became a writer, that interest resulted in *Trapped in Tar: Fossils from the Ice Age*. The book introduces the kinds of fossils found in southern California and presents a picture essay focusing on the treasures found in the George C. Page Museum of La Brea Discoveries.

In Los Angeles Caroline Arnold's husband, a neurobiologist, teaches animal behavior at the University of California at Los Angeles. In 1983 Arthur Arnold was invited to speak at some scientific meetings in Australia. The Arnolds decided to take their son and daughter along and make the trip into a family vacation. They spent part of the trip on Heron Island, on the Great Barrier Reef. Arthur Arnold, an amateur photographer, took so many pictures that when they returned home they realized they had a book. Earlier, Caroline Arnold had met Richard Hewett, a professional photographer, whose wife Arnold had met in a writer's class at UCLA. When Arnold was offered the opportunity to write a book about koalas and kangaroos, she knew exactly where to go. Arnold and Hewett actually traveled to Australia, where they spent two weeks behind the scenes in a wildlife park. In 1987 Clarion published *Koala* and *Kangaroo*. Both books were named Outstanding Science Trade Books. The publisher asked Arnold and Hewett to do more animal books.

As their animal book series has developed, they have tried to write about animals from different parts of the world. Each pair of books is about animals that live on the same continent and in some cases, such as zebras and giraffes, in the same environment. They often choose endangered animals to write about, because Arnold feels that it is important for children to realize the plight of these animals. Because of the time and expense involved, most of the research for Arnold and Hewett's books is done in zoos and wild animal parks. Because the animals are more accustomed to people in those types of places, Arnold and Hewett are able to get closer to the animals. They usually try to research animals when the adult animals are about to give birth, because Arnold often focuses on baby animals in her stories. As their series on animals grows, they are attempting to write about animals from various animal groups: herbivores, carnivores, primates, birds, reptiles, etc.

Once Arnold has chosen a topic, she locates a zoo or wildlife park where Hewett can take photographs. Then she goes to the library to do background research. If they have to travel out of the Los Angeles area, they must know exactly what they are looking for, because they usually spend only two weeks on a research and photography trip. For their animal books Arnold and Hewett work as a team. Arnold writes an outline that tells Hewett what kinds of pictures will be needed. However, often Hewett takes pictures of things they could not predict, and the photographs suggest changes for Arnold to make in the writing. Once the book, text, and photographs are laid out, they submit the book to their editor. Most finished books are very similar to the original layout.

Each book idea has come to Arnold from its own source. Her childhood interest in fossils and later the La Brea tar pits brought about *Trapped in Tar: Fossils from the Ice Age* (Clarion, 1987). When her editor read that book and noted the mention of the fossils found at Dinosaur National Monument in Utah, she suggested to Arnold that she might like to do a similar book about dinosaurs. Another editor read *Pets without Homes* (Clarion, 1983) and suggested she write another book focusing on a dog. That suggestion resulted in *A Guide Dog Puppy Grows Up* (Harcourt, 1991).

Many of the Arnolds' friends are experts on animals. *Electric Fish* (Morrow, 1980) was inspired by the scientific research of a personal friend who is an expert in that area. And when Caroline Arnold realized that the Golden Gate Bridge was going to be celebrating its fiftieth anniversary, she decided to write a book, *The Golden Gate Bridge* (Watts, 1986). She had been interested in the bridge ever since her parents moved to San Francisco in the 1960s. She has to cross the bridge every time she visits them.

Both of Arnold's children, Jennifer and Matthew, play the violin. They inspired the book *Music Lessons for Alex* (Clarion, 1985). Jennifer and Matthew appeared in the photographs for that book and sometimes show up in photographs in other books as well. Matthew's interest in soccer brought about the book *Soccer: From Neighborhood Play to the World Cup* (Watts, 1991). Other books that spun off from this interest were *Pelé* (Watts, 1991), *The Summer Olympic Games* (Watts, 1991), and *The Winter Olympic Games* (Watts, 1991).

Most of Arnold's books are nonfiction, but she has written a fiction book, *The Terrible Hodag* (Harcourt, 1989), which is told from her childhood memories of a campfire story at Camp Hodag. She has written over a dozen books in her animal series, several of which are about dinosaurs and fossils. She has also written books about community helpers, geography, and ceremonies and celebrations. Altogether Arnold has written more than forty books for young readers. Earlier in her writing career she illustrated two of her own books: *Sun Fun* (Watts, 1981) and *The Biggest Living Thing* (Carolrhoda, 1983). But she no longer draws. Most of her books are now illustrated with photographs, often by Richard Hewett.

Caroline Arnold and Arthur Arnold make their home in Los Angeles with a pet cat named Muffie. Their son and daughter are now in college. Arthur teaches at the University of California in Los Angeles; Caroline spends her mornings writing and her afternoons working on other activities necessary to keep her writing going: researching, answering letters, communicating with her editors, etc. In her spare time she enjoys tennis, cooking, movies, and gardening.

SETTING THE STAGE

As a group or class project, search through magazines and newspapers to locate photographs of koalas, kangaroos, giraffes, zebras, llamas, penguins, hippopotamuses, cheetahs, orangutans, wild goats, flamingos, snakes, camels, sharks, pandas, tule elks, and ostriches. Use these pictures to create a wide border on the bulletin board that will feature Caroline Arnold. In the center of the board (inside the border) place a photocopy of Caroline Arnold's poster page and a copy of the large-print information sheet located at the beginning of this chapter. On strips of paper write brief facts about Arnold. For example: "Lives in Los Angeles," "Traveled to Australia to learn about koalas and kangaroos," "Writes nonfiction books," "Researches before she makes a book outline," and "Many books illustrated with photographs." Later, students can add strips with facts about Arnold that they think are interesting.

Once the author's bulletin board is in place, introduce Caroline Arnold and her books. Put up a map of the world, and as the class or groups read about animals, identify the continent or area where those animals would live in nature. If the animals are pictured around the edge of the bulletin board where the map is placed, yarn could be stretched from the animal's picture to its habitat on the map.

Use Caroline Arnold's books as read-alouds and in smaller groups. Culminate the focus on the author by asking individuals to give brief book talks about their favorite Arnold books, or hold an "information fair" where posters about the books and the animals or topics presented are hung and murals and sculptures displayed. Be sure to end the day by snacking on animal crackers.

IDEA CUPBOARD

Arnold, Caroline. *Dinosaurs Down Under and Other Fossils from Australia*. Illustrated by Richard Hewett. Clarion, 1990.

Dinosaur Mountain: Graveyard of the Past. Illustrated by Richard Hewett. Clarion, 1989.

Trapped in Tar: Fossils from the Ice Age. Illustrated by Richard Hewett. Clarion, 1987.

Dinosaurs Down Under is a photo essay depicting the action behind the scenes at a museum and intriguing details about the unique fossils of prehistoric Australian creatures. The photographs for this book were taken as Australia's traveling exhibit arrived and was assembled for display at the Natural History Museum in Los Angeles. *Dinosaur Mountain* focuses on the unique contributions to dinosaur collections found at the Dinosaur National Monument quarry in Jensen, Utah. And the third title, *Trapped in Tar*, describes the kinds of fossils found in southern California tar pits. The photographs include close-ups of scientists working with bones in excavation pits.

1. Build students' knowledge of dinosaurs and fossils by sharing books about dinosaurs by Aliki:

Digging Up Dinosaurs (Crowell, 1981; revised 1988)

Dinosaur Bones (Crowell, 1988)

Dinosaurs Are Different (Crowell, 1985)

Fossils Tell of Long Ago (Crowell, 1972; revised 1990)

My Visit to the Dinosaurs (Crowell, 1985)

Also suitable are the following books in the Knopf Eyewitness series:

Norman, David, and Angela Milner. *Dinosaur*. Knopf, 1989.

Taylor, Paul D. *Fossil*. Knopf, 1990.

2. As part of a career awareness objective, help students investigate the role of a paleontologist. Interview, in person or by letter, a paleontologist at a natural history museum. Inquire about duties, education needed, and positive and negative aspects of the job. Combine the information from the interview and the information gleaned from the books by Arnold, Aliki, and Lasky (see activity 3), and from the Eyewitness titles to make a paleontology career board. This career board would consist of a poster featuring information about becoming a paleontologist and the benefits and duties of the job. Illustrations for the career board might be enlargements of some of Aliki's drawings.

3. More information about the work of a paleontologist appears in Kathryn Lasky's book *Dinosaur Dig*, illustrated by Christopher G. Knight (Morrow, 1990). In Lasky's book five families accompany Dr. Keith Rigby, a paleontologist, on a dig to the Badlands of Montana. Knight's photography captures the families' struggle down the slippery siltstone hills in 100-degree heat, their search for fossils (and rattlesnakes), and their work with sharp-pointed awls—with which they hoped to uncover a dinosaur bone. Write or discuss whether students would or would not like to participate in a dinosaur dig.

4. Other books about dinosaurs can be located by using the subject heading DINOSAURS in your library or media center's catalog. Or consult the booklists under dinosaurs in:

Kobrin, Beverly. *Eyeopeners! How to Choose and Use Children's Books about Real People, Places, and Things*. Penguin, 1988.

Lima, Carolyn W. *A to Zoo*. 3d ed. Bowker, 1990.

McElmeel, Sharron L. *My Bag of Book Tricks*. Illustrated by Deborah L. McElmeel. Libraries Unlimited, 1989.

Arnold, Caroline. *A Guide Dog Puppy Grows Up*. Illustrated by Richard Hewett. Harcourt, 1991.
    This informational book discusses how guide dogs are raised and trained by Guide Dogs for the Blind.

1. Help students investigate the origin of the Guide Dogs for the Blind organization and the Seeing Eye corporation and determine what each of these organizations does to help blind people.

2. Extend students' interest in guide dogs and their use by reading *The Trouble with Tuck* (Doubleday, 1981), Theodore Taylor's account of Helen's beautiful golden retriever, Friar Tuck Golden Boy. Tuck had twice saved Helen's life, so when he becomes blind Helen attempts to find a dog that will guide her dog. The book gives much information about the cost and effort it takes to train a guide dog. Taylor's book is excellent for group reading or to read aloud. Taylor has written a sequel to this book, *Tuck Triumphant* (Doubleday, 1991), which focuses on fourteen-year-old Helen and her family's crises after they adopt a deaf Korean boy. Tuck again displays special abilities, this time in helping to watch over Chok-Do.

Arnold, Caroline. *Juggler*. Illustrated by Richard Hewett. Clarion, 1988.

The text and the black-and-white photographs work together to present professional juggler Jahnathan Whitfield. Readers will be captured in the fun of learning how to juggle as Whitfield gives much practical advice to help beginners get started.

1. After reading *Juggler*, have students practice some of the juggling skills that Whitfield presents in Arnold's book. Incorporate the practice into playground or gymnasium activities.

2. If the book spawns some successful jugglers, hold a "performance" fair where the novice jugglers can show their talents. Other students could be court jesters (using tumbling skills), poetry readers, and mime performers. Utilize each student in some manner. Invite other groups to be the fair audience.

3. Extend students' interest in juggling by sharing some of the following stories about jugglers:

    Cooney, Barbara. *The Little Juggler*. Illustrated by Barbara Cooney. Hastings, 1961; 1982.

    dePaola, Tomie. *The Clown of God: An Old Story*. Illustrated by Tomie dePaola. Harcourt, 1978.

    Pack, Robert. *The Octopus Who Wanted to Juggle*. Illustrated by Nancy Willard. Galileo, 1990.

4. In Arnold's book the juggler is performing in a contemporary time period. Cooney's and dePaola's jugglers are both from a time in the past. Jugglers are found in the circus, at fairs, and in modern-day malls. Discuss the settings of the books read and then have students use favorite art media to create pictures of jugglers. They should be sure to include a background to show the setting (where the juggler is performing), such as a medieval fair, a circus, a modern-day county fair, an amusement park, or their very own living room.

Arnold, Caroline. *Kangaroo*. Illustrated by Richard Hewett. Morrow, 1987.

An informative text and gorgeous pictures combine to make this a book that reads well and gives much information about one of Australia's most famous animals.

1. Brainstorm a list of "facts" that the students think they know about kangaroos.

    a. List all the information without judging its validity or accuracy. Accept all comments.

    b. During a second session, form groups of three to four students to go over the list to identify information they are absolutely sure is correct. At this point the discussion is just that—a discussion; the activity does not involve any research or additional reading.

c. Bring the entire group back together and star all those items that all groups agree are true. If the majority believes the item to be true/correct, put a check mark by it.

d. Put a minus mark by those statements the group feels are inaccurate.

e. Search for information and prove or disprove the checked items on the list.

2. As students set out to verify statements about kangaroos, they will be motivated to read information and stories about these animals. In addition to Arnold's book, some of the following may be helpful. Some of these books are informational; others are fiction stories.

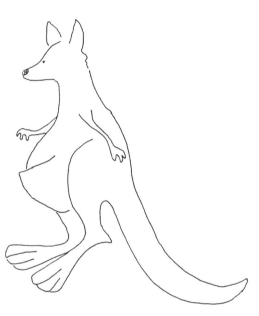

Barry, S. L., et al. *Amazing Animals of Australia*. National Geographic, 1984.

Burt, Denise. *Kangaroos*. Illustrated by Neil McLeod. Houghton, 1991.

Kipling, Rudyard. *The Sing-Song of Old Man Kangaroo*. Illustrated by John Alfred Rowe. Picture, 1990. (Folktale)

Payne, Emmy. *Katy No-pocket*. Illustrated by H. A. Rey. Houghton, 1944.

Schlein, Miriam. *Big Talk*. Illustrated by Joan Auclair. Bradbury, 1990.

Ungerer, Tomi. *Adelaide*. Illustrated by Tomi Ungerer. Harper, 1959.

Wax, Wendy, and Della Rowland. *10 Things I Know about Kangaroos*. Illustrated by Thomas Payne. Calico, 1990.

Arnold, Caroline. *Koala*. Illustrated by Richard Hewett. Morrow, 1987.

Arnold and photographer Hewett traveled to Australia to research the information for this book. For two weeks they observed koalas in a wildlife park to find out how they behave. They found out that koalas mostly eat and sleep. They smell like eucalyptus leaves and have soft fur but needle-sharp claws.

1. Motivate students to read about koalas by using the brainstorming/categorization technique described in the entry for Arnold's *Kangaroo*.

2. Give students the opportunity to learn more about koalas by reading some of the following titles in addition to Arnold's book:

Barry, S. L., et al. *Amazing Animals of Australia*. National Geographic, 1984.

Bright, Michael. *Koalas*. Illustrated with photographs. Gloucester, 1990.

Wexo, John Bonnett. *Koalas*. Wildlife, 1983.

3. Mem Fox has written a story about a small koala that wishes to enter the bush Olympics. She wants to win so that she can hear her mother say, "Koala Lou, I do love you." Read *Koala Lou* by Mem Fox (Harcourt/Gulliver, 1989). Identify and discuss facts about koalas (and Australia) that Fox uses in her story.

4. Caroline Arnold and Richard Hewett have collaborated on a number of other animal books. Each of the books presents a photo essay on the featured animal. In every case the text is well organized and provides a variety of information about the specific animal—information that includes how the animal lives in its natural habitat as well as in captivity. The focus is often on the young of the species. The books in Arnold and Hewett's animal series lend themselves to brainstorming and additional research about animals; they also contain expressive activities for classroom use. Read some of the following animal books by Caroline Arnold:

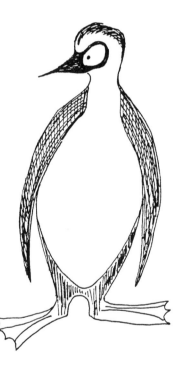

Camel. Illustrated by Richard Hewett. Morrow, 1992.

Cheetah. Illustrated by Richard Hewett. Morrow, 1989.

Flamingo. Illustrated by Richard Hewett. Morrow, 1991.

Giraffe. Illustrated by Richard Hewett. Morrow, 1987.

Hippo. Illustrated by Richard Hewett. Morrow, 1989.

Llama. Illustrated by Richard Hewett. Morrow, 1988.

Orangutan. Illustrated by Richard Hewett. Morrow, 1990.

Ostriches and Other Flightless Birds. Illustrated by Richard Hewett. Carolrhoda, 1990.

Panda. Illustrated by Richard Hewett. Morrow, 1992.

Penguin. Illustrated by Richard Hewett. Morrow, 1988.

Snake. Illustrated by Richard Hewett. Morrow, 1991.

Tule Elk. Illustrated by Richard Hewett. Carolrhoda, 1989.

Wild Goat. Illustrated by Richard Hewett. Morrow, 1990.

Zebra. Illustrated by Richard Hewett. Morrow, 1987.

The following activities could be used with students as they read any of Arnold's animal books:

a. Identify the animal's homeland and mark it on a map of the world. Cut a color transparency to overlay the animal's natural habitat on the world map.

b. Use the index of an encyclopedia to locate articles about the animal.

c. Locate other books on the animal by using the catalog in your school or public library. Use the animal's name as the subject heading.

d. Create a diorama showing the animal's natural habitat. Be sure to include the plants and other animals that inhabit the area. Attempt to show the terrain of the land.

e. Make an information chart detailing information about the animal, in pictorial form. Include average weight/height/length, life span, food source, etc., of the animal.

f. Use favorite media to depict the animal in its natural habitat.

g. Create a papier-mâché model of the animal. Make it either full scale or choose a specific scale—for example, one-half actual size, or one-fourth actual size.

h. ·Locate at least one fiction story that has the animal as part of the story. After reading the story, list the facts about the animal that the fiction writer managed to include in the story.

i. Write a literary folk story explaining how the animal came to have one of its unique characteristics. For example: Why the Giraffe Has a Long Neck, or How the Penguin Got Its Tuxedo Coat. For motivation read some of the "why" stories by Rudyard Kipling.

j. Make a list entitled "Ten things I know about _____." Illustrate your list.

Arnold, Caroline. *Music Lessons for Alex*. Illustrated by Richard Hewett. Clarion, 1986.
The first year of study in a young violin student's life as described in this book introduces readers to the world of music lessons. The photographs portray periods of frustration, hours of concentration, and the resulting enjoyment as the lessons yield success.

1. Have students who are taking music lessons write an essay detailing personal experiences with those lessons. Title the text "Music Lessons for _____."

2. Have other students write why they would or would not like to take music lessons.

3. Establish knowledge and build on background information about musical instruments and the effort it takes to learn to play them by holding a classroom Music Day. Establish a day each month when students or others (parents, grandparents, principal, secretary, etc.) are invited to come to the classroom/library and play their instruments for the group. Encourage students to ask questions about how the person learned to play the instrument, how much one practices, etc.

Arnold, Caroline. *Pets without Homes*. Illustrated by Richard Hewett. Clarion, 1983.
The inner workings of a big-city animal shelter are shown and explained. This is a compassionate essay that is sure to provoke thought and questions about pets without homes in the reader's community.

1. Visit an animal shelter in your community or invite a representative from the animal shelter to talk with your class about how your local animal shelter works.

2. Correlate information about the animal shelter with information about animal shelters and the care of animals as presented in *Zucchini* by Barbara Dana, illustrated by Eileen Christelow (Harper/Zolotow, 1982). The novel could be read aloud to primary-age or intermediate readers. Intermediate readers will also be able to read *Zucchini* independently, perhaps as a common reading. Zucchini is a ferret that was born inside the rodent house at the Bronx Zoo. The personified animal plans his escape and ends up under the care of the American Society for the Prevention of Cruelty to Animals. A young boy, Billy, becomes involved in the animal's welfare.

Arnold, Caroline. *Saving the Peregrine Falcon*. Illustrated by Richard Hewett. Carolrhoda, 1985.
    Once on the brink of extinction, the peregrine falcon is now making a comeback. Insecticide in the parent falcon's system causes the falcon's eggs to be thin-shelled. In order to preserve the species, the eggs are taken from the falcon's nest and hatched. The chicks are fed and returned to the wild or to city skyscrapers, where they are flourishing and restoring their numbers.

1.   Encourage students to learn more about the efforts to save endangered species of birds. Compare the efforts being made to save the falcon to efforts under way to preserve other endangered animals. Use the subject heading ENDANGERED ANIMALS in your school or public library's catalog to locate sources of information about other endangered animals. The following books will be useful.

     Birkhead, Mike. *Animal Habitats: The Falcon over the Town*. Illustrated by Mike Birkhead. Gareth Stevens, 1988.
          Explains how falcons live in their natural habitat and in new locations in the city, how they feed themselves, and how they struggle to survive and reproduce.

     Harrison, Virginia. *Where Animals Live: The World of a Falcon*. Illustrated by Mike Birkhead. Gareth Stevens, 1988.
          Adapted from Mike Birkhead's *Animal Habitats: The Falcon over the Town*.

     Hendrich, Paula. *Saving America's Birds*. Lothrop, 1986.
          Focuses on the people who spend their lives preserving peregrine falcons and other birds of prey.

2.   Invite a local animal conservationist to visit your classroom to discuss with students the efforts being made to preserve the flora and fauna in the local area. This exchange may result in a group project that would contribute to the preservation of plants or animals in the community. A typical long-range project might include establishing a nature preserve or the planting of shrubs to provide a haven for small animals and birds.

Graeme Base

From *An Author a Month (for Dimes)* by Sharron L. McElmeel (Libraries Unlimited, 1992)

Graeme Base

Graeme Base spent his early years in England, where he was born on April 6, 1958. His family moved to Melbourne, Australia, when he was eight. He attended school in Melbourne and received a Diploma of Art from the Swinburne College of Technology. He worked for a while in advertising and then began to create books.

His first book was *My Grandma Lived in Gooligulch*. He spent three years creating his next book, *Animalia*. During this time he also played in a rock band, where he met his wife, Robyn, when she sang with his band. *Animalia*, a very unusual alphabet book, was published in the United States in 1986. His favorite page in the book is the "Horrible Hairy Hogs," but he says that "the Lazy Lions run a close second." In 1987 he traveled overseas to collect ideas for another book, *The Eleventh Hour*. He spent a month in the game parks of Kenya and Tanzania on the African continent taking lots of photographs to help him when he began to create the illustrations.

Graeme Base once considered eating, flying kites, and playing music his hobbies. He still enjoys eating and loves music but doesn't have much time to fly kites. He puts a tiny letter *R* in his illustrations for Robyn's name. After the 1990 birth of their son, James, he also began to include a tiny letter *J*. The family and their cat, China, live in Melbourne.

Chapter

3

Graeme Base

ABOUT THE AUTHOR/ILLUSTRATOR

Graeme Base was born in England on April 6, 1958, and spent his first eight years in that country. The Base family first lived in Beaconsfield, Buckinghamshire, but later moved to Weymouth in Dorset. When Base was eight years old, he moved with his family to Melbourne, Australia, where he has lived ever since. His childhood was very happy except for some rough times he had in primary school. Those rough times came about because he was one of the few English boys in the Australian school. Both his parents were loving and encouraging, so he got through those days okay. They lived in the Box Hill and Parkville sections of Melbourne.

Graeme Base read J. R. R. Tolkien's *The Lord of the Rings* and Kenneth Grahame's *The Wind in the Willows*. He also read books by A. A. Milne. Each had an influence on him. At the age of twelve he started to tell people that he wanted to be a commercial artist. He attended Box Hill High School for three years, studied with the Australian Correspondence School for one year, and spent another two years at the Melbourne High School. During his childhood Base discovered books illustrated by Sir John Tenniel, the illustrator of Lewis Carroll's Alice books, and Ernest A. Shepherd, the illustrator of A. A. Milne's *Winnie the Pooh*. It was during his high school years that Base discovered Salvador Dali. Later he spent three years at the Swinburne College of Technology studying graphic design. After earning a Diploma of Art in 1978, he began working as a commercial artist, but "got sacked ... for incompetencies." He was also playing piano in a rock band. His future wife, Robyn Paterson, sang in the band.

When Base started showing his artwork to publishers, one publisher suggested he do something Australian. He did. He wrote and illustrated *My Grandma Lived in Gooligulch*, which was published in Australia in 1983. In 1990 Abrams published it in the United States. Base showed a publisher the art for the "Hairy Hog" picture that eventually became part of his *Animalia* book. When the publisher expressed interest in the book, Base began work on it. It took a total of three years to complete. Penguin Publishers in Australia printed 11,000 copies, almost double its usual run. But even before the official publication date, they had run 10,000 more copies in a second run. Within a week they printed 10,000 more copies and then decided to run 25,000 copies. In 1989 it had sold nearly a half million copies—and has sold many more since. During a presentation at the International Reading Association's conference in New Orleans, Base told of being at the Frankfurt Book Fair when a representative for his Australian publisher sold the U.S. rights to *Animalia* to a man (from Abrams) who was just browsing and looking over the representative's shoulder. The American man offered $10,000.

While *Animalia* was enjoying great success, Base was asked to do two stories for Macmillan's reading series. One of the stories he illustrated was Lewis Carroll's *Jabberwocky*. Abrams published *Jabberwocky* as a trade book in the United States in 1989. Base then resumed working on a dragon book that he had been working on for several years. But soon another idea emerged—a mystery story in pictures. *The Eleventh Hour* would have all the clues in the illustrations. The original idea was that eleven animals would go to an eleventh birthday party on November 11, play eleven games, and then the lights would go out. Base had two basic ideas for the story at this point. The first was that the dog would be dead; he rejected that idea. The second idea was that the ostrich's jewelry would be stolen. He rejected that idea, too. Instead, he decided to have the animals, at 11 a.m., rush to the feast and find the food missing. To gather images for this book Graeme Base and his wife traveled extensively in Asia, Africa, and Europe. In an interview in 1991, Base commented, "I traveled overseas in 1987 collecting ideas for *The Eleventh Hour*, and spent a month in the game parks of Kenya and Tanzania. It was an incredible experience to travel through herds of zebras and wildebeest and see giraffes, rhinos, elephants, lions, cheetahs, hippos, crocodiles, and even a leopard all running free in the wilds of Africa! I hope to return there one day."

The backgrounds for the animal scenes in *The Eleventh Hour* come from images inspired by Egyptian temples, Scottish castles, and St. Peter's Basilica. The entrance hall in Horace's house is St. Peter's in Rome, the borders were inspired by paintings at the Uffizi Gallery in Florence, Italy, and the rug is one that Graeme Base purchased in Istanbul. The chess game has many Indian motifs. He takes many photographs during his travels and also makes small pencil sketches of the things he sees each day. He uses the photographs and sketches to help him develop original sketches for his books.

Base commented further on his travels, "We also traveled through northern India where we thought we were going to be murdered by a taxi driver but were mistaken, Nepal where we thought we were going to die of exhaustion but finally reached the end of the trek, Europe where we thought we were going to be run over by several crazy European motorists but they missed us, and USA where we thought we were going to die of over-eating but ran out of money."

The Eleventh Hour was published in Australia in 1988. After completing the art for *The Eleventh Hour*, Base returned to the dragon book and decided in early 1989 that twelve dragon pictures would become a calendar.

Graeme Base's art has been influenced by British artists Sir John Tenniel and Ernest A. Shepherd. He is fascinated by the work of Maxfield Parish and the Australian artist Robert Ingpen. He also admires the work of American illustrator Michael Hague. In 1991 he was working on a new book, *The Sign of the Seahorse*, which is planned for publication in 1992. It is set totally underwater and was inspired by "three weeks spent snorkeling and scuba diving in the Galapagos Islands, Martinique and Australia's Great Barrier Reef."

Graeme Base's work schedule is, in his words, "very erratic. Sometimes I work all day, sometimes all night and sometimes not at all." He describes his creative process: "My paintings are done on illustration board with watercolors and transparent inks, using brushes, pencils, technical drawing pens, a scalpel (for scratching). I also use a very special tool called an airbrush which actually sprays colors onto the board (very handy for painting skies and mist and breath from horses' mouths). I do exhaustive rough drawings and detailed designs before embarking on the finished art. I present my concept first, then the dummy, and finally the finished product." In the *Animalia* book, Base put himself in each illustration—as a boy in an orange and yellow striped sweater. He also includes a tiny letter *R*, for Robyn, in most of his illustrations, and since September 1990, he has been including a tiny letter *J*, for his baby son, James.

He describes his present life in Melbourne as "extraordinarily hectic, exciting, exhausting and very rewarding from a creative point of view." He credits his wife, Robyn, with giving him endless support and criticism. She also creates large oil portraits. He describes his son, James, born September 7, 1990, as "incredibly cute." And of his longtime pet cat, China, Base says, "China is getting old and sleepy and has coped far better than we had thought he would with the arrival of James in his well-ordered life."

Base has traveled extensively for the past fifteen years and feels that there is no place he would rather live than Australia, specifically Melbourne. "It has a near perfect balance of everything I consider important—sunshine, seasons, culture, security and an incredibly varied countryside within minutes and hours of the city."

His favorite food is Vegemite. His favorite color is Norway blue, and his favorite animal is the leopard. When he is not working on a book he spends time writing music on his guitar and keyboards. He hopes one day to make a record and perhaps write a musical score for a movie. He likes music so much that he feels that someday music may replace books as his main occupation. Right now his heros are mainly musicians—like Peter Gabriel. He says that whenever he needs a break from his illustration work, he picks up the guitar or picks out a tune on the piano.

SETTING THE STAGE

In your author's corner or bulletin board, place a picture of Graeme Base and information about him as an author and illustrator. If book jackets of his books are available, use those around a map of the world. Label England as Base's birthplace and Melbourne, Australia, as his current home. In 1992 Abrams issued a calendar featuring scenes from *Animalia*; if calendar pages are available from that calendar, those could also be used. Since Base often sketches or photographs the scenes he sees (so that he can remember them when he begins to create his illustrations), a camera and sketchbook might be incorporated into the exhibit. Display books by Graeme Base. As you share information about the places Base has traveled to gather images for his books, mark those locations on the world map. Perhaps small pictures of the animals pictured in *Animalia* and *The Eleventh Hour* could be placed in their native countries.

Codes and ciphers are important in solving the mystery in *The Eleventh Hour*. A code is a system of symbols used in secret writing. Every letter or word has a set meaning. Letters, symbols, etc., are arbitrarily given certain meanings, while a cipher assigns certain values, as in a = 1, b = 2, etc., or a = f, b = g, etc. A ciphered message is a message based on the cipher key. Anyone who figures out the cipher can figure out the message. At the end of *The Eleventh Hour*, Base includes a "Note for Detectives." He says that the note, when "decoded," will reveal the culprit as well as the method used to steal the feast. However, the message is really a cipher, since there is a set value for each letter. Once that series of values is discovered, the mystery message can be *deciphered*. Before introducing the book, give children some practice in deciphering messages. In a prominent place in the author center, display a large sign that says:

Bmvzhz Wvnz

Make no comment about the sign at first. When students inquire about its meaning, discuss the possibility that the phrase is a code or a cipher. Clifford Hicks explains codes and ciphers in chapter 4 of his book *Alvin's Secret Code* (Holt, 1963). Lorna Balian introduces a cipher with *Humbug Potion: An A B Cipher* (Abingdon, 1984). Use these two books to discuss the difference between a code and a cipher. Encourage students to think critically and to figure out the cipher that will allow the deciphering of the sign.

To make your own cipher write each of the twenty-six letters of the alphabet, and then write the alphabet alongside of it, starting with another letter. For example:

letter	A	B	C	D	E	F	G	H	etc.
cipher	F	G	H	I	J	K	L	M	etc.

Every time one writes the letter *a* it will really mean *f*. So *fig* would be written as *adb*. Using this cipher one would write the author's name, Graeme Base, as *Bmvzhz Wvnz*.

After working with ciphers introduce Graeme Base and his books. In your author center place a copy of *The Eleventh Hour*. In that book the title page includes an invitation to Horace's eleventh birthday party. Issue your own invitations to a Graeme Base Mystery Party.

Invitation

Dear _____

    Please come to the author reading center and help solve a curious mystery. Read *The Eleventh Hour* by Graeme Base. To solve the mystery you will have to find the hidden codes and clues. Pay special attention to the clocks. Share your ideas with classmates so that we can work together to find out who stole the food at my birthday party.

                                                           Horace

---

Explain the premise of the book. *The Eleventh Hour* is a story with a mystery. The cipher at the end of the book will reveal the person who stole the feast, but before the cipher can be figured out the names of the guests must be determined and some reasonable idea of who the culprit might be will need to be put forth. At this point go to the entry for *The Eleventh Hour* in the Idea Cupboard and encourage students to explore the clues and book to find the solution to the mystery.

Explore with students the other books by Graeme Base by using the suggestions in the Idea Cupboard. Much of the pleasure in these books will be gained through group interaction, so allow plenty of opportunity for small groups to peruse the books and to discuss the things they find. Each day discuss new things that others have found in Base's books. Keep a cumulative list of information the students gather.

Culminate the focus on Graeme Base by having an eleventh-hour feast. Ask for volunteers to bring eleven items (eleven chocolate chips, eleven slices of apple, eleven carrot sticks, eleven celery sticks, etc.) to share at the feast. During the feast read for eleven minutes.

IDEA CUPBOARD

Base, Graeme. *Animalia*. Abrams, 1986.

This is a most unusual alphabet book in which all the letters of the alphabet are represented by wonderfully imaginative collages of people, animals, and things. The collages bring to mind many words and images that contribute to the alliterative mood of the collage. For example, the *L* page shows lazy lions lying on a library table in a library surrounded by many library books with titles such as *Lassie*. There are many other images that bring the *L* sound into focus. And of course there is Base's favorite page showing the Hairy Hogs.

1. Discuss alliteration. Share other selections that illustrate the alliterative technique. Read aloud "The Pirate Don Durk of Dowdee" by Mildred Plew Meigs or "Godfrey Gordon Gustavus Gore" by William Brighty Rands. Both poems are available in May Hill Arbuthnot's *The Arbuthnot Anthology of Children's Literature*, 3d ed. (Scott, Foresman, 1971). In *Aster Aardvark's Alphabet Adventures* (Morrow, 1967), Steven Kellogg also uses alliterative sentences as he discusses Aster Aardvark's aversion to the alphabet. Aunt Agnes is not happy with Aster's attitude so she arranges for an airplane to aide Aster's academic advancement ... and all assemble to applaud Aster's amazing aptitude for alliterative aerial acrobatics. Encourage students to use a similar technique to describe, alliteratively, more of the action in Base's illustrations for each letter of the alphabet.

2. Find Graeme Base in each picture. He is pictured as a young boy in a yellow and orange striped sweater. Write a sentence describing the boy's location in each picture. Ask a classmate to locate Base quickly by using your description of his location.

3. As a long-range project, immerse the readers in other alphabet books and then use their familiarity with the various types of alphabet books to identify a format for writing an alphabet book of their own. Alphabet books can be created by individuals or by pairs of students. A booklist of alphabet books can be found in *My Bag of Book Tricks* (Libraries Unlimited, 1989), and those available in a specific library or media center can be located by using the subject heading ALPHABET BOOKS.

Base, Graeme. *The Eleventh Hour*. Abrams, 1989.

The story begins, "When Horace (an elephant) turned Eleven he decided there should be/ Some kind of celebration. 'For my friends,' he said, 'and me./ For though I've been the age of eight and nine and six and seven,/ This is the very first time that I've ever been Eleven.'" Horace invites every guest and makes a list of "eleven sorts of food that Elephants like best." He even decides on eleven games for everyone to play. The feast promises to be fantastic, with cheesecake full of strawberries and cream, pastries, and chocolate supreme. The ten guests include a pig that comes as an admiral, a punky zebra, an astronaut rhino, a swan, a Bengal tiger, a musketeer mouse, a cat, Sam the crocodile, and twin giraffes. The ten guests plus Horace make eleven friends to share the party fun. In each illustration is a hidden message. Three basic methods can be used to solve the mystery:

a. The final page will give many insights into the clues readers should have been looking for, but readers should try to figure out the more obscure clues first; it'll be more fun.

b. Each page has a clock somewhere. The clocks will help pinpoint the time that the theft occurred. And those with good eyesight will be able to pinpoint and deduce the identity of the thief.

c. Hidden messages appear on each page, and the borders almost always offer some sage advice. And there is a multitude of other messages as well, some misleading — true red herrings. Graeme Base says that a "little knowledge of ancient Egypt could also prove useful here."

Of course, a great deal of intuition cannot hurt, and if you get frustrated enough you can always break the seal on the "Top Secret" section at the end of the book, which gives page-by-page information about the clues found on each page. And, of course, the thief's identity is all but revealed.

1. The obvious activity is to attempt to find the thief's identity. Work as a group. List the clues that are being found. Collaborate and discuss the implications. For example, on the first page, which shows Horace's study, notice the pencils in the gray border that give the message, "Drawing conclusions from sketchy clues may lead you astray, so sharpen your eyes and your wits — get the point?" Another clue is in the pencil border. At the end of each pencil is another single letter within a small rectangle. Reading clockwise the message reads, "It was not Max." Thus, Max the tiger can be eliminated as a suspect.

2. The sketch for the illustration of the hide-and-seek game page perhaps suggests that that page will offer an important clue to solving the mystery. But that first page is filled with many other interesting items. There is a button on the bulletin board bearing the numerals *986* — forward or backward (if turned upside down) the button reads the same. It is a palindrome, a word, a phrase, or sentence that reads the same backward or forward. Hannah is a name that is a palindrome. A palindrome year is 1991. "Name no one man" is also a palindrome. It *may* be a clue.

    a. Make a list of interesting things found on each page. Those interesting things may be clues for solving the mystery.

    b. Build vocabulary by listing as many palindromes as students can identify.

3. Develop visual acuity by looking for, and recording, the occurrences of eleven on each page. On the first page, the border holds eleven pencils, there are eleven objects pinned on the bulletin board, and *eleven* is written both as a word and as a numeral on the tires on the car in the picture hanging on the wall.

4. Each illustration also has some hidden mice in it, (for a book total of 111, to be exact). Within a small circle somewhere in each picture is a numeral giving the number of mice that can be found in that particular illustration. In the first picture, in a small circle inside the desk's open lower righthand door, is the numeral *18*. This is a clue telling readers that there are eighteen mice in the picture. In this case the mice can all be found huddled together in the pink and green part of the stained glass window above Horace's desk. Find the numeral in each illustration and make a list of the location of the mice in each picture.

5. Each picture gives some clue as to the time the activity is taking place. Note those times. Knowing the time each event takes place will help formulate hypotheses about the thief.

6. The guests play several games: sack racing, musical chairs, a card game, snakes and ladders (a board game), cricket, pool, blind man's bluff, tennis, hide-and-seek, chess, and tug o' war—eleven games in all. Create a party game book. Include the rules for each game, learn the games, and play a game or two.

7. In each illustration is the letter *R* for Robyn, Graeme Base's wife. Find the *R* in each picture. Write a sentence describing where the *R* is located and then share your descriptive sentence with a partner. See if he or she can quickly find the *R* by using your directions.

8. In mystery terminology a "red herring" is a clue that is designed specifically to throw off track those who are trying to solve the mystery. After discussing the term, find the references Base makes to a red herring in his illustrations.

9. Following Base's model for using the number eleven, use your own age to draw a picture incorporating as many items or ideas representing that number as you can. Write sentences to accompany the illustrations. For example: I got up at eight o'clock and put on eight items of clothing. My shirt had eight buttons on it and I tried to tie my shoelaces eight times before I finally got them tied correctly. I pulled my bedspread up to make the bed. (The bedspread has eight dinosaurs on it.)

10. As a last question Base asks if readers have discovered the name of the swan. Base doesn't give the answer to that one in his solutions section. In fact, can you list all the eleven animals' given names? The following are the ones I figured out:

Elephant	Horace
Mouse	Kilroy
Tiger	Maxwell
Rhinoceros	Thomas
Zebra	Eric
Crocodile	Sam

Pig	Oliver
Giraffe (1)	Cora
Giraffe (2)	
Cat	Alexandra
Swan	

As you can see, I could not find the swan's name nor could I determine the name of the second of the giraffe twins. Can you?

Carroll, Lewis. *Jabberwocky*. Illustrated by Graeme Base. Abrams, 1989.

Carroll was a master of nonsense verse. Much of it was included in his stories *Alice's Adventures in Wonderland* and *Through the Looking-Glass*. "Jabberwocky," from *Through the Looking-Glass*, contained language that Carroll invented—portmanteau words. Portmanteau words are formed by combining the meaning and parts of two words to create a new one. *Slithy* is made up of lithe and slimy. *Mimsy* is a combination of flimsy and miserable. He used other words such as *brillig* and *borogoves*. But according to information referenced by Myra Cohn Livingston in her *Poems of Lewis Carroll* (Crowell, 1973), even Carroll could not explain the meaning of *vorpal blade* or *tulgey wood*. But he thought that *uffish thought* might suggest a state of mind when the voice was gruffish, the manner roughish, and the temper huffish. He also noted that *burble* might be made up of parts of *bleat*, *murmur*, and *warble*. But he went on to say that he could not distinctly remember having made it that way.

1. Compare the conceptualization of Carroll's poem "Jabberwocky" as presented in Base's illustrated version with *Jabberwocky*, illustrated by Jane Breskin Zalben (Warne, 1977). Zalben's version is illustrated with watercolors.

2. Paul Coltman, a British poet, has written a wonderfully spooky narrative poem using nonsense words much as Carroll did in his "Jabberwocky." In the story *Tog the Ribber; or Granny's Tale*, Granny relates a childhood experience to explain "Why her hair is white/ And ... why she don't speak right." It seems that one night as she was coming home alone, the ghostly bones of Tog the Ribber chased her. Coltman's daughter has illustrated the verse in deliciously spooky and eerily beautiful full-color pictures. The pages are filled with threatening shapes of worms, insects, spiders, snakes, owls, bones, and disembodied faces. Granny ends up in her "cosly bed." Compare the language in *Tog the Ribber* by Paul Coltman, illustrated by Gillian McClure (Farrar, 1985), with the vocabulary Carroll uses in "Jabberwocky."

3. Make up some words of your own. Tell what they mean and then use them in a story or a sentence.

4. Each person who illustrates Carroll's poem views the poem in a different manner. After reading "Jabberwocky" draw some of your own illustrations for the poem.

5. Compare the pictures Base imaginatively creates for this poem with the images created by English illustrator Anthony Browne for his version of *Alice's Adventure in Wonderland* (Knopf, 1988). Discuss how the illustrations establish the setting for the story.

Base, Graeme. *My Grandma Lived in Gooligulch*. Illustrated by Graeme Base. Abrams, 1990.

This story poem tells of Grandma's many strange adventures with a menagerie of Australian animals. Grandma is eccentric and convincing as she relates how she'll ride a kangaroo around town and dine with emus. Subdued sepia-toned illustrations alternate with vibrantly colored, very detailed double-page spreads. The illustrations combine realism and exaggeration. The poem is outrageous and immeasurably fun to read aloud.

1. Compare Grandmother's deeds with those of McBroom in Sid Fleischman's McBroom series. The McBroom series is published by Little, Brown and includes, among other titles, *McBroom's Zoo* (1982) and *McBroom and the Great Race* (1980).

2. Read a story of Amelia Bedelia by Peggy Parrish and compare Amelia Bedelia's behavior to Grandmother's behavior. The Amelia Bedelia stories include *Amelia Bedelia Goes Camping* (Greenwillow, 1985), *Amelia Bedelia* (Harper, 1963), and *Amelia Bedelia Helps Out* (Greenwillow, 1979).

3. Discuss how true events can be stretched and become exaggerated to create unusual and humorous events. Write a brief paragraph telling about a true event. Write the story again, but this time stretch all the facts until the story becomes an outrageous and humorous account of the event. The story could be illustrated.

4. Base's story takes place in Australia. To build background and knowledge about that country, list the animals that Grandmother tames. Discuss (and list) other details that Base uses to show that the story takes place in Australia. Some of the details about Australia may have to be investigated to determine if they are true.

5. Have students gather and share with classmates information about the kangaroo, the emu, and the other animals that Grandmother tames. An informational mural about each animal could provide the vehicle for sharing. The mural should give significant information detailing the animal's average size, the food it eats, where in Australia (and the world) it lives, its enemies, etc. If the animal has unique characteristics, that information should also be included. Excellent sources of basic information about two animals are books by Caroline Arnold: *Kangaroo* (Morrow, 1987) and *Koala* (Morrow, 1987). These books are discussed in chapter 2. Information about the other animals in Base's book can be located by using the school or public library's catalog, the encyclopedia index, and the indexes of books about Australia.

Byrd Baylor

Byrd Baylor

From *An Author a Month (for Dimes)* by Sharron L. McElmeel (Libraries Unlimited, 1992)

Byrd Baylor

Byrd Baylor lives in the southern part of Arizona just a few miles from Mexico. She lives in an adobe house that her friends helped her build. Once the walls were up she could not stand to put in inside walls, so they left it as one room with a greenhouse. Her bathroom is in the greenhouse. Her bathtub looks like a little rock spring in a mountain pool. From her door she can see hawks' nests and rocky cliffs. She has no electricity or telephone.

Often she wanders through the desert with a backpack, searching for pieces of ancient pottery, grinding stones, and turquoise beads. She celebrates special days such as Green Cloud Day and Coyote Day. She calls herself a desert person and thinks the desert is the perfect place to write.

Byrd Baylor was born in San Antonio, Texas, on March 28, 1924. She grew up on a south Texas ranch, where she listened to her grandfather tell stories on their long walks together. When it was time for her to enter first grade, instead of sending her to school, her mother read her stories and let her explore the countryside. Her favorite book was Rudyard Kipling's *Jungle Book*. Later the family moved to Arizona and Byrd went to school in Tucson. She spent her summers in Mexico, where she and her brother roamed the deserts on the backs of burros. She grew to love the land and the animals that lived there.

Chapter

4

Byrd Baylor

ABOUT THE AUTHOR

Byrd Baylor lived her first ten years in Texas, where she was born on March 28, 1924. Her grandfather herded angora goats and farmed the land. Byrd and her grandfather often took long walks while he told her stories. Byrd Baylor often tells audiences about her formative years. Byrd's mother did not like the school that was nearest, so when it was time for Byrd to go to first grade, her mother kept her home for the year and read to her.

Byrd became an avid reader of such books as *David Copperfield* and *The Jungle Book*, and she enjoyed poetry. Her favorite poet was Edgar Allan Poe. Encouraged to explore, she found a "wonderful ditch" to investigate. On some afternoons her mother would drive her to that favorite spot and return for her several hours later. After her year at home, Byrd went to school and read "dull" things. She loved to memorize and at a very young age memorized Longfellow's poem *Hiawatha*. Byrd was ten when the family moved to Arizona. The family's home was just a few miles from the Mexican border. Her father worked in Mexico, in a gold mine. Byrd and her brother spent most of their summer days in Mexico. They attended school in Tucson, where Byrd remembers being allowed to study under a mesquite tree.

Byrd Baylor attended the University of Arizona for a short while but married before she earned her degree. She wrote her first books under the name Byrd Baylor Schweitzer. She and her husband had two sons. For a time she lived in Washington, D.C., but she became lonely for the desert and the wide open spaces. She returned to the Southwest and for a time worked as a reporter for an Arizona newspaper. Later, in Tucson, she was an executive secretary for the Association of Papago Affairs. In the early 1960s she began to use her writing skills to create children's books. Her first book was *Amigo*, illustrated by Garth Williams (Macmillan, 1963). It was a story about a Mexican boy whose father worked in the gold mine. Her next book, *One Small Blue Bead*, illustrated by Symeon Shimin (Macmillan, 1965), is the story of a cave boy, living in prehistoric times, wondering if there were other tribes out in the wilderness somewhere. In the July 1987 issue of *City Magazine* (Tucson), Baylor tells of a young boy who wrote to her. In his letter Louis said, "That book really seems close to me. I've read it seven times already. The reason I like it so much is that I'm a lot like that boy myself, only I live in an apartment and I'm fatter and Jewish." In 1992, Scribner's reissued *One Small Blue Bead* with new illustrations by Ronald Himler.

Byrd Baylor has written more than forty books. Her stories always reflect a sensitivity to the earth and its creatures and plants. Because of the subject matter of her books and the moods she evokes, she is often thought to be of Native-American ancestry. She is not. But in her work she reflects a philosophy of respect that is kindred to that of Native Americans.

She doesn't like the sound of mechanical things so she writes all her manuscripts on paper with a pencil. Besides, she says, she writes so slowly it would be an insult to a word processor. She usually has paper and pencil with her wherever she goes. Her books result from the notes she makes as she travels and observes her surroundings. Baylor thinks the desert is a perfect place to write. When she goes hiking she takes her paper, pencil, and binoculars. She writes and thinks about the generations that preceded her. She says she has been known to have "floated a whole manuscript down the Rio Grande." Her books reflect her life in the desert. Her association with the Papago Indians inspired *The Desert Is Theirs*. *When Clay Sings* was brought about by the many fragments of pottery shards she found on desert walks. And a thousand-year-old shell bracelet and many turquoise beads resulted in the beginnings of *Everybody Needs a Rock*. Her love and respect for animals and all things in nature shine through the words of all of her writing.

One day when Baylor was driving her truck in New Mexico, on her way to Santa Fe, she decided to take the southern route between Deming and Hatch. During the drive she noticed the "incredible skies" above her. In those skies was a great green cloud. She stopped her truck and got out to look. Soon another truck, with seven or eight children, stopped to look with her. They watched the cloud turn into a parrot. One of the children said that they should all come back at the same time next year and have a party. That would have been fine, but the children lived just 10 miles away and Baylor lived 450 miles away. But in spite of that, February 6 became a celebration for the green cloud. Coyotes are celebrated on September 28. She began to add these celebrations to her first celebration for Dust Devil Days, and soon she had 108 celebrations that she included in *I'm in Charge of Celebrations* (Macmillan, 1986).

Kipling's *Jungle Book* was one of her favorite books when she was a child and it still is. But she "dislikes people who take books like *Jungle Book* and make them into a movie." She also campaigns against those who destroy other living things. She feels that the human animal is no more important than any other animal. She tries to live no more destructively than any other animal, even when strange things come into her house. She has become rather adept at removing them, including the occasional rattlesnake, without doing them in. In the area where she lives there is a lot of trapping, so Baylor spends a lot of time going from trap to trap and releasing the animals. She also destroys the traps she finds. She works to keep trapping off government land. Her respect and love for animals comes through in all of her books.

One of her next books will be about the monarch butterfly. When she was working on research for that book, she found that there was an organization in Mexico City dedicated to protecting the monarch butterfly. Many believe that the butterfly holds the souls of the dead. She went to Mexico City and visited with the members of the organization. She was entranced with the sight of 10,000 butterflies that had flown to a Mexican mountain.

Baylor lives her life very simply. She is known for her statements supporting efforts to prevent tampering with the earth around us. For example, she once told an audience at the University of Arizona that "walking around on cement too much will make you crazy." She feels that it is much healthier to walk on dirt. Many modern conveniences are unnecessary and simply pollute the earth and destroy the natural habitat of animals and other small creatures.

Baylor's adobe home, without telephone or electricity, is located near a little town, Arivaca, in Pima County, Arizona. Her two sons are grown and she lives alone. She does not get her mail regularly; she picks it up when she happens to be in town or friends drop it off if they're coming past her house. It takes at least thirty minutes to travel the eight-mile dirt road leading to her house.

Baylor spends her days in the mountains and the desert, where she celebrates her surroundings and writes poetic texts for us to read. As to other things that she does, she says: "I read a lot as a child. I also lied a lot. I still read a lot." But mostly Byrd Baylor just enjoys her life in the desert.

SETTING THE STAGE

Place a map in the center of a bulletin board and mark the area where Byrd Baylor now lives — near Arivaca, in Pima County, Arizona. Search for pictures from magazines that depict that area of the country. Include, near the board, books about Arizona's geography. Complete the bulletin board by including a copy of the poster pages for Byrd Baylor and book jackets from her books. If book jackets are not available, write the titles of her books on appropriately shaped pieces of paper. For example, on a stone-shaped piece of gray paper write the title *Everybody Needs a Rock*, and on an outlined silhouette of a hawk write the title *Hawk, I'm Your Brother*.

Then set the mood to introduce Baylor and the things that have inspired her writing by reading a book by Jean Craighead George, *One Day in the Desert* (Crowell, 1983). The book begins at daybreak in the desert. A wounded mountain lion limps toward a Papago Indian hut. A young Indian girl, Bird Wing, and her mother are also headed toward their hut seeking refuge from the sun as it rises higher and higher. The temperature reaches 121 degrees, and shortly after, a thunderclap brings a deluge from Mount Scorpion. This July 10th is a memorable day.

Follow the reading of George's book with a reading of any of Baylor's books. Her poetic text will reflect the spirit of that same land, a respect for the animals, and the beauty of the surroundings. Share information about the house where Baylor lives and her philosophy about walking on dirt, trapping for animals, and her efforts to live undestructively. Then make available as many of her books as possible.

IDEA CUPBOARD

Baylor, Byrd. *And It Is Still That Way: Legends Told by Arizona Indian Children*. Scribner, 1976.

Baylor has collected traditional tales told to her by Native-American children. Native Americans traditionally have had a high regard for storytellers. The stories in the collection are told with a feeling that they are not out of the past and finished but rather that "it is still that way." The stories are illustrated by the children who told them. Children on the reservation were asked to choose the best story they had ever heard told to them by someone in their tribe. Those stories are the ones collected here.

1. Build a background of knowledge concerning the tales told by Native Americans by reading selections from the following collections.

   Baylor, Byrd. *A God on Every Mountain Top: Stories of Southwest Indian Sacred Mountains*. Illustrated by Carol Brown. Scribner, 1981.

   Bierhorst, John. *A Cry from the Earth: Music of the North American Indians*. Four Winds, 1979.

   Bierhorst, John. *The Sacred Path: Spells, Prayers, and Power Songs of the American Indians*. Morrow, 1983.

   Coatsworth, Emerson, and David Coatsworth, compilers. *The Adventures of Nanabush: Ojibway Indian Stories*. Illustrated by Francis Kagige. Atheneum, 1980.

Curtis, Edward S. *The Girl Who Married a Ghost and Other Tales from the North American Indian*. Edited by John Bierhorst. Four Winds, 1978.

Grinnell, George Bird. *The Whistling Skeleton: American Indian Tales of the Supernatural*. Edited by John Bierhorst. Illustrated by Robert Andrew Parker. Four Winds, 1982.

Harris, Christie. *Mouse Woman and the Vanished Princesses*. Illustrated by Douglas Tait. Atheneum, 1976.

Harris, Christie. *The Trouble with Adventurers*. Illustrated by Douglas Tait. Atheneum, 1982.

Robinson, Gail. *Raven the Trickster: Legends of the North American Indians*. Illustrated by Joanna Troughton. Atheneum, 1982.

Wallas, James. *Kwakiutl Legends*. Recorded by Pamela Whitaker. Hancock House, 1981.

Whitaker, Muriel, editor. *Stories from the Canadian North*. Illustrated by Vlasta Van Kampen. Harwig, 1980.

2. Use Baylor's collection of stories told by children to motivate students to interview their older relatives and to record stories told in their families. This project will have to be accomplished over an extended period of time, as students will need to identify relatives to interview, collect and record the stories told, and finally retell the stories in written form to share with others. If the stories are to be put in book form, a method of binding will have to be decided upon. A spiral binder, if available, might be the quickest and simplest option. Other methods include stapling, placing in a three-hole binder, and making a cloth-covered binder for the story. The story will make a welcome gift to the original storyteller or to any other member of the family for whom the story has significance. (If multiple copies are to be made, ask students to use only black-and-white illustrations so that they will reproduce on the duplicating machines available in most schools/libraries. Color could be added after the copies are made.) This project will provide an opportunity to put into action the writing steps: draft, revision, editing, rewriting, final revision and editing, and final copy.

Baylor, Byrd. *Before You Came This Way*. Illustrated by Tom Bahti. Dutton, 1969.
Baylor's poetry describes the Native-American petroglyphs, created in ancient times, on the canyon walls of the Southwest.

1. Use an unabridged dictionary to help define *petroglyph*. Find out as much information as possible about petroglyphs. What are they and where have they been found?

2. Read Gloria Skurzynski's *Trapped in Slickrock Canyon* (Lothrop, 1984) as a group reading for intermediate-age readers or as a read-aloud for younger students. The book deals with thieves who attempt to remove a petroglyph from the wall of a canyon and are discovered by Justin and Gina. Justin thinks his rich, spoiled brat cousin, Gina, will get in his way during the summer that Gina and her father visit Justin's family in the mesa country of Arizona. But on the day the two cousins decide to go into the canyon, they come across the thieves attempting to remove a valuable petroglyph from the canyon wall. The cousins find themselves being pursued by the thieves through the dangerous canyon and trapped by a flash flood. In the course of telling an exciting story, Skurzynski gives the reader considerable information about petroglyphs and their importance in recording the history of the southwestern region of the United States.

Baylor, Byrd. *The Best Town in the World*. Illustrated by Ronald Himler. Scribner, 1983.

This book is set in a small Texas town where the blackberries are tastier, the dogs smarter, and the creek water clearer and colder.

1. Many people would consider wherever they are currently living the "best place in the world." Describe your "best place/town in the world." What makes the place special for you? The special place may be the town where you live now or a town where you would like to live.

2. As a group, brainstorm a list of attributes that would make your school "the best school in the world." Use the list to evaluate your school—is it the "best school in the world"? Why or why not? What can the group do to help the school achieve "best school in the world" status?

Baylor, Byrd. *Coyote Cry*. Illustrated by Symeon Shimin. Lothrop, 1972.

Antonio and his grandfather hear many coyote cries as they herd their sheep; but one cry is different—it is the call of a female who has lost her puppies. When the coyote steals a puppy from the sheep dog, Antonio recognizes the maternal instinct of this predator he had always regarded as an enemy. The most poignant moment in this book comes when the coyote sneaks back into the camp to see the puppy one last time. They touch noses and say good-bye.

1. While the coyote is often portrayed as mean and menacing in the folklore of other cultures, in the legends of Native Americans the coyote is often honored and revered. After reading other stories about the coyote, use a character web (see example following booklist) to describe the attributes those stories give the coyote.

Baker, Betty. *And Me, Coyote!* Illustrated by Maria Horvath. Macmillan, 1982.

Baker, Betty. *Partners*. Illustrated by Emily Arnold McCully. Greenwillow, 1978.

Baylor, Byrd. *Moon Song*. Illustrated by Ronald Himler. Scribner, 1982.

Bernstein, Margery, and Janet Kobrin. *Coyote Goes Hunting for Fire: A California Indian Myth*. Illustrated by Ed Hoffernan. Scribner, 1974.

Carrick, Carol. *Two Coyotes*. Illustrated by Donald Carrick. Houghton, 1982.

Character Web

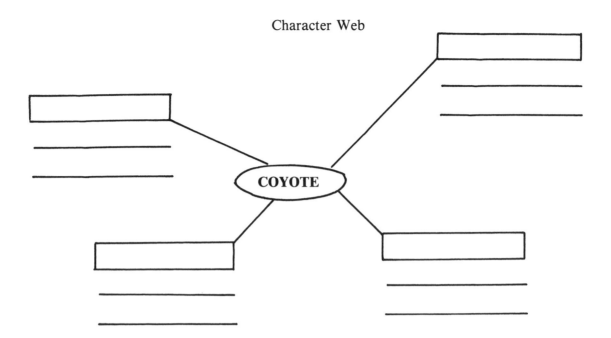

As books about the coyote are read, determine characteristics that you would attribute to the coyote, in general. Those characteristics should be placed in the rectangles. On the lines below the rectangles cite the passages, lines, or phrases that support your choice of characteristic trait.

2. As a group, brainstorm information about the coyote. Use a technique similar to that described in chapter 2 in the first activity for *Kangaroo*. After investigating and confirming the information gathered in brainstorming, make a chart, or other visual display, sharing information about the coyote.

Baylor, Byrd. *The Desert Is Theirs*. Illustrated by Peter Parnall. Scribner, 1975.
   Parnall's sparse full-color drawings contribute to the simplicity of this lyrical prose poem of the "strong brown Desert people." Baylor speaks of the Papagos, who try not to disturb their animal brothers, and of selected flora and fauna found in the desert.

1. Write about why a person would or would not like to live in the desert.

2. The Papagos, a Native-American tribe, live in the southwestern part of the United States. Use reference books in the library/media center to learn more about this group of people. There may not be entire books about the Papagos, so be sure to check sources that tell about various Native-American tribes, and locate information specifically about the Papagos by using the index in those books.

3. The Association of Papago Affairs, 6542 W. Indian School Road, Tucson, AZ 85200, is an agency specifically concerned with the Papago tribe. Write a business letter requesting information about the Papagos. Be sure to include a self-addressed 9"-×-11" manila envelope, stamped with sufficient return postage.

4. Extend the mood of *The Desert Is Theirs* by reading Baylor's *Desert Voices*, illustrated by Peter Parnall (Scribner, 1981).

Baylor, Byrd. *Everybody Needs a Rock*. Illustrated by Peter Parnall, Scribner, 1974.

Parnall's sparse semi-abstract black-and-white drawings, highlighted with touches of brown and ocher, complement Baylor's concrete poetic form as she relates the ten rules for finding a special rock. Only the owner will know if it is "easy in your hand" or "jumpy in your pocket when you run."

1. Rocks come in many different shapes and sizes. Their shapes may suggest a certain "personality." Go on a walk and find a rock that is appealing. Explain how you knew it was *just the right rock*.

2. Read other books about rocks or pebbles and discuss why that rock or pebble is just right for the person who has it.

   Lionni, Leo. *Alexander and the Wind-up Mouse*. Illustrated by Leo Lionni. Pantheon, 1969.

   Lionni, Leo. *On My Beach There Are Many Pebbles*. Illustrated by Leo Lionni. Astor-Honor, 1961.

   Steig, William. *Sylvester and the Magic Pebble*. Illustrated by William Steig. Windmill, 1969.

3. Develop students' creative thinking by asking them to work in pairs or small groups to add their own rules to the list of rules for finding that special rock. Or make a list of rules for finding other special objects: a type of flower, a hat, a cane, a pencil, etc.

Baylor, Byrd. *Hawk, I'm Your Brother*. Illustrated by Peter Parnall. Scribner, 1976.

This narrative poem describes the taming and freeing of a boy's hawk. Rudy Soto's selfishness in confining the hawk is gently dealt with in a nonjudgmental manner. Rudy discovers that no one can be free if others are not allowed to be free. It is unclear whether this story is intended to be Native American or Chicano, and that seems intentional on the author's part. Baylor focuses more on the values of these groups of people rather than on their color, living style, traditions, or other obvious aspects of their culture. The theme is unity between human beings and nature. The illustrations capture the glorious sweep of a hawk in flight and help to interrelate the sky and human beings.

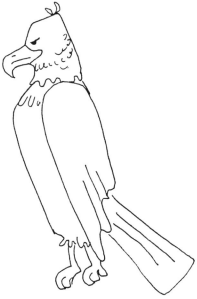

1. This book gives readers a feeling for the magnificence of the hawk. Locate information about the hawk. What areas of the world does it inhabit? How wide is its wing span? Motivate an investigative activity by making a collective list of things students know or would like to know about hawks. Mark those statements that are questionable or about which the group needs more information, then invite the students to research those statements. Locate books about birds and use the indexes to locate specific information about the hawk. There may also be books dealing specifically with the hawk. Those can be located by using the catalog of the school or public library.

2. Parnall's sepia illustrations appear to have been created using a soft-leaded drawing pencil. Suggest that students create illustrations of their own; the drawings should reflect respect for the hawk and its surroundings. If several students create illustrations, display them in a grouping with the heading "Hawk, We're Your Brothers."

Baylor, Byrd. *Moon Song*. Illustrated by Ronald Himler. Scribner, 1982.
    This is a Pima Indian legend. Coyote and his descendants gather on the hills and sing their longing song to the moon. The moon fills them with mysterious power.

1. Native Americans and members of other cultures have given moon names to the moon during specific months or seasons. Some of the more common names found in literature are:

    January—Old Moon, Moon After Yule, Wolf Moon, Winter Moon, Deep Snow Moon

    February—Snow Moon, Hunger Moon, Wolf Moon, Trapper's Moon, Crust of Snow Moon

    March—Sap Moon, Crow Moon, Lenten Moon, Fish Moon, Worm Moon, Snowshoe Breaking Moon

    April—Grass Moon, Egg Moon, Sprouting Grass Moon, Pink Moon, Planter's Moon, Maple Sugar Moon

    May—Planting Moon, Milk Moon, Mother's Moon, Flower Moon, Budding Plant Moon

    June—Rose Moon, Flower Moon, Strawberry Moon, Stockman's Moon

    July—Thunder Moon, Hay Moon, Buck Moon, Summer Moon, Midsummer Moon

    August—Green Corn Moon, Grain Moon, Sturgeon Moon, Harvest Moon

    September—Harvest Moon, Fruit Moon, Fall Moon, Wild Rice Moon

    October—Hunter's Moon, Dying Grass Moon, Harvest Moon, Falling Leaves Moon

    November—Frosty Moon, Beaver Moon, Hunter's Moon, Freezing Moon

    December—Long Night Moon, Moon Before Yule, Cold Moon, Christmas Moon, Descending Cold Moon

    Each of the moons has a story behind it. For example, Native Americans called the February moon the Hunger Moon because of the sparsity of animals and food available for hunting or gathering during this month. A Harvest Moon is usually a full moon during the harvest season. It is during this time that the moon offers light for the hunter or farmer who works late into the night. Other names indicate humans' concern or fear about snow, wolves, and starvation.

    a. Write a story about how a full moon (or any of the other moons) came to have the name it does.

    b. Suggest another name for a full moon and explain why the moon should have that name.

2. Focus on the stages of the moon by reading other moon stories:

    Asch, Frank. *Happy Birthday, Moon!* Illustrated by Frank Asch. Prentice, 1982.

    Asch, Frank. *Moon Bear*. Illustrated by Frank Asch. Scribner, 1978.

Asch, Frank. *Mooncake*. Illustrated by Frank Asch. Prentice, 1983.

McDermott, Gerald. *Anansi the Spider: A Tale from the Ashanti*. Holt, 1972.

Sleator, William. *The Angry Moon*. Illustrated by Blair Lent. Little, 1970.

Thurber, James. *Many Moons*. Illustrated by Marc Simont. Harcourt, 1990.

Willard, Nancy. *The Nightgown of the Sullen Moon*. Illustrated by David McPhail. Harcourt, 1983.

Baylor, Byrd. *One Small Blue Bead*. Illustrated by Ronald Himler. Scribner, 1992. (Originally published by Macmillan in 1965 with illustrations by Symeon Shimin.)
   The story of a prehistoric boy is told in verse. The people of the boy's tribe believe that they are the only humans in existence. An old man sets out on a quest to answer his questions about that belief. "Boy" volunteers to take the old man's place in the tribal community. Months later, the old man returns with living proof that others exist. With the old man is another boy, a stranger from another tribe, who brings with him a turquoise bead. The bead becomes a symbol of the tribe's connection to other human beings.

   1. If the original edition (with Shimin's illustrations) is available, compare and contrast the effect the illustrations and book design have on each other and the mood evoked, as well as the subtle differences or similarities in feeling and empathy, for example. In the Scribner edition the text is crowded onto fewer pages. The boy in the story has not contributed much to his tribe up to the time he volunteers to take the old man's place. In Himler's illustrations the boy seems to be much older than the very young child portrayed in the Shimin depictions. The depiction of the boy as older brings to question how he had avoided working as a member of the tribe. Shimin's pictures are basically one color, but Himler's seem more vital, with brilliant blue skies and clear, cool earth colors. Although there are differences in the illustrations, the similarities are also striking — Himler's illustrations, in composition, subject matter, and placement of figures and poses, seem to be based on Shimin's ideas. However, Himler has added a depth of elaboration with detail and color. The figures in Shimin's work seem to be lithe and graceful, and Himler's figures appear blocky and stiff.

   2. The notion that one tribe is the only group of human beings on earth is similar to the notion that we earthlings are the only civilization in the universe. Discuss the possibility of intelligent life in other parts of the universe. Investigate theories about life on other planets.

   3. The small blue bead becomes a symbol for the connection between human beings. Many groups have symbols for their unity or connection. For example, some fraternal lodges have a special handshake, sports teams have a special color or uniform, and other groups have a flag or insignia. Make a list of icons that signify a connection between individuals in your community.

Baylor, Byrd. *They Put on Masks*. Illustrated by Jerry Ingram. Scribner, 1974.
   Indian and Eskimo masks and ceremonies are the subject of this book. The verses tell about the uses and meanings of masks. Illustrations are flat, colorful, stylized portrayals of masks in green, yellow, blue, pink, and mauve. Five masks are shown on each double-page spread.

   1. Investigate the significance of the masks and learn about the ceremonies and songs that accompany the masks. Either of the following books may help.

Alkema, Chester Jay. *Masks*. Sterling, 1971.

Hunt, Kari, and Bernice Carlson. *Masks and Mask Makers*. Abingdon, 1961.

2. Experiment with making masks. The masks can be used as decorative objects or for story-telling. The following books may be useful.

Payne, G. C. *Adventures in Paper Modeling*. Warne, 1966.

Ross, Laura. *Mask-Making with Pantomime and Stories from American History*. Lothrop, 1975.

Baylor, Byrd. *The Way to Start a Day*. Illustrated by Peter Parnall. Scribner, 1978.
This book describes the way the cave dwellers, the Peruvians, and the people of Africa, Egypt, and China welcomed the new day with their song, gift, or blessing.

1. Start the day by going outdoors and welcoming the sun. Write special welcome verses for the day.

2. Design a welcoming day poster. Use colors that will reflect how you want the day to be—yellow for bright and sunny, red for bright and exciting, blue for calm and cool, etc. Before making the poster decide as a group what mood each color represents, then use those colors appropriately in your poster. Mary O'Neill's *Hailstones and Halibut Bones* (Doubleday, 1961; 1989) may be helpful.

Baylor, Byrd. *When Clay Sings*. Illustrated by Tom Bahti. Scribner, 1972.
This is a lyrical treatment of archaeology and the art of the Native Americans that live in the Southwest. The pen-and-ink drawings of Bahti, by accurately representing the primitive figures and designs found on the pottery, bring to life the prehistoric period and its people. Baylor's text describes both the artifacts from the past and the people who created them.

1. Compare the images of art objects in Baylor's book with the images in Shirley Glubok's *The Art of the North American Indian* (Harper, 1964). Glubok's book shows, through photographs, many examples of the art created by Native Americans in North America.

2. Have students make coil pots and carve their own design into the side of the pots. Dry the pots in the sun and fire them if a kiln is available. If your school has an art teacher, ask her or him if this project might meet objectives in the art curriculum. If so, work together to integrate this project into both the art class and the language arts period.

3. Compare the pottery created by Native Americans with the pottery/ceramics made in Gail Gibbons's *The Pottery Place* (Harcourt, 1987). Gibbons's book gives a simplified view of the work of a rural potter. After the potter mixes her clay and throws it, she bisques, glazes, fires, packs, and delivers her pots.

4. Invite a potter to visit your class and describe the art of making pottery today.

5. After visiting with a potter or investigating the length of time it takes to complete a pot, make a timeline showing the process.

6. The November 1982 issue of *National Geographic* contains an article titled "Pueblo Pottery." If the article is available, use it to compare the prehistoric pottery with the pottery made by the same tribes today.

Baylor, Byrd. *Your Own Best Secret Place*. Illustrated by Peter Parnall, Scribner, 1979.

A young girl describes her own secret places and those of her friends. Included are a barn, a sand dune, and a pear tree. Each of the places was special to someone, much as Baylor's "wonderful ditch" was a special place to her during her growing-up years.

1. Build readers' familiarity with the theme of secret or special places by reading other books or selections about special places:

   Burnett, Frances Hodgson. *The Secret Garden*. Adapted by James Howe. Illustrated by Thomas B. Allen. Random, 1987.

   Burnett, Frances Hodgson. *The Secret Garden*. Harper, 1962. (Novel)

   deRegniers, Beatrice Schenk. *Little House of Your Own*. Illustrated by Irene Haas. Harcourt, 1954.

   Livingston, Myra Cohn. *I'm Hiding*. Illustrated by Erik Blegvad. Harcourt, 1961.

   Paterson, Katherine. *Bridge to Terabithia*. Crowell, 1977. (Novel)

2. Describe "your own best secret place." Where is it? What do you do there? Why is it so special? Write about it or show the special place in an illustration.

Jan Brett

Jan Brett

From *An Author a Month (for Dimes)* by Sharron L. McElmeel (Libraries Unlimited, 1992)

Jan Brett

Jan Brett was born on December 1, 1949, in Hingham, Massachusetts, a seacoast town. She often read books and drew pictures of horses and the many animals she had as pets. One of her pet chickens, Delly, used to ride on her shoulder.

Jan Brett still has a quarterhorse, Westminster. "Westy" is sometimes stubborn, just like the reindeer in *The Wild Christmas Reindeer*. Her Siberian husky, Perky Pumpkin, has one brown eye and one blue eye. Her smallest pet is a mouse, Little Pearl II, who appears in *The Mitten*. When Jan Brett's daughter, Lia, was young, she wanted a wolf or a moose for a pet. Jan Brett put that idea in *Annie and the Wild Animals*.

Drawing illustrations filled with animals and images from her travels is considered by Jan Brett to be the best part of telling a story. She observed hedgehogs in England and visited the Ukrainian section of New York City before creating *The Mitten*. She traveled to Martinique in the Caribbean before illustrating Edward Lear's *The Owl and the Pussycat*, to Bavaria before illustrating *Berlioz the Bear*, and to Norway to see the beautiful designs on blankets, sleighs, and harnesses in folk museums before illustrating *The Wild Christmas Reindeer*.

Jan Brett and her husband, Joe Hearne, live in Norwell, Massachusetts. In the summer they move to a cabin in the Berkshire Mountains where she paints and her husband plays with the Boston Symphony at its summer festival home in Tanglewood, in western Massachusetts.

Chapter

5

Jan Brett

ABOUT THE AUTHOR/ILLUSTRATOR

When Jan Brett was growing up in Hingham, Massachusetts, she had many animals. She spent a lot of time drawing animals and reading. She especially liked horses and drew them over and over again, trying to perfect her drawings. The animals she had while growing up—horses, dogs, cats, guinea pigs, rabbits—often show up in her illustrations.

In the late 1960s Jan Brett enrolled in the New London Academy (now Colby-Sawyer College), and in 1970 she attended the Boston Museum of Fine Arts School. She spent much time in the museum and marveled at the huge landscapes, the stone sculptures, the delicately embroidered kimonos, and the ancient porcelain. Her illustrations are filled with the images and animals she has gathered during extensive travel and research.

In 1970 she married Daniel Bowler, whom she divorced in 1979. They had one daughter, Lia. *Woodland Crossings* by Stephen Krensky (Atheneum, 1978) was illustrated by Brett under the name Jan Brett Bowler. Her later books have been published under the name Jan Brett. In 1980 she married Joseph Hearne, a musician with the Boston Symphony Orchestra.

Brett's daughter's desire for a pet wolf or moose planted the seed for Brett's illustrated story *Annie and the Wild Animals*. The story tells of a little girl whose pet cat disappears in the woods. Over a period of days the girl is visited by a succession of wild animals. Through the story Brett is able to explore the differences between wild animals and friendly pets.

Ideas for other of her books came from experiences in her life. Jan Brett once met a little girl, Miriam, who was very unusual. Brett thought that the face of this curious child could have come out of the past and wanted to put her into a book. Miriam's sense of adventure brought about Brett's version of *Goldilocks and the Three Bears*. She used Miriam as her model for both Goldilocks's spunky personality and physical features. Brett's pet mouse, Little Pearl II, was a model for a mouse that readers can find in *Goldilocks and the Three Bears* and for the mouse that appears in *The Mitten*.

Three teacher friends suggested that Brett retell *The Mitten* because they thought she would like to draw the animals and the snowy scenery that are part of the story. When she began to search for the story, she talked with a Ukrainian woman named Oxana Piaseckyj, who helped Brett by translating eight different versions of the tale into English. One of the versions had the animals crawl into an old pot, which breaks into bits when too many animals squeeze in. Another version, this one with a violent ending, told of a hunter who when he finds his lost glove filled with animals blasts it with his gun in order to have food for his family's dinner. After hearing different versions, Jan Brett created a retelling that included the important aspects of the tale but gave the story a new twist at the end. Since the story was Ukrainian in origin, Jan Brett and her husband, Joe Hearne, went to the Ukrainian section of New York City to find out what a Ukrainian house looked like and to gather other bits of information about the Ukrainian culture. One of the guides at the museum suggested that the clothes should look too big since clothes were often handmade and had to last a long time. Also, clothes were usually handed down from one wearer to another. Brett also learned that Ukrainians often hang a water jug on their fence to tell those passing by that they are welcome to help themselves to a cool drink. A stork's nest on the cottage roof was thought to bring good luck.

Brett had to decide whether or not to have the animals wear clothing and talk. She felt that she could not have the little boy talk if the animals did. She decided to use a hedgehog in the story, but hedgehogs live only in Europe and they are nocturnal animals, so other animals might not have ever seen a hedgehog. Brett traveled to England, where she visited the St. Tiggywinkles wildlife hospital, a hospital that has one entire wing devoted to the care of hedgehogs. She learned that hedgehogs roll up when they sense danger. They forage at night for insects, and many experts believe that hedgehogs just naturally turn over objects looking for bugs. Many gardeners like hedgehogs because they eat destructive bugs. Brett found she liked them because they are gentle and determined, are covered with prickles, and have a nice shape—she especially likes their noses. Brett observed their distinctive walk. She describes their walk as "not a waddle, and it's not a scurry; it's more like a scuttle." At the hospital Brett and her husband sponsored three hedgehogs: Ryeship, Julie, and Mowgli. Each of them needed special care but were eventually released back into the wild.

Brett's art director suggested that using a model for characters in her book would help her avoid drawing the same person over and over. The model for the little boy, Nicki, in *The Mitten* was one of Brett's neighbors, Tad Beagley, who seemed full of energy. Tad climbed trees, jumped walls, and leaped into the air so that Brett could take pictures. Baba's model was Jan Brett's mother, Jean Brett. Brett changed her mother's shiny brown hair to snowy white. She also used her artistic license to put a long braid on her mother's head. In the illustrations Brett was able to include traditional ceramics, a fireplace, and coral beads, all of which might have been found in an ordinary, traditional Ukrainian home. Some of Brett's research indicated that Ukrainian women would have worn a head scarf, so Brett put a head scarf on Baba. However, Brett felt that Baba did not look friendly with the head scarf, so she put the scarf on a peg. Later she was told that wearing a head scarf was an old-fashioned custom that some considered sexist, so Brett was glad that she did not leave the scarf on Baba's head. She did put a ceramic jug upside down on a fence as an invitation for strangers to dip into the stream, and she put a stork's nest on the roof. Brett also dressed Nicki in handmade clothes that were slightly too large.

After deciding to illustrate Edward Lear's *The Owl and the Pussycat*, Jan Brett traveled to Martinique to gather ideas and take pictures for her illustrations. Her choice of settings was influenced by a friend who had sailed to the area intending to stay a short while; he stayed for ten years. The Caribbean was filled with images and style. Colors that were common for Martinique fishing boats, such as pink and azure blue, would not have been found in New England. While in Martinique Brett observed that many women wore white blouses and skirts with lots of white petticoats. They also wore brightly colored turbans, tied in a traditional fashion. Turbans tied with one point indicated that the wearer was single, two points that she had a boyfriend, three points that she was married, and four points that she was married but loved attention. When the illustrations for *The Owl and the Pussycat* were completed, Brett had depicted the owl as a sugar cane plantation worker who had just been paid. The pussycat is shown as owning her own little shop, a shop similar to many of the shops that are on Martinique. Pussycat is surprised at Owl's proposal. They go to sea in a pea-green boat with the name "Promise" on its side. Beneath the boat Brett depicts a pair of yellow fish who have their own story. In Lear's original manuscript for *The Owl and the Pussycat*, the "Bong tree" was called a "palm tree," so Brett wanted to find a real tree to use as a model to depict a bong tree. Eventually she discovered a tree that looked as if it had ping pong balls all over it. Piggy, who was to marry Owl and Pussycat, is depicted as a beachcomber (one who used to have a nine-to-five job). The turkey is shown as a pompous individual. The scene includes palm trees and the terra-cotta jugs that are often seen on local plantations. The traditional turban, sometimes with one point, sometimes with three points, sits on Pussycat's head. Many details about the setting and story are included in the four-sided borders.

For *The Wild Christmas Reindeer*, Jan Brett began with an idea about the North Pole. Her image of Santa Claus was one of a toymaker who loved to make toys for children. To help him she imagined elves who at one time actually existed and who now live in a secret place known as Santa's Winterfarm. She knew she would love to draw the reindeer. She wanted the reindeer to be important to the story, so she began to think about the problems elves might have if Santa asked them to get the reindeer ready to fly on Christmas Eve. She thought about her own problems with her horse, Westminster. Sometimes when Westy would not do what she wanted him to do, Brett got angry and lost her temper. That only made things worse. Brett soon learned that if she remained calm, things improved. She had the very same thing happen to the elf girl, Teeka, and the reindeer. Teeka's image was modeled after a very special girl named Natalie. Natalie acted out all of the things that Brett imagined Teeka would do in the story. Brett watched Natalie's movements, took photographs, and drew sketches so that she could create realistic illustrations. The original drawings of Teeka depicted her with the same long hair and graceful curls that Natalie had. But Brett's editor suggested that the long hair made Teeka look too modern, so Brett redrew the images to show Teeka with shorter hair.

Many of the decorations in *The Wild Christmas Reindeer* came from images Jan Brett and her husband saw when they visited folk museums in Norway. They saw beautiful designs on sleighs, clocks, spoons, harnesses, and blankets. Brett discovered that the caribou in North America and the reindeer in Europe are varieties of the same animal. To learn how to draw reindeer Brett and her husband paid a visit to the University of Maine, where scientists were studying caribou. Brett was able to get very close to the caribou and was able to find out what the tummy of a caribou looked like so that she could show Lichen, one of the reindeer that appear in the book, upside down. She decided that the reindeer she was writing about were probably the great-great-grandchildren of the ones that Clement Moore wrote about in his poem "A Visit from St. Nicholas." So she was able to name the reindeer and give each one his or her own personality. Tundra liked being first and saw himself as a noble leader. The pure white and chubby reindeer was named Snowball. Crag was sometimes called "Crab" when he was too grumpy. Twilight was dark and mysterious, and Heather was easily frightened. She had big, brown eyes. Brett discovered that each caribou or reindeer's antlers are different, so she created each of the reindeer with its own distinctive antlers. Bramble was named for the shape of his antlers. Because the seventh reindeer often forgot to stop once he got started, he was named Windswept. The last reindeer was named Lichen because of the mossy-like markings on his coat.

Berlioz the Bear was inspired by Brett's pleasure in the Boston Symphony. Her husband, Joe, plays the double bass, and one day Brett began to wonder what would happen if something very small crawled into his bass and began to play. Later she learned that weather sometimes affects musical instruments. Joe's three-hundred-year-old bass produces a loud and annoying buzz when it becomes too dry. Eventually Brett developed a story line about an orchestra composed of bears that have a problem getting to a town festival. They get stuck because the driver of their mule-drawn cart is distracted by a buzzing coming from his bass. Once stuck, the mule becomes stubborn and will not pull the cart out; finally a bee flies out from the bass and stings the mule. The orchestra arrives at the town square just in time for the concert. To gather the images for the illustrations for this book, Brett and Hearne, while on a Boston Symphony Orchestra tour to Europe, took a side trip to Bavaria. They went on May Day in hopes of being able to observe a town festival, the kind often held in the town square. They were fortunate to find a concert in Grunwald. Brett sketched and photographed the costumed Bavarians as they raised the May Pole, the orchestra as it played, and the people as they danced. Brett and Hearne also enjoyed eating weisswurst. They searched for a decorated bandwagon similar to the ones they had seen depicted on posters and carvings, but they could not locate a real one until they visited the village of Bad Tolz. The folk museum in that village had a real cart. They took many photographs. When Brett returned to Massachusetts, she had a scale model of the cart constructed so that she could use it as she painted her illustrations. She found an especially endearing plowhorse in Bavaria, one that looked as if it really wanted to be in her book. The schnauzer that appears in the book was found near her home. The dog is her neighbor's pet, Gretchen. When it came to the bear characters, Jan Brett looked toward the Boston Symphony. In her drawings she lengthened her husband's nose, rounded his ears, covered him with fur, and made him Berlioz—the star of the book. The reddish bear was modeled after the symphony's clarinetist, Tom Martin, who is tall and lanky. The trombonist, Norman Bolter, became the dark bear with the expressive eyes; the blond drummer, Tom Gauger, became the blond bear; and the Boston Symphony's cellist, Martha Babcock, became a French horn-playing bear, while her husband, Harvey Seigel, became a violin-playing bear.

When Jan Brett creates a book, she starts with what she feels is the hardest part—writing the story. In each of her stories something happens that causes a change. In *The Mitten* it is a sneeze that creates the change. In *The Wild Christmas Reindeer* it is Teeka's change from bossy to helpful that causes the change in the reindeer's behavior. In *Berlioz the Bear* it is a bee sting that causes the stubborn mule to get the bandwagon to the festival on time. After the story line is completed, Brett creates a book dummy, a simple version of the book. She uses a cartoon style that doesn't take too much time. The dummy gives her a first impression of what her book will look like. During the process of creating the book, changes take place that contribute to the final version. After planning spaces for the words, Brett creates a pencil sketch for the final version. Often she uses photographs to help her construct the paintings. For *Berlioz the Bear* she asked the symphony members she intended to feature as bears in her book to attend a photo session, where each was photographed as they went through the actions that take place on each frame of the dummy. By using her photographs of characters, photographs of the settings from her travels, and her preliminary sketches, Brett was able to paint the characters in their setting. Her art tools are simple: pen and ink, small brushes, watercolors, good light, and imagination. She uses a very small amount of water on her brushes to keep the colors from running together.

Brett creates many of her books with borders. The borders give her an opportunity to add images and ideas that she cannot easily put into the main frame of the story. For example, in *The Mitten* the borders show Nicki trudging through the woods, while the main picture focuses on the animals and their efforts to squeeze into the lost mitten. In the border art Brett shows Nicki scaring different animals out of their hiding places. On the following page in the book, the animal Nicki has scared out appears in the mitten scene. Since the animals grow in size throughout the book, the green branches serve as a marker to indicate the animals' size. The borders of *The Wild Christmas Reindeer* show the activity in Santa's workshop as the calendar marks the days during the time Teeka is training the reindeer. The borders of *Annie and the Wild Animals* tell a second story by showing the cat and what is happening to her in the woods while Annie is trying to lure a new pet to her yard by placing corn cakes at the edge of the woods. The borders eventually show the kittens that are born and mature in the hollow tree. In the final pages of the book, the cat and her kittens move from the hollow tree (and the border story) to arrive back in Annie's yard (and the main story frames), where Annie welcomes them all home. The side borders for *Berlioz the Bear* depict the authentically dressed concertgoers as they arrive in the town square. The top border shows the animals as they set up the town square for the festival and the concert.

Brett's art is quite intricate, and it takes her an hour to do one inch, or about two days to complete a page. The art for *The Mitten* took four months to complete, and the art for *The Wild Christmas Reindeer* took five months. She tells young artists that some artists can draw some things better than others. She says she cannot draw motorcycles or bridges very well. But she especially enjoys drawing animals and is proud of them. Her books are filled with animals and intricate designs.

Jan Brett lives with her husband, Joe, in Norwell, Massachusetts. During the summer months they move to a cabin in the Berkshire Mountains where Brett is able to paint in a setting near a shimmering lake surrounded by birds and wild animals. Joe is a musician with the Boston Symphony Orchestra, and during the summer the orchestra's festival home is in Tanglewood, in western Massachusetts, near the family's summer cabin. Joe plays the double bass as does Berlioz in *Berlioz the Bear*. Brett and Hearne's combined family includes three grown daughters.

SETTING THE STAGE

Create a Jan Brett bulletin board divided into interest sections. In one section place colorful boats (silhouette cutouts similar to the boat in *The Owl and the Pussycat*) and children's drawings of an owl and a pussycat. In another section feature pictures of animals, mitten shapes, and paper snowflakes. In a third section feature pictures of a double bass, a French horn, a trombone, a drum, and a violin, along with drawings of bears. Feature other titles illustrated by Jan Brett in a similar fashion in additional sections on the bulletin board. Tie the sections together with a center section bordered by book jackets from books Brett has illustrated. In the center of that section, place a copy of the author poster pages from this book.

Since Jan Brett uses watercolors, set up a watercoloring center near the bulletin board. Encourage children to experiment with the medium by making paintings of animals they like, pictures of the three bears, pictures of the owl and the pussycat's pea-green boat, or brightly decorated mittens.

Introduce children to Jan Brett by reading aloud one of the books she has illustrated and by sharing information about her life and her books. Brett seems to have a fascination for hedgehogs. Look through her books and find where she managed to include them. In *Goldilocks and the Three Bears* she included a couple of tiny wooden hedgehogs. The hedgehog is a main character in her retelling of *The Mitten* and also appears in her *The Wild Christmas Reindeer*. Hedgehogs live in northern Europe and Asia, Asia Minor, southern and eastern Africa, and New Zealand, so even though hedgehogs seem to be Brett's favorite animal she includes them only in books set in the appropriate locations. As readers enjoy Brett's books, encourage them to notice other clever illustrative touches that she includes in her pictures: the word on the mule's harness (in *Berlioz the Bear*), the figure on top of the double bass (*Berlioz the Bear*), the pussycat's turban (*The Owl and the Pussycat*), the wooden bedstead carved in the shape of a bear (*Goldilocks and the Three Bears*), and the two mice with bulging stomachs fast asleep under an overflowing jar of honey (*Goldilocks and the Three Bears*). Discuss Brett's illustrative style and notice the variety of borders and the type of information she includes in her borders. Suggest that books written and illustrated by class members might utilize borders on the cover or on some or all of the pages of the books. Make sure that rulers and other measuring devices, which might assist in making borders, are included in the illustration center.

IDEA CUPBOARD

Brett, Jan. *Annie and the Wild Animals*. Illustrated by Jan Brett. Houghton, 1985.

Annie's beautiful golden-haired cat, Taffy, disappears on a snowy day. Annie attempts to find a new animal to tame by putting corn cakes at the edge of the forest. She is successful in attracting a moose, a bear, a wildcat, a stag and his family, and a gray wolf. She does not think any of them are suitable for taming. Finally, the snow melts, the sun comes out, and Taffy emerges from the green forest. And behind her are three cuddly soft kittens. Brett uses her characteristic borders to full advantage as she foreshadows the action that is to come on the following pages. The birth of the young kittens and their emergence weeks later with their eyes open are depicted in selected border scenes well before they appear in the main illustrations.

1. Visually this book brings to mind another of Brett's books, *The Mitten*. Compare the illustrations in the two books, particularly noting the animals and the settings. Are the stories set in the same area? Defend your answer.

2. Discuss whether this story could really have happened. Why or why not?

3. Research information about each of the animals in the story. Would any of the animals eat corn cakes? What would the animals eat if Annie had not fed them corn cakes?

Brett, Jan, reteller. *Beauty and the Beast*. Illustrated by Jan Brett. Clarion, 1989.
This retelling remains faithful to the traditional tale first retold by Madame deBeaumont.

1. Compare and contrast this complex story to Kathleen Hague and Michael Hague's retelling of a French tale, *East of the Sun and West of the Moon*, illustrated by Michael Hague (Harcourt, 1980), or to the Scottish tale "Black Bull of Norroway," retold in Flora Annie Steel's *English Fairy Tales*, illustrated by Arthur Rackham (Macmillan, 1962 [1918]).

2. Compare the retelling and the illustrations, particularly the manner in which the beast is depicted, in Brett's illustrated version of "The Beauty and the Beast" with one or more of the following retellings. Goode depicts the beast in her story as a lion-maned beast, while other versions show the beast as a cat or an ogre.

   Apy, Deborah. *Beauty and the Beast*. Illustrated by Michael Hague. Holt, 1983.

   deBeaumont, Madame. *Beauty and the Beast*. Translated and illustrated by Diane Goode. Bradbury, 1978.

   Harris, Rosemary, reteller. *Beauty and the Beast*. Illustrated by Errol Le Cain. Doubleday, 1979.

   Hutton, Warwick, reteller. *Beauty and the Beast*. Illustrated by Warwick Hutton. Atheneum, 1985.

Mayer, Marianne, reteller. *Beauty and the Beast.* Illustrated by Mercer Mayer. Four Winds, 1978.

Provensen, Alice, and Martin Provensen, retellers. "The Beauty and the Beast," in *The Provensen Book of Fairy Tales.* Illustrated by Alice Provensen and Martin Provensen. Random, 1971.

Brett, Jan. *Berlioz the Bear.* Illustrated by Jan Brett. Putnam, 1991.

This cumulative tale has Berlioz so worried about the buzz in his double bass that he guides his mule-drawn bandwagon right into a mud hole. Several animals—a rooster, a cat, a billy goat, a plowhorse, and an oxen—try to pull the wagon out of the hole. Finally, a bee flies out of the bass, stings the mule, and the wagon begins careening toward the village square where the orchestra is to play at the gala festival. At the end Berlioz prepares to play Rimsky-Korsakov's "The Flight of the Bumblebee."

1. End an oral reading of *Berlioz the Bear* by playing a recording of "The Flight of the Bumblebee." That selection is included on an inexpensive cassette produced by Polygram Records, *Flight of the Bumblebee and Other Favorites from Old Russia.*

2. Encourage students to learn more about the orchestra and the instruments that are part of the orchestra. Use the catalog in your school or public library to locate books about music and instruments. One source that may be helpful is a volume in the Knopf Eyewitness series, *Music* by Neil Ardley (Knopf, 1989).

3. Create a story map showing the cumulative nature of this story.

4. Suppose the buzzing had not been made by a bee inside the bass. Discuss or write about what else might have made the noise and how that would have changed the story.

5. Berlioz the Bear was named for the nineteenth-century French composer Louis-Hector Berlioz (1803-1869). Considered by many a genius of orchestration, Berlioz is known for his uninterrupted melodies. His symphonies include *Symphonic Fantastique* (1830) and *Romeo and Juliet* (1839). He also write an oratorio, *The Childhood of Christ* (1854), and a cantata, *The Damnation of Faust* (1846). His operas include *Benvenuto Cellini* (1837), *The Trojans* (1858), and *Beatrice and Benedict* (1862). Learn more about the composer Berlioz and search out some of his music to enjoy.

6. On the final page Berlioz is about to play "The Flight of the Bumblebee." That song is from the opera *Tsar Sutan* by Russian composer Nikolay Rimsky-Korsakov (1844-1908). Rimsky-Korsakov was known for his brilliant orchestration. He wrote fifteen operas, but only excerpts have enjoyed enduring popularity. Those excerpts, in addition to "The Flight

of the Bumblebee," include "Song of India" from *Sadko* and "Hymn of the Sun" from *The Golden Cockerel*. He wrote three symphonies, some choral works, and a book on instrumentation. He was largely a self-taught composer whose professional standing was the result of self-discipline. He was a professor of orchestration and composition at the Conservatory of Saint Petersburg, where the composer Igor Stravinsky studied under him. Listen to a recording of "The Flight of the Bumblebee" and some of Rimsky-Korsakov's other compositions.

Brett, Jan. *The First Dog*. Illustrated by Jan Brett. Harcourt, 1988.
This is an account of how humans domesticated the dog during the Ice Age. The borders framing each double-page spread include many examples of cave drawings from the Ice Age.

1. Compare and contrast the story and illustrations in Brett's book with the explanation given in Pauline Baynes's *How the Dog Began*, illustrated by Pauline Baynes (Holt, 1987).

2. The domestication of the dog brought about significant changes in the way humans were able to function in society. Compare the impact of dog (wolf) domestication with the impact that resulted from the introduction of the horse into the culture of Native Americans. The story of the first horse is told in Paul Goble's *The Gift of the Sacred Dog*, illustrated by Paul Goble (Bradbury, 1980).

Brett, Jan. *Goldilocks and the Three Bears*. Illustrated by Jan Brett. Putnam, 1987.
In this retelling of a traditional tale, Brett uses her creative art to feature unusual designs and intricate patterns. Small acorns adorn the bedposts, and other pieces of furniture feature carved bear figures. Floral endpapers give the book a finishing touch.

1. Locate versions of "The Three Bears" in folklore anthologies. Make a bibliography of all the versions located. The book information should come from the title page. The date is usually on the back side (verso) of the title page. Alphabetize the entries by the author or editor's last name.

Last name author/editor, first name. *Title of Book*. "Story Title." Illustrated by (name of illustrator). Publisher, date. pp. (page numbers of the story that you have cited).

2. Compare and contrast versions of "The Three Bears" you have located. Various versions of the story will have the obvious similarities in basic story grammar and setting. Note similarities and differences in the stories' conclusions, illustrations, time period, and character portrayal. Assess how the reteller and the illustrator convey their message about each character's personality.

   One of the earliest versions of "The Three Bears" was related in 1837 by Robert Southey, who tells about a little old woman who comes to the house and first looks in the window and later peeps in the keyhole. When the bears return, the old lady leaves and the bears never see her again. In 1850 Joseph Cundall retold the tale in his *Treasury of Pleasure Books for Young Children*. In his retelling the intruder becomes a little silver-haired girl. In Joseph Jacob's version, retold in *More English Fairy Tales* (1894), a fox is the intruder. It seems that not until 1904 was the intruder called Goldilocks, when *Old Nursery Stories and Rhymes*, illustrated by John Hassall, was published. In some versions the "wee" bear becomes the baby bear, the middle-sized bear becomes Mama Bear, and the great, huge bear becomes Father Bear or Papa Bear. As readers share the different versions of "The Three Bears" (see list in activity 4), note the various styles of bowls, chairs, and beds depicted in the different books. A variety of information about Goldilocks and the three bears is given in the introductory section of each story. The physical settings in some versions of the story are very distinctive, such as the Ukrainian setting in Brett's illustrated retelling. The specific locations of other settings often cannot be ascertained. Common to most settings is a wooded area, but time period and location are more often depicted by the style of the house and the characters' clothing. The bears' house varies from a stone house with a castle-style turret to a cozy white frame cottage in the woods. As for clothing, sometimes the three bears wear nothing at all, and sometimes they wear elaborate costumes; one book shows Papa Bear in a plaid shirt with suspenders and pants, Mama Bear in high heels, a dress, and a pearl necklace, and Baby Bear in overalls and tennis shoes.

3. After reading Brett's version of *Goldilocks and the Three Bears*, discuss how the story is similar to or different from some of the original elements of the story. Discuss how the book might have been changed had the intruder been a fox, an old woman, or Silverlocks.

4. Examine several retellings of the tale and discuss the text and the illustrations. Discuss which version the group likes best. Make miniature book jackets representing each version of the story that the group has read and place the book jacket along the bottom of a graph grid. As each child selects his or her favorite version, glue a copy of the child's school picture (or a hand-drawn image) above the appropriate jacket to create a picture graph of the favorite-version poll. Use the picture graph to make a bar graph, with each student's picture (or vote) representing one inch on the graph. The following versions may be useful for the class comparison sessions:

   Cauley, Lorinda Bryan. *Goldilocks and the Three Bears*. Illustrated by Lorinda Bryan Cauley. Putnam, 1981.

   Eisen, Armand, reteller. *Goldilocks and the Three Bears*. Illustrated by Lynn Bywaters Ferris. Knopf, 1987.

   Galdone, Paul. *The Three Bears*. Illustrated by Paul Galdone. Clarion, 1972.

   Jacobs, Joseph. "The Three Bears." In *Tomie dePaola's Favorite Nursery Tales*. Edited and illustrated by Tomie dePaola. Putnam, 1986.

   Marshall, James, reteller. *Goldilocks and the Three Bears*. Illustrated by James Marshall. Dial, 1988.

Rockwell, Anne. *The Three Bears and 15 Other Stories*. Illustrated by Anne Rockwell. Crowell, 1975; Harper Trophy, 1984.

Spowart, Robin. *The Three Bears*. Illustrated by Robin Spowart. Knopf, 1987.

Stevens, Janet. *Goldilocks and the Three Bears*. Illustrated by Janet Stevens. Holiday, 1986.

Watts, Bernadette. *Goldilocks and the Three Bears*. Illustrated by Bernadette Watts. Henry Holt, 1988.

5. After reading several versions of "The Three Bears," discuss the location of the houses relative to the woods, etc. Build a three-dimensional model. Use the model as the first step toward creating a map with symbols representing the trees, the houses, the path, etc.

6. Because of the repetitive language of the bears, this story is an excellent first experience with drama. Young students will enjoy reenacting the play in live action. Scripting the story will give more mature elementary students experience in identifying the role of each character and that of the narrators. These students will also enjoy reenacting the story by using transparency figures to perform on a theater stage (overhead projector). The transparency figures can be made by using black line drawings on white paper to create a transparency. Add color to the characters with permanent felt-tip markers. Cut the characters out of the transparency.

7. View the filmstrip version of Lorinda Bryan Cauley's *Goldilocks and the Three Bears* or a video or 16mm film version of James Marshall's *Goldilocks and the Three Bears*; both titles are available from Weston Woods®. Compare the nonprint version with the book on which the video or film is based.

8. Make full-scale drawings of the three bears. Use butcher paper to construct the figures. Three-dimensional figures can be made by stapling two cutouts together and stuffing lightly with crumbled newspaper. Discuss the concept of big, bigger, biggest.

9. Build on the readers' knowledge of the traditional story by reading reverse or fractured versions of the tale from the following list. After reading the fractured versions discuss how the author "played" with the tale.

    Ahlberg, Allan. *Ten in a Bed*. Illustrated by André Amstutz. Viking, 1989.

    Dahl, Roald. *Roald Dahl's Revolting Rhymes*. Illustrated by Quentin Blake. Knopf, 1982. (Note: Please read this account prior to using it with children.)

    Turkle, Brinton. *Deep in the Forest*. Illustrated by Brinton Turkle. Dutton, 1976. (A wordless reverse version of the tale.)

10. Extend students' interest in "Goldilocks and the Three Bears" by creating a celebration for bears—"another celebration for a day, a week, or here and there any day of the year." Suggestions for celebrating bears for a day, a week, ... can be located in Sharron L. McElmeel's *My Bag of Book Tricks* (Libraries Unlimited, 1989), pp. 44-48.

Brett, Jan. *The Mitten*. Illustrated by Jan Brett. Putnam, 1989.

A boy name Nicki wants his new mittens made from wool as white as snow. His grandmother does not want to knit white mittens. "If you drop one in the snow you'll never find it." But Baba finally makes them for her grandson. He goes off to play and before long one of his new mittens drops in the snow and is left behind. While the mitten is lost in the snow, a mole, rabbit, hedgehog, owl, badger, fox, and bear settle into the mitten. They squeeze and wiggle into the mitten, but Baba's good knitting holds fast. Then a very small meadow mouse settles on the bear's nose and causes him to give an enormous sneeze. The bear's sneeze causes all the animals to be pushed out of the mitten and scattered in all directions. The sneeze also causes the white mitten to fly high into the air where it is silhouetted against the blue sky. Nicki is able to see the mitten, recovers it, and returns home, where Baba holds it and seems to wonder why it is stretched so big.

1. Compare and contrast Brett's version to *The Mitten*, retold by Alvin Tresselt, illustrated by Yaroslava (Lothrop, 1964). The story grammar in the two stories is quite similar. In Tresselt's version a young boy loses his yellow leather, fur-trimmed mitten. Into the mitten squeezes a little mouse, a green frog, an owl, a rabbit, a fox, a wolf, a wild boar, a bear, and a little black cricket.

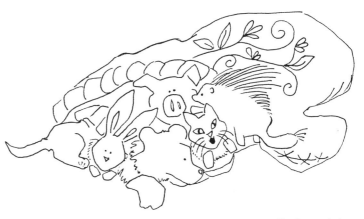

   The mitten stretches and stretches, straining the mitten at its seams, until the cricket squeezes in and the mitten bursts at its seams. When the boy (who is not given a name in the story) returns, he finds his mitten in pieces and goes home with only one mitten. In contrast, the Brett version has Nicki going outside with his newly knitted pair of mittens and losing one of them. A mole, rabbit, hedgehog, owl, badger, fox, and bear squeeze into the mitten. It stretches and stretches. A mouse comes along and sits on the bear's nose. The mouse's whiskers tickle the bear's nose making the bear sneeze. All the animals and the mitten go flying into the air. Nicki sees the mitten flying high in the air, recovers it, and returns home with both mittens—one stretched to a larger size.

2. Write an original version of "The Mitten." Younger children might list the animals that would have squeezed into their glove or mitten. With older children share information about the versions that Brett says she encountered while researching her retelling. After discussing the story grammar of each story, plot out the essential elements of the story. Then discuss details that might be changed without altering the basic story grammar. Illustrate the sentences or the complete story.

3. Discuss the Ukrainian origin of the story and how its origin influences the setting and the animals that are part of the story. How would the story change if it were set in Australia? If it were set in Alaska or Hawaii?

Lear, Edward. *The Owl and the Pussycat*. Illustrated by Jan Brett. Putnam, 1991.

Lear's poem is lushly illustrated and put in a brightly colored Caribbean island setting. The setting is based on pictures the illustrator took in Martinique, where women wear skirts with lots of white petticoats and white blouses. The pussycat's turban reflects the tradition of using the points on the turban to indicate a woman's marital status. The two yellow fish that swim beneath the boat seem to have their own story.

1. Read Edward Lear's "The Owl and the Pussycat." It can be found in *The Random House Book of Poetry for Children*, edited by Jack Prelutsky and illustrated by Arnold Lobel (Random, 1983), and in *Wider Than the Sky: Poems to Grow Up With*, collected and edited by Scott Elledge (HarperCollins, 1990). Ask students to draw their own interpretations of the poem.

2. Discuss terms such as *six-pound note, shilling, runcible spoon, elegant fowl, pea-green.*

3. Read Brett's version of *The Owl and the Pussycat*. Compare her illustrations with those created by the students. Notice the tropical scenes of fruits, flowers, and basketry borders, as well as the concurrent underwater story of a small fish who seems to be searching for a mate.

4. In a listening and viewing center place the filmstrip/cassette (or use the video or 16mm film) of *The Owl and the Pussy-cat* based on Barbara Cooney's illustrated version of Lear's poem (Little, 1961; 1969). The nonprint versions of Cooney's version are available from Weston Woods®.

5. Compare and contrast Brett's version of *The Owl and the Pussycat* with some or all of the following versions:

   Knight, Hilary. *Hilary Knight's The Owl and the Pussy-Cat*. Illustrated by Hilary Knight. Macmillan, 1983.

   Lear, Edward. *The Owl and the Pussycat*. Illustrated by Ron Berg. Scholastic, n.d. (Scholastic has published a big book edition of this title. This version is unique in that the pea-green boat is a steamship.)

   Lear, Edward. *The Owl and the Pussy-cat*. Illustrated by Barbara Cooney. Little, 1969. (Weston Woods has a filmstrip/cassette and video of this title.)

   Lear, Edward. *The Owl and the Pussycat*. Illustrated by Helen Cooper. Dial, 1991.

   Lear, Edward. *The Owl and the Pussy-cat*. Illustrated by William Pène Du Bois. Doubleday, 1961.

   Lear, Edward. *The Owl and the Pussy-cat*. Illustrated by Gwen Fulton. Atheneum, 1977.

   Lear, Edward. *The Owl and the Pussycat*. Illustrated by Paul Galdone. Clarion, 1987.

   Lear, Edward. *The Owl and the Pussycat*. Illustrated by Janet Stevens. Holiday, 1983.

   Lear. Edward. *The Owl and the Pussy-cat and Other Nonsense*. Illustrated by Owen Wood. Viking, 1979.

Bunting, Eve. *Scary, Scary Halloween*. Illustrated by Jan Brett. Clarion, 1986.
Eyes in the night stare through the dark. Vampires prowl and witches and devils stalk past. A sheeted creature thumps his feet on the steps and drags his claws across the floor. In the end the green almond-shaped eyes are revealed to belong to a mother cat and her kittens.

1. Scary things are not only for Halloween; children love scary experiences all year long. Connect prose with poetry by reading Beatrice Schenk deRegniers's poem "When I Tell You I'm Scared" in *The Way I Feel Sometimes* (Clarion, 1988). Then extend the idea of scary things by reading titles from the following booklist:

    Calhoun, Mary. *The Night the Monster Came*. Illustrated by Leslie Morrill. Morrow, 1982.

    Crowe, Robert L. *Clyde Monster*. Dutton, 1976.

    Howe, James. *There's a Monster under My Bed*. Illustrated by David Ross. Atheneum, 1986.

    Martin, Jacqueline Briggs. *Bizzy Bones and Uncle Ezra*. Lothrop, 1984.

    Ross, Tony. *I'm Coming to Get You!* Dial, 1984.

2. Cut cat faces from construction paper. Add the cat's facial features, including whiskers and green almond-shaped eyes. Put the collection of cats on a door and make a "watch out for cats" sign.

Brett, Jan. *The Twelve Days of Christmas*. Illustrated by Jan Brett. Putnam, 1986; miniature edition, 1990.

This traditional carol is joyously illustrated by Brett. Each of the Christmas gifts is brought alive in two-page spreads surrounded by a menagerie of animals in the borders. Music is included in the book. Although traditionally the "twelve days of Christmas" are the days between Christmas Day and the Epiphany (January 6), Brett illustrates the twelve days *before* Christmas. The twelve days culminate with the objects being hung on the Christmas tree.

1. Compare and contrast Brett's version with other versions of this traditional carol:

    Kent, Jack. *Jack Kent's Twelve Days of Christmas*. Illustrated by Jack Kent. Parents, 1973.

    Knight, Hilary. *Hilary Knight's The Twelve Days of Christmas*. Illustrated by Hilary Knight. Macmillan, 1981.

    The Twelve Days of Christmas. Illustrated by Ilonka Karasz. Harper, 1949.

    The Twelve Days of Christmas. Illustrated by Ilse Plume. HarperCollins, 1990.

    The Twelve Days of Christmas. Illustrated by Erika Schneider. Alphabet Press, 1984.

2. After reading several of the books on the preceding list, discuss the idea that Brett's twelve days of Christmas takes place during the twelve days *before* Christmas Day, while traditional versions of the twelve days of Christmas depict the twelve days *after* Christmas. As a group project create a class-illustrated edition of this traditional verse.

3. Extend the appreciation of this music form by reading Elizabeth Lee O'Donnell's *The Twelve Days of Summer*, illustrated in watercolors by Karen Lee Schmidt (Morrow, 1991). It is a story spawned from the traditional verse "The Twelve Days of Christmas." A child finds an array of animals on the beach while her parents doze away. Use this innovative text to motivate some experimentation with the form — perhaps *The Twelve Days of Halloween*, *The Twelve Days of My Birthday*, or *The Twelve Days of School Vacation*.

Brett, Jan. *The Wild Christmas Reindeer*. Illustrated by Jan Brett. Putnam, 1990.

This holiday fantasy for the Christmas season is set in an arctic wonderland. Teeka prepares the reindeer for their annual trek with Santa. After a week of yelling and fussing, she decides that it is her fault that the reindeer have misbehaved and decides she should help instead of yell. The reindeer — Heather, Lichen, Crag, Tundra, and the others — cooperate and come prancing in just in time. Side panels show the elves preparing the Christmas gifts before December 24, when Santa loads up. Borders focus on holiday symbols and a calendar countdown. The reindeer are stubborn and Teeka is intelligent and persistent. Each page is filled with details.

1. Read this tale in conjunction with other stories of the Christmas trek, notably Chris Van Allsburg's *The Polar Express* (Houghton, 1985).

2. Extend the giving and sharing aspect of the holiday season by reading titles from the following list:

   Andersen, Hans Christian. *The Fir Tree*. Adapted and illustrated by Bernadette Watts. North-South, 1990.

   Branley, Franklyn. *The Christmas Sky*. Revised edition, illustrated by Stephen Fieser. Crowell, 1990.

   Bulla, Clyde Robert. *The Christmas Coat*. Illustrated by Sylvia Wickstrom. Knopf, 1990.

   Collington, Peter. *On Christmas Eve*. Illustrated by Peter Collington. Knopf, 1990.

   Day, Alexandra. *Carl's Christmas*. Illustrated by Alexandra Day. Farrar, 1990.

   Denton, Kady MacDonald. *The Christmas Boot*. Illustrated by Kady MacDonald Denton. Little, 1990.

   Ehrlich, Amy. *The Story of Hanukkah*. Dial, 1989.

   Harvey, Brett. *My Prairie Christmas*. Illustrated by Deborah Kogan Ray. Holiday, 1990.

   Kimmel, Eric A. *The Chanukkah Guest*. Illustrated by Giora Carmi. Holiday, 1990.

   Lagerlof, Selma. *The Legend of the Christmas Rose*. Retold by Ellin Greene. Illustrated by Charles Mikolaycak. Holiday, 1990.

McKenna, Colleen O'Shaughnessy. *Merry Christmas, Miss McConnell!* Scholastic, 1990. (Novel)

Murphy, Shirley Rousseau. *The Song of the Christmas Mouse*. Illustrated by Donna Diamond. Harper, 1990.

Say, Allen. *Tree of Cranes*. Illustrated by Allen Say. Houghton, 1991.

Schotter, Roni. *Hanukkah!* Illustrated by Marylin Hafner. Joy Street/Little, 1990.

Tyler, Linda Wagner. *The After-Christmas Tree*. Illustrated by Susan Davis. Viking, 1990.

Anthony Browne

From *An Author a Month (for Dimes)* by Sharron L. McElmeel (Libraries Unlimited, 1992)

71

Anthony Browne

Anthony Browne was born in England on September 11, 1946, and grew up in Hipperholme, near Halifax in Yorkshire, England. As a child he drew funny pictures. He enjoyed reading *Alice's Adventures in Wonderland*, fairy tales, and comics. His heroes were all sportsmen—soccer players, rugby players, cricketers—and a character he invented and called "Big Dumb Tackle."

He attended Whitcliffe Mount Grammar School and in 1963 entered Leeds College of Art. For a while he worked as a medical illustrator but found that in that job he had to suppress much of his imagination. So he began to illustrate books. One of his first books, *Gorilla*, was awarded England's Kate Greenaway award.

The illustrations in Anthony Browne's books are filled with surprises: birds and cats come to life and scamper out of pictures, roses turn into pigs, books become butterflies, and gorillas pop up almost everywhere. Some of his stories are about things he did as a child. The children in *The Tunnel* are similar to Anthony and his brother, Michael, and there was a real tunnel. And he says that the family in *Piggybook* is in some ways like his own family.

Anthony Browne lives in Kent, England, with his wife, Jane, and their two young children, Joseph and Ellen. He enjoys sharing time with his family, being in the fresh air, reading, going to the cinema, and playing cricket.

Chapter
6
Anthony Browne

ABOUT THE AUTHOR/ILLUSTRATOR

Anthony Edward Tudor Browne was born on September 11, 1946, in Sheffield, England, to Jack Holgate Browne and Doris May (Sugden) Browne. He grew up in Hipperholme, near Halifax in Yorkshire, England, where his father was a teacher. His father spent many hours drawing pictures and playing drawing games with Anthony and his older brother, Michael. Anthony drew, too. He was always drawing funny pictures—and lots of pictures of battles. He even put humor in his battle scenes—surrealistic jokes, perhaps. He entered Whitcliffe Mount Grammar School in 1957. In 1963, after leaving Whitcliffe, Browne enrolled in Leeds College of Art, where he studied until 1967. His father died while he was still in college, leaving Anthony with a great sense of loss. When he left Leeds he became a medical illustrator, a job that did not allow him to express his humor, imagination, and creativity. From there he entered the world of advertising. It was a very boring, high-pressure job, and still he was not able to draw a "happy" picture. He then turned to the greeting card industry, where he learned how to do "happy teddy bears and happy cats." A friend in the card industry suggested that he stablize his income by taking up magazine illustration or perhaps children's books. Publisher Julia MacRae saw promise in his work and *Through the Magic Mirror* (Julia MacRae, 1976) was eventually published.

Browne's illustrative trademarks include creative use of color, finely drawn details, and inventive surreal humor. Some of the things he read as a child came back to him when he began to illustrate books. *A Walk in the Park*, *Bear Hunt*, *Look What I've Got*, and *Bear Goes to Town* began to bring Browne critical acclaim. As a child he had enjoyed *Alice's Adventures in Wonderland* and he later illustrated a version of the story. He had also read many fairy tales and later had the opportunity to illustrate *Hansel and Gretel*. His love of comic books probably contributed to the "Super Gorilla" image that he used in *Gorilla*. *Gorilla*, which started as a greeting card featuring a gorilla holding a teddy bear, later became a complete book. But how did it get from greeting card to book? Brown says that it is "impossible to really remember how the idea (for a book) came about, I just try to make my books as rich as possible—to have more than one level." So perhaps the development of *Willy the Wimp* and *Willy the Champ* came from Browne's awareness of sports heroes and what makes them real heroes. At one time Browne commented that the family he portrayed in *Piggybook* was based on a real family—to some extent like the one in which he was raised. And Mrs. Piggott bears an interesting resemblance to his wife, Jane. And the children in *The Tunnel* have definite similarities to Anthony and his brother. And there really was a tunnel that they went through.

There is a gorilla in most of his books—such as *Willy the Champ*, *Willy the Wimp*, and *Changes*—but not quite all. In fact, Browne states that at times he makes a conscious effort to keep gorillas out, but he doesn't always succeed. The gorilla shows up in the illustrations he created for *Kirsty Knows Best* by Annalena McAfee. There are plenty of other interesting things as well. Throughout the book Browne foreshadows the ending of the story by placing a round shape with antenna-like projections on almost every page. There is a flying mouse with butterfly wings, a child's picture that comes alive, and a black shadow that is really the gorilla. Familiar fairy tales are incorporated into *The Tunnel* through the illustrations. The trees are formed as composites of other strange and interesting shapes—which is where the gorilla shows up in this book. The *Piggybook* is filled with visual images that slowly transform almost everything into a pig symbol. The gorilla makes his entrance early in this book, appearing as a picture in the newspaper in one of the first double-page spreads. Sally Grindley's *Knock, Knock! Who's There?* is a wonderful vehicle for Browne's ingenuity. Each time a knock is heard at the door, the little girl imagines it is one frightening creature after another. The ever-changing wallpaper gives ample clues as to who will be the next creature at the door (of course, the gorilla was the first to frighten her). But in the end it is just Father with a cup of hot chocolate. Browne's forte is his ability to create very imaginative illustrations.

Browne often incorporates elements of fairy tales into the books he illustrates. For example, in *The Tunnel* one can find a great deal of similarity to Hansel and Gretel and their trek through the woods to the witch's cottage. And Browne heightened the idea of that comparison by placing in the illustrations several images from fairy tales. When Browne illustrated his version of *Hansel and Gretel*, he placed the story in a contemporary setting, bringing the story from the past into the present. His British publisher has asked him to illustrate a large collection of fairy tales. He has started on "Beauty and the Beast," but so far it isn't feeling quite right. He is, however, optimistic about the project.

After receiving many letters from readers asking him to write another "Willy" book, he complied by creating *Willy and Hugh*. When he wrote *Willy and Hugh* he felt that the time was right to do another light, funny book. His collaboration with Gwen Strauss on *Trail of Stones*, a book for older readers, led him to collaborate on a picture book for young children. *The Night Shimmy* was published by Knopf in 1992. It is the story of Eric and his relationship with an imaginary companion, "the night shimmy." One of his next books is tentatively titled "Funny Things." It will be about sayings grown-ups use, funny sayings like "My mum says that Rex, our dog, is driving them up the wall." And, "When Dad came home from work today, he said it was raining cats and dogs." When this book is available, plan to use it in conjunction with several titles by Fred Gwynne. Response suggestions for Gwynne's *A Chocolate Moose for Dinner* are included in Sharron L. McElmeel's *My Bag of Book Tricks* (Libraries Unlimited, 1989).

Browne works at home. His book schedule is fairly normal—he usually works from 9:30 a.m. until about 6 p.m. When he is working on the early stages of a book, he considers it less like writing a story and more like planning a film. So he makes a storyboard and then works out how to tell the story in thirty-two pages (actually twenty-nine "shots"). He uses mostly watercolors but occasionally chooses gouache for overpainting or inks and crayons for a lighter effect, as he did for the "Willy" books.

Browne is married to Jane Browne and they live in a historic seventeenth-century house in the county of Kent, England, close to the sea. The Brownes have two young children, Joseph and Ellen. They also have a dog, Gilbert, and a cat, Tom. Jane is a musician and music teacher so the house is filled with music. Both children play musical instruments—the piano, violin, and cello. The children also write stories and paint pictures. In 1991 Crown publishers released a song book by Jane Browne. The book, *Sing Me a Story: Action Songs to Sing and Play*, includes thirteen songs with words and music to share with young children. Each of the songs relates to a nursery rhyme or fairy tale—from "Sing a Song of Sixpence" to "Sleeping Beauty." Among Anthony Browne's favorite things are the cinema, reading, being by the sea, playing cricket, the color blue, fresh bread, and the number *4*. Among his own books, he says *Gorilla* is his favorite, but he receives far more letters from children about *Willy the Wimp* and *Willy the Champ*. One letter from Jan Brett in Australia was addressed to Willy: "Dear Willy, you don't have to be big and strong, just watch where you're going."

SETTING THE STAGE

Include a world map in an author's corner featuring Anthony Browne. On the map mark his place of birth, Sheffield, England, and Nicholas—at—Wade, Kent, England, where he now lives. As a prelude to introducing Anthony Browne, use the encyclopedia to learn something about the Greenaway and Caldecott awards and the English illustrators for whom the awards were named: Kate Greenaway and Randolph Caldecott. The Caldecott award is given in the United States for the best-illustrated book published during the preceding publishing year. The Kate Greenaway award is a similar award given in England. After discussing the awards, introduce Anthony Browne as having won a Kate Greenaway award for *Gorilla*. His creative illustrations are recognized for their originality and imagination. Browne has also won a *Horn Book* Fanfare citation and a *New York Times* Best Illustrated Book award. Some critics feel that Browne's imagination transcends cultural boundaries, while others cite his surreal illustrative style as reflecting subtle English humor.

Browne's artistic medium is usually watercolor that is semi-moist or concentrated liquid. He does not use tubes of paint. His work has been influenced by Maurice Sendak and surrealists René Magritte, Max Ernst, and, to some extent, Salvador Dali. Browne describes surrealists as being very interested in juxtaposing seemingly normal objects. Browne uses bold, rich colors and clear outlines that are often set against white backgrounds. His images mix the realistic with the fantastic. Display in an art center reproductions of paintings by Sendak, Magritte, Ernst, and Dali. Encourage students to experiment with watercolors to create their own pseudosurrealistic illustrations.

Toward the end of the focus on Anthony Browne and his work, extend the experience by sharing books written and illustrated by other English authors and illustrators. Discuss the similarities and differences in the book creators' sense of humor and style. Use the card catalog in your school or public library to locate books by the following authors and illustrators: Quentin Blake, John Burningham (who is married to Helen Oxenbury, another English author/illustrator), Jane Hissey, and Peter Collington—all current residents of England.

Culminate the unit by holding a Gorilla Day. Ask children to bring in stuffed primate pets, statues, or pictures from magazines. Display the gorillas and their cousins in a special center. Then enjoy a read-and-feed. Share books about all kinds of primates. For a treat, serve bananas or dried banana chips. Consider including some of the following books in the read-and-feed session:

Arnold, Caroline. *Orangutan*. Illustrated by Richard Hewett. Morrow, 1990.

Bright, Michael. *Mountain Gorilla*. Watts/Gloucester, 1989.

Bunting, Eve. *Monkey in the Middle*. Illustrated by Lynn Munsinger. Harcourt, 1984.

Galdone, Paul. *The Monkey and the Crocodile*. Illustrated by Paul Galdone. Seabury, 1969.

Harrison, David Lee. *Detective Bob and the Great Ape Escape*. Illustrated by Ned Delaney. Parents, 1980.

Hazen, Barbara Shook. *The Gorilla Did It!* Illustrated by Ray Cruz. Atheneum, 1974.

Hazen, Barbara Shook. *Gorilla Wants to Be the Baby*. Illustrated by Jacqueline Bardner Smith. Atheneum, 1978.

Hoff, Syd. *Julius*. Illustrated by Syd Hoff. Harper, 1959.

Hurd, Edith Thacher. *The Mother Chimpanzee*. Illustrated by Clement Hurd. Little, 1978.

Irvine, Georgeanne. *Raising Gordy Gorilla at the San Diego Zoo*. Simon, 1990.

Knight, Hilary. *Where's Wallace?* Illustrated by Hilary Knight. Harper, 1964.

Krahn, Fernando. *The Great Ape: Being the True Version of the Famous Saga of Adventure and Friendship Newly Discovered*. Illustrated by Fernando Krahn. Viking, 1978.

McNulty, Faith. *With Love from Koko*. Illustrated by Annie Cannon. Scholastic, 1990.

Meyers, Susan. *The Truth about Gorillas*. Illustrated by John Hamberger. Dutton, 1980.

Morozumi, Atsuko. *One Gorilla: A Counting Book*. Illustrated by Atsuko Morozumi. Farrar, 1990.

Schertle, Alice. *The Gorilla in the Hall*. Illustrated by Paul Galdone. Lothrop, 1977.

Schlein, Miriam. *Gorillas*. Atheneum, 1990.

Selsam, Millicent E., and Joyce Hunt. *A First Look at Monkeys*. Illustrated by Harriett Springer. Walker, 1979.

Zimelman, Nathan. *Positively No Pets Allowed*. Illustrated by Pamela Johnson. Dutton, 1980.

IDEA CUPBOARD

Browne, Anthony. *Bear Hunt*. Illustrated by Anthony Browne. Atheneum, 1979; Doubleday, 1980.

Two hunters stalk Bear through the preposterous jungle. Bear, a portly teddy in a red-spotted bow, lays his escape by using his pencil and drawing his way out of each new peril. The bear's pencil makes black line drawings on a white background, providing a very visible contrast between the danger and escape scenes. The hunting scenes hold the magic, however: a teacup, an egg, and a glove become flowers; lips, shoes, and fishes become leaves. This is a simple text that will appeal to the emerging reader.

1. Compare and contrast the following books with *Bear Hunt*. During the comparison explore which titles have the drawn object given life for the amusement of the other characters in the story and which titles present drawings that are given life in an effort to save their creator from danger or from grave circumstances. Also note how the illustrations distinguish between the "drawing" and the objects and animals once they become "real."

   Alexander, Martha. *Blackboard Bear*. Illustrated by Martha Alexander. Dial, 1969.

   Bang, Molly Garrett. *Tye May and the Magic Brush*. Adapted and illustrated by Molly Garrett Bang. Greenwillow, 1981.

   Demi. *Liang and the Magic Paint Brush*. Illustrated by Demi. Holt, 1980.

   Gackenbach, Dick. *Mag, the Magnificent*. Illustrated by Dick Gackenbach. Clarion, 1985.

2. Read other bear books:

   Asch, Frank. *Bear Shadow*. Illustrated by Frank Asch. Prentice, 1985.

   Asch, Frank. *Mooncake*. Illustrated by Frank Asch. Prentice, 1984.

   Banks, Kate. *Alphabet Soup*. Illustrated by Kate Banks, Knopf, 1988.

   Bird, E. J. *How Do Bears Sleep?* Illustrated by E. J. Bird. Carolrhoda, 1990.

   Bunting, Eve. *The Valentine Bears*. Illustrated by Jan Brett. Clarion, 1983.

   Carlstrom, Nancy White. *It's About Time, Jesse Bear: And Other Rhymes*. Illustrated by Bruce Degen. Macmillan, 1990.

   Carlstrom, Nancy White. *Jesse Bear, What Will You Wear?* Illustrated by Bruce Degen. Macmillan, 1987.

   deRegniers, Beatrice Schenk. *How Joe the Bear and Sam the Mouse Got Together*. Illustrated by Bernice Myers. Lothrop, 1990.
   (This is a newly illustrated edition of a text first published in 1965 by Parents.)

   Hale, Irina. *Brown Bear in a Brown Chair*. Illustrated by Irina Hale. Atheneum, 1984.

   Hissey, Jane. *Little Bear's Trousers (An Old Bear Story)*. Illustrated by Jane Hissey. Philomel, 1987.

   Hofmann, Ginnie. *The Runaway Teddy Bear*. Illustrated by Ginnie Hofmann. Random, 1986.

Martin, Bill, Jr. *Brown Bear, Brown Bear, What Do You See?* rev. ed. Illustrated by Eric Carle. Holt, 1992.

Martin, Bill, Jr. *Polar Bear, Polar Bear, What Do You Hear?* Illustrated by Eric Carle. Holt, 1991.

McPhail, David. *Lost!* Illustrated by David McPhail. Little/Joy Street, 1990.

Yektai, Niki. *Bears in Pairs*. Illustrated by Diane deGroat. Bradbury, 1987.

Yolen, Jane. *The Three Bears Rhyme Book*. Harcourt, 1988.

3. Use the subject heading BEARS in the catalog of your school or public library to locate additional titles. *My Bag of Book Tricks* by Sharron L. McElmeel (Libraries Unlimited, 1989) includes a section "Bears—Another Celebration for a Day, a Week, or Here and There Any Day of the Year" (pages 44-48). Those pages include a more comprehensive booklist and celebration suggestions.

Browne, Anthony. *Changes*. Illustrated by Anthony Browne. Knopf, 1990.
At first reading, this book seems to be a book about strange changes: teakettles become cats and sneak away, a sofa becomes a reptile, a pillow becomes an imposing gorilla, garden hoses change into snakes, and a bicycle tire transforms into an apple. Each page foreshadows something that will happen one or two pages later. But in the end, readers see the story as one showing the anxiety that a child feels when his or her parents bring home a baby. When Joseph sees his father, mother, and the baby, he smiles because he knows that this is the change his father had talked about.

1. Read the book once, without interruption, and then reread the story, this time stopping to discuss and think about the changes that students noticed in each of the illustrations.

2. Extend the theme of developing relationships between a child and a new sibling by sharing some of the following books. After reading several of the books, discuss similarities in the relationships or conflicts within sibling relationships. Compare and contrast the relationships in the various books with those that exist within the readers' families.

Adorjan, Carol. *I Can! Can You?* Illustrated by Miriam Nerlove. Whitman, 1990. (Originally published as *Someone I Know* [Random, 1968])

Birdseye, Tom. *Tucker*. Holiday, 1990. (A 112-page read-aloud novel)

Blume, Judy. *The Pain and the Great One*. Illustrated by Irene Trivas. Bradbury, 1984; Dell, 1986.

Boyd, Lizi. *Sam Is My Half Brother*. Illustrated by Lizi Boyd. Viking, 1990.

Dunrea, Olivier. *Eppie M. Says...*. Illustrated by Olivier Dunrea. Macmillan, 1990.

Greenfield, Eloise. *She Come Bringing Me That Little Baby Girl*. Illustrated by John Steptoe. Lippincott, 1974.

Henkes, Kevin. *Julius, the Baby of the World*. Illustrated by Kevin Henkes. Greenwillow, 1990.

Hutchins, Pat. *The Very Worst Monster*. Illustrated by Pat Hutchins. Greenwillow, 1985.

Hutchins, Pat. *Where's the Baby?* Illustrated by Pat Hutchins. Greenwillow, 1988.

Keats, Ezra Jack. *Peter's Chair*. Harper, 1967.

Kellogg, Steven. *Much Bigger Than Martin*. Illustrated by Steven Kellogg. Dial, 1976.

Moss, Marissa. *Want to Play?* Illustrated by Marissa Moss. Houghton, 1990.

Pomerantz, Charlotte. *The Half-Birthday Party*. Illustrated by D. DiSalvo-Ryan. Houghton, 1984.

Sharmat, Marjorie, and Mitchell Sharmat. *The Day I Was Born*. Illustrated by Diane Dawson. Dutton, 1980.

Steptoe, John. *Stevie*. Illustrated by John Steptoe. Harper, 1969.

Stevenson, James. *Worse Than Willy*. Greenwillow, 1984.

Viorst, Judith. *I'll Fix Anthony*. Illustrated by Arnold Lobel. Harper, 1969.

Walter, Mildred Pitts. *My Mama Needs Me*. Illustrated by Pat Cummings. Lothrop, 1983.

Browne, Anthony. *Gorilla*. Illustrated by Anthony Browne. Knopf, 1983.

Hannah loves gorillas. Everything around her has some relationship to a gorilla, but she has never seen a real one. Her father has very little time to be with her. From the empty picture frame on her father's desk one might conclude that the mother has gone. Father seems totally involved with work, and Hannah is lonely and totally involved with gorillas. She is given a toy gorilla but it isn't quite what she wants. She wishes for a trip to the zoo to see the gorillas. Then one night her imagination takes over. Her toy gorilla becomes a real part of her life. Dressed in a trench coat, the gorilla escorts her through the air to an adventurous evening. And when Hannah rushes downstairs the next morning, her dad is waiting with a gorilla-decorated birthday cake and an offer to take her to the zoo. And they walk off hand in hand, father in the trench coat and Hannah with her toy gorilla dangling from her hand.

1. Reading this story is joy enough—and looking for all the gorilla images hidden here and there is a magical search that everyone will want to share. Make a list of all the gorillas and where they were found in the book.

2. On the page where Hannah is pictured in a dark room, there is, in one brightly lit corner, one bit of information about gorillas—the map of Africa on the wall. According to *The Animal Atlas* by Barbara Taylor and illustrated by Kenneth Lilly (Knopf, 1992), the gorilla is most prevalent in the tropical rain forests of Africa in "a broad band from West Africa to the edge of the Great Rift Valley." The mountain gorilla is considered to be endangered. Taylor says, "[T]here are probably only about 300 mountain gorillas left in Central Africa. They are threatened mainly by the destruction of their forest habitat." Make a map and mark the locations where gorillas can be found.

3. Locate other information about gorillas. Investigate the gorilla population in Zaire (formerly the Belgian Congo) and other parts of Africa, including the famous mountain gorillas of Rwanda. Make an information chart. One excellent resource is Miriam Schlein's *Gorillas* (Atheneum, 1990), which covers habitat, lineage, community life, rearing young, animals in captivity, and preservation.

4. Cut out pictures of gorillas from magazines, newspapers, and original drawings to make a gorilla collage.

Grimm, Jacob, and Wilhelm Grimm. *Hansel and Gretel*. Illustrated by Anthony Browne. Knopf, 1981.

This version of "Hansel and Gretel" is put into a contemporary setting. In the family's living room a bare light bulb hangs from the middle of the peeling ceiling, and a modern airplane is shown on a television in the dining room. Although the scene is one of apparent poverty, there is no shortage of amenities for the mother of the family, whose sinister selfishness is highlighted by her flashy red high-heeled shoes, her spotted leopard coat, and an array of cosmetics, including a bottle of Oil of Olay®, on the bedroom dresser. The text is basically faithful to the story grammar in the Grimm brothers' original version – the twist is in the illustrations.

1. Gather together as many versions of "Hansel and Gretel" as you can locate. After reading with students several of the versions, have them compare and contrast the versions. The discussion notes after the following booklist will assist in the comparison activity.

Alderson, Brian, translator. *The Brothers Grimm: Popular Folk Tales*. "Hansel and Gretel." Illustrated by Michael Foreman. Doubleday, 1978.

Edens, Cooper, selector. *Hansel and Gretel*. Green Tiger, 1990.
This collection includes standard retellings illustrated by a variety of artists: Jessie Wilcox Smith, Arthur Rackham, Kay Nielsen, Wanda Gag, and others. Valuable to adults who want to gain experience with different interpretations of the tale, but the book might be used successfully with older readers as well.

Ehrlich, Amy, translator. "Hansel and Gretel." In *The Random House Book of Fairy Tales*. Illustrated by Diane Goode. Random House, 1985.

Galdone, Paul, reteller. *Hansel and Gretel*. Illustrated by Paul Galdone. McGraw, 1982.

Grimm, Jacob, and Wilhelm Grimm. *Hansel and Gretel*. Illustrated by Adrienne Adams. Translated by Charles Scribner, Jr. Scribner, 1975.

Grimm, Jacob, and Wilhelm Grimm. *Hansel and Gretel*. Illustrated by Antonella Bolliger-Savielli. Adapted from *Grimm's Fairy Tales*. Oxford University Press, 1969; 1981.

Grimm, Jacob, and Wilhelm Grimm. *Hansel and Gretel*. Illustrated by Susan Jeffers. Translated from the German by Mrs. Edgar Lucas and originally included in the collection *Fairy Tales of the Bros. Grimm* (Lippincott, 1902). Dial, 1980.

Grimm, Jacob, and Wilhelm Grimm. *Hansel and Gretel*. Adapted and illustrated by Arnold Lobel. Delacorte, 1971.

Grimm, Jacob, and Wilhelm Grimm. *Hansel and Gretel*. Illustrated by John Wallner. Simon, 1985.

Grimm, Jacob, and Wilhelm Grimm. *Hansel and Gretel*. Illustrated by Lisbeth Zwerger. Translated from the German by Elizabeth D. Crawford. Morrow, 1979.

Lesser, Rika, reteller. *Hansel and Gretel*. Illustrated by Paul O. Zelinsky. Putnam, 1989.

Marshall, James, reteller. *Hansel and Gretel*. Illustrated by James Marshall. Dial, 1990.

In retellings of traditional tales, the illustrator often takes a major role in setting the mood or tone of the story. In most retellings the story grammar follows the same plot structure as traditional retellings, but the illustrations change the mood. Illustrations can depict the parents as cold and harsh, or loving but poor. In retellings of "Hansel and Gretel" the witch is most often a menacing hag, but in some versions she is more than menacing—she is vile and wicked. The portrayal of the witch's death can increase the foreboding or decrease it for the child, depending on how the death is visualized. The same is true for how the stepmother's disappearance is presented. Many have defended the gruesomeness of the Grimms' tales, such as "Hansel and Gretel," by saying that the tales obviously take place in the past. Anthony Browne did away with that defense when he created a contemporary setting. Some feel that the contemporary setting brings the story too close to the present and makes the story more threatening to the younger reader. But the variation makes the story all the more interesting for critical reading by the older reader.

Lisbeth Zwerger keeps the time element in the distance by portraying her characters and scenes in a brown wash, which gives the feeling of long ago. Paul O. Zelinsky uses dark, somber but lush oil paintings to create a dense dark forest and the interior of the poor woodcutter's home, and suggests a more traditional setting. Zelinsky's characters are in period dress. Meticulous detail is one characteristic of Susan Jeffers's forest scenes; leaves on trees and feathers on birds are individually painted, and the result is exquisite. Her illustrations do not distinguish between those experiences in the forest and those with the witch. She is also one of the artists to pictorially suggest that the stepmother and the witch are one and the same. In Jeffers's illustrations the witch is wrapped in a shawl identical to the stepmother's. Anthony Browne makes the same suggestion by using a mole on each woman's cheek. He includes other pictorial symbols in his illustrations. Pages are filled with reflected images, symbols of cages and flight, and the triangle shape representative of the witch's hat. For example, in the third double-page spread, the triangle shape reoccurs several times—in the picture of the church steeple hanging on the bedroom wall, as the gap created by the curtains not fully drawn across the window, in a mouse's hole in the baseboard, as a shadow on the chest of drawers, and as an object partially seen on the top of the wardrobe.

A second example of pictorial symbols Browne uses is birds. Traditionally birds play a role when they eat the bread crumbs Hansel puts down, but Browne introduces more through his illustrations. Hansel is shown to have a pet dove, a white bird guides Hansel and Gretel to the gingerbread house, and a white duck carries the two children back across the water when they are ready to return. And the bird in the cage, on the title page, will be associated with the passive children pictured sitting in the living room. On the first full page a pattern of bars is used for the first time—as the bars in a chair's back. The pattern is repeated at least four more times: the vertical bars on the headboard of the parents' bed, the lines formed by trees behind the roof of the family home, the vertical bars on the front door, and the bars on the cage that Hansel is in.

Browne draws in readers through his unique illustrations. He has spiced his pictures with the kind of details children enjoy looking at. For example, Gretel's dolly wears a dress of the same fabric as Gretel's dress; Hansel has socks of two different colors; and the previously mentioned bars at windows or cages reoccur throughout the book, as does the triangular shape. Compare these details with the type of details other illustrators slip into their retellings.

Compare and contrast story grammar, and discuss the change in the story, if any, brought about by the setting depicted. Other storytelling elements might be identified and discussed. Several versions, including the Scribner translation and the versions illustrated by Browne and Zwerger, retain the storyteller's coda or verse that traditionally ends the story. The Browne version ends the story with this coda:

> My tale is done; see the mouse run;
>
> Catch it if you would, to make a fur hood.

Chart the story grammar for each tale on the form on page 83 and use it to compare and contrast the setting, characterization, and basic plot of the stories.

2. After comparing and contrasting several versions of the story, write a group or class retelling of the story. Add a coda at the end. Make copies for each child. Leave space on each page or on a blank page opposite the text so that students can illustrate their copy. Compare the illustrations created.

3. Visit another classroom and read versions of "Hansel and Gretel," or read copies of the retold version created in activity 2.

Browne, Anthony. *I Like Books*. Illustrated by Anthony Browne. Knopf, 1989.

Billed as a book for preschoolers, this book is very useful for that age group and older. A little chimpanzee shows all the different kinds of books he likes—funny books, scary books, fairy tales and comic books, books about dinosaurs and monsters. The book focuses on the love of reading.

1. Use this book to encourage each child to bring his or her favorite book to class to give a one-minute oral advertisement for the book. Label the half-hour "I Like Books."

2. Categorize favorite books. Devise the categories and then sort the books according to those attributes. This might lead into the development of an organizational scheme for the books in your classroom.

3. Following activity 2, ask the library media specialist to share information about how books are categorized in the school's library or the public library.

4. To extend the celebration of reading and books, share poems from Lee Bennett Hopkins's collection of poems *Good Books, Good Times!* Illustrated by Harvey Stevenson (Harper, 1990).

McAfee, Annalena. *Kirsty Knows Best*. Illustrated by Anthony Browne. Knopf, 1987.

This is a very nontraditional tale of how one child deals with the school bully. Kirsty handles the problem by bringing new situations into view through her imagination. In the end Nora, the bully, has been dealt with when she flies off as a butterfly. The title page and the last page of the book summarize the theme—metamorphosis of a personality. The title page shows a caterpillar, the last page a butterfly.

1. Look for the reoccurring symbols and shapes that are tucked in the illustrations throughout the book. One of the most used is the antenna-like projections.

2. Talk about how other people deal with class bullies. Then choose one of the following novels to read aloud and discuss. More able readers might use one (or more) of the books as a common reading, after which they could discuss the book in a student-led discussion group.

PLOTTING STORY GRAMMAR

A Story Map

for _____ by _____

(Story title)   (author/illustrator name)

Setting/time

Main characters

Problem _____
_____
_____

First attempt to resolve the problem _____
_____
_____

Second attempt to resolve the problem _____
_____
_____

Third attempt to resolve the problem _____
_____
_____

Resolution/problem solved _____
_____
_____

Conclusion/climax _____
_____
_____

Byars, Betsy. *The 18th Emergency*. Viking, 1973.

Marv Hammerman is one of the biggest, strongest kids in school. Benjie, better known as "Mouse," makes the grave error of taking him on. Although Mouse's buddy has several emergency plans worked out for almost any event, Mouse is sure that Marv is going to get him, and he does everything he can to avoid another confrontation.

Carrick, Carol. *What a Wimp!* Illustrated by Donald Carrick. Clarion, 1983.

Barney's divorced mother has had to move herself and her two sons, Barney and Russ, to the little town of Hillside. Barney presents an opportune target for the sixth-grade bully, Lenny. At first he "borrows" Barney's sled but fails to return it. Lenny hassles Barney at every opportunity. After a near accident Barney decides that he will not fight but will stand his ground.

Mauser, Patricia Rhoads. *A Bundle of Sticks*. Atheneum, 1982.

Day after day, Ben Tyler comes home from school black and blue. He does not know how to fight or retaliate against Boyd and Boyd knows it. Ben's mother convinces Ben that attending kajukenbo school will give him the confidence he needs to face Boyd. Ben doesn't want to fight and doesn't understand how learning to fight will help him cope with Boyd.

Stolz, Mary. *The Bully of Barkham Street*. Harper, 1963.

Edward has to cope with a bully that runs the neighborhood. Martin finds he has to deal with more than just being the bully when Edward discovers how to cope with him.

3. Discuss the concept of metamorphosis and how Browne used the theme in his illustrations for *Kirsty Knows Best*, and how McAfee used the concept to build the text of the story. Identify other books that focus on metamorphosis.

Grindley, Sally. *Knock, Knock! Who's There?* Illustrated by Anthony Browne. Knopf, 1985.

In a delightfully illustrated version of a child's game, a girl is snuggled in her bed with a big teddy bear when she hears "Knock, knock! Who's there?" Fingers grasp the edge of the closed door and the wallpaper has bananas interspersed between the roses. When readers turn the page, they see that "who is there" is a great big gorilla. But he does have on patterned slippers, which may foreshadow action on later pages. With the next knock, the door is nudged open with a pointy black hat. This time the wallpaper has black cats situated between the roses. Opening the door is a witch. The witch has on the same patterned slippers. Further episodes show a ghost, a dragon, and a giant — all wearing the patterned slippers. With the last door knock, her "big cuddly daddy with a mug of hot chocolate and a story to tell" arrives, and he's wearing those same patterned slippers.

1. As a class note the wallpaper and the hand or object squeezing through the door and how they connect with the person/thing that is behind the door when it is opened.

2. Using the information gathered in activity 1, brainstorm a list of other people/things that could show up behind the door. Add ideas for the wallpaper and the hand or object that begins to squeeze through the door.

3. After the brainstormed list is created, give each child two pieces of manila drawing paper. On one piece cut a door so that it folds open. Place that piece on top of the uncut piece of paper and make a pencil mark on the bottom piece to outline the door size. Separate the two pieces of paper. On the uncut paper, but within the pencil lines for the door, ask each student to draw the person or thing that shows up at the door when it is opened. On the piece of paper with the cutout door, create the wallpaper around the door and draw in the details of the door and any "parts" that are squeezing through. Once the drawing is

completed, glue the piece of paper with the cut doorway onto the uncut piece of paper in such a way that the doorway can be folded back to reveal the visitor behind the door. Use these pages to add episodes to the story. Write the dialogue and add the pages for *Knock, Knock! Who's There? Part II.*

4. Another tale that might evoke the same emotions is Tony Ross's *I'm Coming to Get You!* Illustrated by Tony Ross. Dial, 1984. Compare Ross's story with Browne's. A loathsome monster is eating his way through all the planets in the galaxy. He finds "little Tommy Brown on its radar." The monster roars that he is coming to get him. The monster's spaceship nears Earth and the monster finds out where Tommy lives. Tommy has just listened to a book about scary monsters, so when he creeps to bed he searches the stairs (and even the toilet). But in the morning the end of this tale brings an interesting and surprising climax, when "in the daylight Tommy felt silly for having been so scared of monsters. Then, with a terrible roar, the monster pounced.... But Tommy just walked right by." Ross's humor-filled illustrations show that the monster doesn't even reach the shoelaces on Tommy's green and white sneakers. (American School Publishers has a video edition of this story.)

Strauss, Gwen. *The Night Shimmy*. Illustrated by Anthony Browne. Knopf, 1992.

The Night Shimmy speaks for Eric, so he doesn't have to; and he doesn't. One day he meets someone he wants to talk to and play with. The two of them have wonderful adventures together, but the Night Shimmy disappears and Eric realizes that he must choose between him and his new real friend. Browne's colorful, surreal illustrations draw readers into the story and help them explore the theme of imaginary playmates.

1. Extend the theme of imaginary playmates by reading some of the following books:

    Alexander, Martha. *And My Mean Old Mother Will Be Sorry, Blackboard Bear*. Illustrated by Martha Alexander. Dial, 1972.

    Bogart, Jo Ellen. *Daniel's Dog*. Illustrated by Janet Wilson. Scholastic, 1990.

    Dauer, Rosamond. *My Friend, Jasper Jones*. Illustrated by Jerry Joyner. Parents, 1977.

    Greenfield, Eloise. *Me and Nessie*. Illustrated by Moneta Barnett. Crowell, 1975.

    Hazen, Barbara Shook. *The Gorilla Did It!* Illustrated by Ray Cruz. Atheneum, 1974.

    Josse, Barbara M. *The Thinking Place*. Illustrated by Kay Charao. Knopf, 1983.

    Krensky, Stephen. *The Lion Upstairs*. Illustrated by Leigh Grant. Atheneum, 1983.

    Noble, June. *Two Homes for Lynn*. Illustrated by Yuri Salzman. Holt, 1979.

    Rovetch, Lissa. *Trigwater Did It*. Illustrated by Lissa Rovetch. Morrow, 1989.

2. The illustrations in this book have been described as "surreal." Investigate what that means and decide what elements in Browne's illustrations fit that definition.

Browne, Anthony. *Piggybook*. Illustrated by Anthony Browne. Knopf, 1986.

Right from the beginning this book promises visual puns and lots of humor. The cover shows Mrs. Piggott carrying her husband and two sons piggyback—an obvious pun on the word *piggybook*. The story concerns the Piggott family. The family consists of Mr. and Mrs. Piggott and their two sons, Simon and Patrick. The males in the household are "very important" and do "very important" things. They demand breakfast and attention at every turn. After they leave for work and school, Mrs. Piggott washes the dishes, makes the beds, vacuums the carpets, and goes off to work. That evening things begin to change. Almost immediately one sees the unobtrusive evidence of the transformation to real "pigs." First it is only Mr. Piggott's shadow and a few pig images here and there. But in the end, before Mother returns, even the wallpaper's rose blooms have changed to pigs. Browne's masterful use of color sets the tone for each segment of the story. At first Mrs. Piggott is drawn in drab detail, left in the shadows. In the end, illustrations show Mrs. Piggott in a small, bright setting like those scenes depicting the males. The males in the household have discovered the joys of helping with the housework, and Mrs. Piggott repairs the car. And, of course, only Anthony Browne knows if it is mere coincidence that Mrs. Piggott resembles his wife, Jane.

1. After reading the book, take another look at the illustrations and note all the subtle (and not-so-subtle) signs of pigs. In addition to the transformation to pigs, there are references to "the three little pigs" and "the big bad wolf." Notice the shadow of the wolf through the window of the dining room and, of course, the license plate in the last illustration that reads (backwards) 123 PIGS. My favorite transformation, however, is the change from roses on the wallpaper to pigs, and back to roses again in the end.

2. Discuss any message that Browne is trying to convey through his book. Intermediate/ middle school students may wish to debate the merits of Browne's message.

3. Make your own illustration of the Piggott family and include some pigs in nonobvious places.

4. The name "Piggott" lent itself to the symbol of becoming "pigs." Use either your given name or your family surname and identify a symbol that might represent your name. Then draw an illustration of a room in your house, including that symbol in as many places as possible. If your name does not lend itself to this activity, use your school's name and its mascot. Draw a picture of your school classroom and include your mascot in as many places in your schoolroom as possible.

Browne, Anthony. *Things I Like.* Illustrated by Anthony Browne. Knopf, 1989.
The same little chimp that appears in *I Like Books* now catalogs the *things* he likes. He puts them into categories as quiet, active, or imaginative play.

1. Follow the chimp's lead and categorize the activities that the class engaged in during the previous morning or day.

2. Make a book of other things that can be categorized. The chimp has categorized books and activities—you can categorize favorite sandwiches, kinds of clothes, etc.

3. Write your own book "Things I Like."

Strauss, Gwen. *Trail of Stones*. Illustrated by Anthony Browne. Knopf, 1990.

This book of provocative poems is appropriate for the more mature reader—use discretion with younger readers. However, older students will find the comparison to the originals fodder for much discussion about viewpoint and characterization. Each of Strauss's poems is illustrated with a black-and-white illustration created by Browne.

Browne, Anthony. *The Tunnel*. Illustrated by Anthony Browne. Knopf, 1989.

Jack and Rose are siblings who argue whenever they are together. This is the story of their transformation from best enemies to best friends. This literary fairy tale about contemporary children brings to mind the story of Hansel and Gretel.

1. Compare Jack and Rose's mother and her motives to the motives of Hansel and Gretel's mother.

2. Compare Hansel and Gretel to Jack and Rose.

3. Discuss how this story compares to a fairy tale. Note that a fairy tale by definition is part of the larger body of literature classified as folklore. These stories are passed down from generation to generation and retold in the words of the storyteller. A literary tale is one that is written in a particular style (as in the style of a fairy tale or legend) but has been originated by a contemporary author.

4. This book also examines sibling relationships. Refer to the booklist in the entry for *Changes*. Read some of those titles and compare the different types of sibling relationships.

Browne, Anthony. *Willy and Hugh*. Illustrated by Anthony Browne. Knopf, 1991.

Willy, the mild-mannered chimpanzee from *Willy the Champ* and *Willy the Wimp*, literally runs into a gorilla named Hugh Jape. What happens? They immediately become friends and do everything together: they watch joggers, go to the zoo (to see people in cages), and visit the library. When Willy's archenemy, Buster Nose, appears, Buster finds that there is a surprise in store for him. It's a great story of friendship for every child who's ever felt he or she didn't fit in.

1. Explain why you think Willy and Hugh Jape become friends.

2. Explain in writing why you would or would not like Hugh Jape for a friend.

3. At the end of the story Willy is able to help Hugh Jape. Read any version of the fable "The Lion and the Mouse." Versions are available in many collections of Aesop or La Fontaine fables. After reading the fable discuss how the ending of Browne's tale compares with the message in the fable.

Browne, Anthony. *Willy the Champ*. Illustrated by Anthony Browne. Knopf, 1985.

Willy doesn't seem to be good at anything. But he always tries, even though everyone makes fun of him. Then Buster Nose shows up. He throws a punch at Willy. Willy ducks. Buster Nose stands up and comes underneath Willy's chin. Willy is the champ.

1. This book has Willy dealing with the neighborhood bully. Refer to the entry for *Kirsty Knows Best* and correlate the responses for McAfee's book with this title by Browne.

2. Collect information about chimpanzees. Compare the information you find with the information you gathered about gorillas. (See the entry for *Gorilla*.)

Browne, Anthony. *Willy the Wimp*. Illustrated by Anthony Browne. Knopf, 1984.

Willy would not hurt a fly. All the suburban gorillas call him Willy the Wimp. Willy reads an advertisement for information that would keep him from being a wimp. He sends his money in and promptly gets a package. It tells him to exercise, to jog, to go on a special diet (mountains of bananas), and to go to aerobics class. It makes other suggestions that are supposed to help him become bigger. He follows the directions for months but doesn't get any bigger; but he gains confidence. He saves a woman from being harassed by a group of suburban gorillas, and then he promptly runs into a light post—BANG! He apologizes to the post.

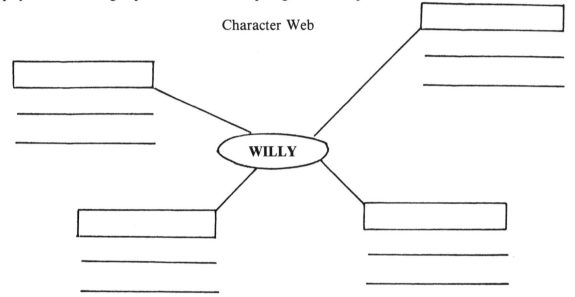

Character Web

As books about Willy are read, determine characteristics that you would attribute to Willy. Those characteristics, such as helpful or friendly, should be placed in the rectangles. On the lines below the rectangles cite the passages that support your choice.

1. Discuss what makes a person a "wimp." List the characteristics on the character web above.

2. Is Willy really a wimp? Discuss how Willy changes, if he does, from the beginning of the book to the end.

3. Would you like to have Willy for a friend? Why or why not?

Joanna Cole

Joanna Cole

From *An Author a Month (for Dimes)* by Sharron L. McElmeel (Libraries Unlimited, 1992)

Joanna Cole

Joanna Cole still has her copy of a book she remembers reading as a child, *Bugs, Insects, and Such*. During her growing-up years, she read that book over and over again. She found plants and animals in her family's small backyard, where she spent a lot of time watching insects, wasps, bees, crickets, and other bugs.

Joanna Cole was born in Newark, New Jersey, on August 11, 1944, and grew up in nearby East Orange, where she went to elementary school. Her favorite subjects in school were science and writing. When she started writing children's books in 1969, she wanted to write books like those by Herbert Zim and Millicent Selsam. She has written many books about animals and books on a variety of science topics, including the Magic School Bus books, which Bruce Degen illustrates.

Joanna Cole's husband, Philip, is a retired psychotherapist who sometimes collaborates with her on books. One of their recent titles is *Big Goof and Little Goof*. The family places a high value on humor, and this book makes readers laugh.

Joanna Cole and her family lived in New York City for many years, but in 1989 they moved to Sandy Hook, Connecticut, with their dog, Muffy, and their four guinea pigs, Isabel, Louise, Shirley, and Chuck. Rachel, the Cole's teenage daughter, spends a lot of time riding horses. And Joanna Cole explores her backyard, enjoys her garden, and writes books.

Chapter

7

Joanna Cole

ABOUT THE AUTHOR

Joanna Cole was born Joanna Basilea on August 11, 1944, in Newark, New Jersey, to Mario and Elizabeth Basilea. She grew up nearby in East Orange. As a young child she was fascinated with science and enjoyed hunting for bugs, insects, and all sorts of crawly creatures. Her family's small backyard, filled with ferns, poison ivy plants, and mulberry trees, was her haven for exploration. But other than a profound curiosity about her surroundings, her childhood was really quite ordinary. Her father had a housepainting business and her mother was a secretary. From her father she learned to be enterprising and from her mother she learned a sensitivity for language. Often during mealtimes either Joanna or her sister was sent to get the dictionary to check a word. Their neighborhood was filled with children—fifty on her street alone. All summer long they played street games until it was too dark to see the ball.

The elementary school was just around the corner. Joanna loved school reports and still has some she wrote. She liked to read, especially science books. One of her favorite books, *Bugs, Insects, and Such*, was a gift from an aunt and uncle. She read it over and over again. Her interest in science and in writing continued through school, and after graduating from high school she entered the University of Massachusetts. She later attended Indiana University before graduating in 1967 from the City College of New York with a degree in psychology. Two years before graduation she met her future husband, Philip Cole, literally on a street corner. They had known each other as teenagers, and within a month of their meeting again they married and moved to New York City, where Joanna worked part time at *Newsweek*, attended City College, and enjoyed the atmosphere of the city.

Cole continued her studies with graduate courses in education, and she spent a year as a librarian in a Brooklyn elementary school, P.S. 46. She spent all of her time there sharing books with children. That experience made her want to write children's books, and since many of the children in the school had reading difficulties, she decided to commit herself to writing easy-to-read books. During presentations where she explains her writing style, she says that she always tries to make her text as simple as possible and still make it interesting while saying exactly what she needs and wants to say. Those goals have made writing a real challenge for her and has forced her to make her writing very clear. Cole says, "[The effort] is worth it ... [when I] know that almost every child can read most of my books."

After her year as a librarian, Cole became a letters correspondent at *Newsweek* and later a senior editor at Doubleday Books for Young Readers. Soon she was writing children's books of her own. She knew she wanted to write the type of books written by Herbert Zim and Millicent Selsam, whose work she greatly admired. Cole's father told her about an article he had read in the *Wall Street Journal* about cockroaches. The article referred to the cockroach as a living fossil. Since Cole had always been interested in insects, she researched the subject thoroughly and wrote a manuscript.

An editor at William Morrow Publishers, Connie Epstein, accepted the manuscript and encouraged her to keep writing children's books. The book, *Cockroaches*, with illustrations by Jean Zallinger, was published in 1971 by Morrow. She worked at Doubleday for about ten years, while continuing to write. In the early 1980s she left her editor's job and became a full-time writer.

Cole does not write about events in her life but rather about subjects that interest her. Most of her information books were inspired by her intellectual curiosity. From her interest in growth and change came *My Puppy Is Born* (Morrow, 1973), *A Chick Hatches* (Morrow, 1976), and other books dealing with birth and growth. Her interest in growth and change brought her to animal adaptation and evolution. From that interest she researched and wrote *A Snake's Body* (Morrow, 1981), *A Bird's Body* (Morrow, 1982), and several other similar books focusing on frogs, horses, and cats. Sometimes editors call and suggest topics. One suggestion led to *Anna Banana: 101 Jump Rope Rhymes* (Morrow, 1989), and another suggestion led to *Hungry, Hungry Sharks* (Random, 1986), a book in Random House's Step into Reading series. But even if the topic is suggested by someone else, it must be interesting to Cole. She feels strongly that good nonfiction grows out of an author's own interest in a subject.

Cole's fiction writing is about characters who figure out how to get along with others and at the same time make their lives more satisfactory to themselves. Sometimes the stories are adventurous and somewhat scary. That is the case with Cole's *Bony-Legs* (Morrow, 1983; Scholastic, 1986), a Russian tale about a girl who escapes from a horrible witch, and *Doctor Change* (Morrow, 1986), where a boy outwits a mean wizard. Some of her funny books include *Norma Jean, Jumping Bean* (Random, 1987), another Step into Reading book, and *Monster Manners* (Scholastic, 1985), a story about a young monster who does not act monstrous. Instead, she acts sweet and is a great disappointment to her parents.

In 1985 an editor at Scholastic called Cole and suggested that she combine her talent for writing fiction with her interest in nonfiction. The editor, Craig Walker, suggested that a story be woven around the idea of a class field trip. The trip would be humorous but the information would be presented during the field trip. Joanna Cole loved the idea right from the start. She realized how the humor and science would mesh. She could envision the teacher being completely in character as she lectured about science *and* for the school children to react with the usual moans and groans. Immediately she began working on *The Magic School Bus at the Waterworks*. At the time, she did not know that Bruce Degen would be the illustrator, nor did she know what Ms. Frizzle would look like. She didn't even know that there would be an "Arnold" in the book. But when she sat down to write the book, she had already done extensive research on water systems. She was alone in her office with a blank piece of paper and a need to create a coherent science book that would make kids laugh. The idea that had seemed possible when Cole and Walker had discussed the idea over lunch now seemed like an impossible task. She did everything she could to avoid beginning the task. Cole said, "I did everything else but write: I answered mail, I went shopping. I even cleaned my apartment—which shows how truly desperate I was! Finally, one morning I said to myself, 'Okay, Joanna, this is it. Today you *must* start this book!' I sat down and wrote these words:

'Our class really has bad luck.

This year we got Ms. Frizzle,

the strangest teacher in school.

We don't mind Ms. Frizzle's strange dresses,

Or her strange shoes.

It's the way she acts that really gets us.'"

Cole says she knew how Ms. Frizzle would act. She was to be a science enthusiast who encouraged her classes to learn science through hands-on activities. The students would build models, do experiments, and read science books. She really had no idea exactly what the strange dresses and shoes would be like. So she had to think about it. Eventually she came up with the idea that "the Fritz" would wear dresses with outlandish patterns on them, and shoes with "weird ornaments."

Joanna Cole begins every Magic School Bus book by going to the library to read, read, and read. She consults scientists, takes notes, and organizes the material. As she writes she makes a blank book dummy in which she tapes the text, the word balloons, and, of course, the school reports. She writes the school reports, by hand, on yellow lined paper. When the dummy is ready she meets with Bruce Degen, the illustrator, and the editors at Scholastic. Usually authors and illustrators do not meet to discuss their book. Each creates his or her own part by working with the appropriate editor at the publishing house. However, in this situation Cole and Degen do meet and work very closely together on the final book. Speaking about this collaboration, Cole says, "Our working relationship has turned out to be the best thing about the Magic School Bus. We humorously banter to each other the whole time a book is in progress. He makes suggestions for the text. I put in my two cents worth about the pictures. He says there are too many words and not enough room for illustrations. I say he has to squeeze everything in anyway. He says I take too long with the writing. I say he has to make up the time by working extra hard. And, meanwhile, the editors are having a cow wondering if the book will ever be done. In the midst of this, we all genuinely like and respect each other—and eventually the books do come out."

Cole and Degen's first collaboration resulted in the publication of *The Magic School Bus at the Waterworks* (Scholastic, 1986). Even though Scholastic editor Craig Walker, Cole, and Degen were all hoping for success, Cole says, "The most amazing thing about The Magic School Bus series is the way kids, parents, and teachers have reacted to it. The books bring out creativity in everyone. Teachers dress up as Ms. Frizzle, classes decorate their rooms to look like the Magic School Bus, and everywhere kids are writing their own Magic School Bus books, complete with wonderful pictures and jokes."

Joanna Cole enjoys getting mail and has a whole collection of *bus* books sent to her by artist-author children. During a joint presentation at the International Reading Association's conference in Las Vegas in May 1991, Bruce Degen expressed equal pleasure with the volume of mail. He said, "The best compliment is when someone uses something you've created to create something else." *The Magic School Bus at the Waterworks* proved to be so popular that a special edition of the books was requested. Cole and Degen revised the book so it specifically related to the waterworks system in New York City. The book is used in the New York City Schools.

When Bruce Degen first met Joanna Cole she had a frizzy perm, so Cole surmised that Ms. Frizzle's looks evolved from that first image. In reality, however, Degen says he based Ms. Frizzle's physical appearance on his tenth-grade geometry teacher. She had blond frizzy hair and a face that beamed with the thought of the pure logic of the material she was presenting to her class. Degen does not stop with illustrating the obvious impressions. He often attempts to sneak little things into the illustrations. In *The Magic School Bus inside the Human Body* he attempted to put "Burp" on the sign on the front of the bus. The editors asked him to remove the word. Degen, Cole, and Walker also had discussions about the color of the "goosh" inside the stomach of a person and how the children should get out of Arnold's body. (Arnold never did realize that he was the field trip.) Craig stipulated that there be no toilet scenes to get the children out of Arnold's body. Other suggestions were to have Arnold bleed, sweat, or burp, but they finally decided on the nose and a sneeze. The editors requested nothing green in the paintings.

The Magic School Bus books tell of field trips to the waterworks, inside the earth, inside the human body, and through the solar system. At the end of each book, Ms. Frizzle's dress and shoes foreshadow the next field trip (and Magic School Bus book). For example, at the end of *The Magic School Bus inside the Human Body*, Ms. Frizzle's dress is patterned with rocket ships signaling the trip through the solar system. In *The Magic School Bus Lost in the Solar System*, Ms. Frizzle finishes the lecture and field trip in rain gear, suggesting the next book, *The Magic School Bus on the Ocean Floor*.

During the nearly twenty-three years the Coles lived in New York City, they lived quite close to the Museum of Natural History, where Cole did much of her research. She also frequented bookstores, went to movies, saw friends, and wrote. Her husband, Philip, is now retired and has become an abstract artist. Together they have written *Hank and Frank Fix Up the House* (Scholastic, 1988) and *Big Goof and Little Goof* (Scholastic, 1989). As she did during her childhood, Joanna enjoys her backyard and garden. Joanna writes her own jokes for the Magic School Bus books, but her daughter, Rachel, has contributed a few. But Rachel spends most of her time riding horses near Sandy Hook, Connecticut, where the Coles now live with their dog and guinea pigs.

SETTING THE STAGE

Joanna Cole has written many fiction and nonfiction books. Gather as many as possible for a display in your author center. On a bulletin board place an enlargement of a school bus. If miniature wallet-sized pictures of individuals in your class or group are available, use a picture of each student (or a photocopy of the photograph) and place the picture in the window of the school bus. Place a large-sized drawing of Ms. Frizzle in the lower left-hand corner of the bulletin board. Then set your class's sights on a Magic School Bus trip through the books by Joanna Cole. In another spot on the board feature a copy of the author picture page and the large-print information page from this book.

Begin by introducing the Magic School Bus books to your students. Scholastic has a big book edition of *The Magic School Bus at the Waterworks*. Share some of the other information about the author and her work by retelling some of the details contained in the "About the Author" section in this chapter. Introduce other books by Cole and encourage students to read them. As students read the books, they might record the stories onto a cassette tape. Those tapes could be made available for other students to listen to. Cole's retelling of a Baba Yaga tale from Russia, *Bony-Legs*, is available on a read-along cassette from American School Publishers. The cassette might be put in a listening center along with copies of the book and the student-made tapes.

Joanna Cole writes the school reports that she includes in the Magic School Bus books on yellow legal tablets. In your writing center include yellow writing tablets along with a variety of other materials that will encourage children to write their own reports or information-filled books. Provide drawing paper for illustrations, covers for books, and plenty of paper and writing utensils.

As children read books by Joanna Cole, ask them to make comments about the books. The comments should be written on 3"-×-5" cards and put in a "comments" section on the author bulletin board. Other readers can read the comments, decide what books they might like to read, and make comments of their own.

IDEA CUPBOARD

Cole, Joanna. *Bony-Legs*. Illustrated by Dirk Zimmer. Macmillan, 1983; Scholastic, 1986.

Bony-Legs is another name for Baba Yaga. Sasha meets the witch who lives in a house that stands on chicken legs. Sasha's kindnesses to a cat, a dog, and a squeaky gate return to her as the cat, dog, and gate help her to escape being eaten by the wicked witch.

1. Discuss this story's story grammar and then compare the story and its corresponding details with some of the Baba Yaga tales:

   Kimmel, Eric A., reteller. *Baba Yaga: A Russian Folktale*. Illustrated by Megan Lloyd. Holiday, 1991.
   Marina is cursed with a horn in the middle of her forehead and is harassed by her stepsister and stepmother. When Marina's stepmother commands her to go into the forest and borrow a needle and thread from Baba Yaga, Marina is obliged to obey. Heeding advice she was given by a frog, Marina aids a tree, a gate, a dog, and a cat. When Baba Yaga threatens Marina, her kindnesses to others return to her.

Silverman, Maida. *Anna and the Seven Swans*. Illustrated by David Small. Morrow, 1984.

Anna attempts to find her wandering little brother. On her journey she stops to pull cherry dumplings from a pleading oven and to bail milk from a river that is about to overflow its jelly banks. Later when Anna attempts to hide from Baba Yaga, those that she helped come to her aid. Illustrations are watercolors washed in brown tones.

Small, Ernest. *Baba Yaga*. Illustrated by Blair Lent. Houghton, 1966.

In this version Baba Yaga, the traditional witch of Russian folklore, is portrayed as a fascinating and harmless witch who likes to eat only bad children. Blair Lent's illustrations give her a considerably more frightening appearance.

2. Compare the Baba Yaga/Bony-Legs tale to the "Hansel and Gretel" tale. The witch in "Hansel and Gretel" is similar in personality and motive to Baba Yaga. Additional "Hansel and Gretel" retellings are cited in the booklist in the entry for Anthony Browne's *Hansel and Gretel* in chapter 6.

Grimm, Jacob, and Wilhelm Grimm. *Hansel and Gretel*. Illustrated by Anthony Browne. Knopf, 1981.

Grimm, Jacob, and Wilhelm Grimm. *Hansel and Gretel*. Illustrated by Susan Jeffers. Translated from the German by Mrs. Edgar Lucas and included in the collection *Fairy Tales of the Bros. Grimm* (Lippincott, 1902). Dial, 1980.

Grimm, Jacob, and Wilhelm Grimm. *Hansel and Gretel*. Adapted and illustrated by Arnold Lobel. Delacorte, 1971.

Marshall, James, reteller. *Hansel and Gretel*. Illustrated by James Marshall. Dial, 1990.

Cole, Joanna. *Bully Trouble*. Illustrated by Marylin Hafner. Random, 1989. (A Step into Reading book: Step 2)

Big Eddie is a bully. He trips Arlo and makes him fall into a puddle, takes his potato chips, throws Robby's mitt away, and steals Arlo and Robby's soda. Arlo and Robby cannot let Eddie continue to bully them, so they decide to give him something to think about. They fix a special soda and a chili sauce sandwich and take the soda and sandwich to the park. When Eddie comes along and takes their lunch, he gets a hot mouth from biting into the sandwich. And when he grabs the soda for relief, he takes a swig of a special "Bully Soda" that the boys have concocted.

1. Use this story to introduce the following novels about a similar problem: How does one deal with the neighborhood or school bully?

   Byars, Betsy. *The 18th Emergency*. Viking, 1973.

   Carrick, Carol. *What a Wimp!* Illustrated by Donald Carrick. Clarion, 1983.

   Mauser, Patricia Rhoads. *A Bundle of Sticks*. Atheneum, 1982.

   Stolz, Mary. *The Bully of Barkham Street*. HarperCollins, 1963.

2. Discuss why bullies pick on other children. How could classmates help a bully become more likable and get rid of his or her bully tendencies?

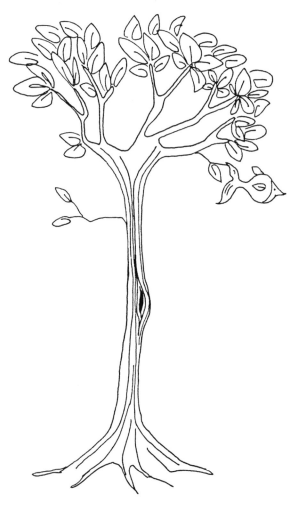

Cole, Joanna. *Don't Tell the Whole World*. Illustrated by Kate Duke. Crowell, 1990.

Emma is a lovable wife but she just cannot keep from telling everything she knows. John doesn't like her telling the whole world, but he usually doesn't stay mad for very long. However, one day John finds a treasure buried in his farm field. He knows that Emma would not be able to keep the treasure a secret and that if the news got out, their greedy landlord would want the gold. So John devises a plan to create several absurd situations and then to uncover the gold in front of Emma. When she tells the landlord of finding a smoked fish growing in a tree, a yellow weed that grows jugs of cider, and stones that taste like molasses candies, he decides that all of it is a dream, including the idea that John has found money in his field.

1. Compare the strategy used by John with the trick the farmer's wife plays on the lazy farmer in *A Treeful of Pigs* by Arnold Lobel, illustrated by Anita Lobel (Greenwillow, 1979).

2. What did John mean when he said, "Good luck *visits* a lot of people but it only *stays* with the ones who use their brains!"

3. *Don't Tell the Whole World* is filled with absurd happenings. Compare the events in that book with those in Wanda Gag's "The Husband Who Was to Mind the House" in *The Arbuthnot Anthology of Children's Literature*, 3d ed., edited by May Hill Arbuthnot (Scott, Foresman, 1971). The story is also available as a single-edition tale retold by Wanda Gag in *Gone Is Gone* (Coward, 1935).

Cole, Joanna. *Evolution: The Story of How Life Developed on Earth*. Illustrated by Aliki. Crowell, 1987; Trophy, 1988.

This book develops the concept of fossils, how they are formed, and how the study of location and type of fossil can lead to conclusions concerning the origin of earth and life on earth. It is a simple summary of the development of life, from simple cells to plants and animals that are living today.

1. This book highlights the importance of studying fossils and builds the connection between fossils and life on earth. Extend the study of fossils by reading the following books:

    Aliki. *Fossils Tell of Long Ago*. Illustrated by Aliki. Crowell, 1972; rev. ed., 1990.

    Taylor, Paul D. *Fossil*. Illustrated with photographs. Knopf, 1990. (An Eyewitness book)

2. Follow the directions in Aliki's *Fossils Tell of Long Ago* and make a "one-minute-old fossil"—a clay imprint of a hand. The directions suggest using clay, but a similar and more permanent "fossil" can be made by using plaster of paris.

Cole, Joanna. *Find the Hidden Insect*. Photographs by Jerome Wexler. Morrow, 1979.

Photographs show insects concealing themselves in their environment. The black-and-white photos emphasize how the insects camouflage themselves by shape and pattern.

1. Extend the concept of camouflage by sharing *Backyard Insects* by Millicent E. Selsam and Ronald Goor, with full-color photographs by Ronald Goor (Four Winds, 1983). The text explains how color and shape camouflage common garden insects. Twenty insects are featured.

2. Read Nancy Winslow Parker and Joan Richards Wright's *Bugs* (Greenwillow, 1987). After gathering information about other insects/bugs from the following books, write an innovation on Parker and Wright's book. Be sure to include information about the insect or bug's ability to camouflage itself.

    Cole, Joanna. *An Insect's Body*. Illustrated by Jerome Wexler and Raymond A. Mendez. Morrow, 1984.

    Mound, Laurence. *Insect*. Illustrated with photographs. Knopf, 1990. (An Eyewitness book)

    Selsam, Millicent. *Where Do They Go? Insects in the Winter*. Illustrated by Arabelle Wheatley. Four Winds, 1982.

Cole, Joanna. *It's Too Noisy*. Illustrated by Kate Duke. Crowell, 1989.

A man lived in a little house with his wife, grandmother, grandfather, lots of children, and a little bitty baby. Because the house was very noisy and the farmer wanted quiet, he went to the Wise Man for advice. The Wise Man suggested that he bring into his house his rooster and chickens. When the house did not get quiet, the Wise Man told him to bring in his pigs, sheep, donkey, and cow. But the house only got noisier. At last the Wise Man advised the farmer to take all the animals out of the house. He did. There still was the noise of the children and the people in the house, but since there was no clucking, crowing, oinking, baaing, mooing, or braying, the house now seemed very quiet.

1. Compare and contrast *It's Too Noisy* with Margot Zemach's *It Could Always Be Worse* (Farrar, 1976). Zemach's tale is cited as being a Yiddish tale. A poor man lives in a one-room hut with his mother, wife, and six children. The house seems overcrowded and is filled with crying and quarreling. When the poor man seeks advice from the rabbi, he receives essentially the same advice that was given to the farmer in Cole's retelling. The rabbi tells the man to take a chicken or two into his house. Soon the man has goats, chickens, geese, and a cow in his hut. Finally the rabbi's advice is to let all of the animals out of the hut. He does and the house seems much quieter and more spacious. In both Cole's and Zemach's stories, the situation at the beginning has the man feeling that the house is too noisy and overcrowded. The end of the story has the man in the same situation (number of occupants, etc.), but now the man perceives the situation as being much better. Discuss why this is true.

2. Compare the situation and outcome in Cole's and Zemach's stories with the situation and turn of events in *Could Anything Be Worse?* by Marilyn Hirsch (Holiday, 1974).

Cole, Joanna. *Large as Life Animals: In Beautiful Life-Size Paintings*. Illustrated by Kenneth Lilly. Knopf, 1985; 1990. (Originally published in 1985 as two volumes: *Large as Life Daytime Animals* and *Large as Life Nighttime Animals*)
Each animal is drawn exactly the size it is in real life. Readers can measure the pictures to compare the size of the red squirrel, the common tree frog, the brown hare, the wood mouse, and sixteen other animals. Each is featured in a full double-page painting accompanied by a brief but interesting paragraph or two that highlights information about the animal. The final pages contain "Nature Notes" that give more statistical and scientific information about each animal.

1. Compare the sizes of the twenty animals featured. Create a bar graph showing the comparative lengths of the animals.

2. The animals included in this book are Red Squirrel, Little Blue Penguin, Queen Alexandra's Birdwing Butterfly, Common Tree Frog, Lesser Spotted Woodpecker, Eastern Chipmunk, Black-tailed Prairie Dog, Bee Hummingbird, Squirrel Monkey, Ermine, Brown Hare, Greater Indian Fruit Bat, Chinchilla, Wood Mouse, Giant Toad, Royal Antelope, Fennec Fox, Elf Owl, Lesser Mouse Lemur, and Western European Hedgehog.

   a. Research more information about each animal.

   b. Choose other animals that interest students. Incorporate mathematical measurement skills by creating life-size pictures of the animals researched. Some full-size illustrations may not fit on a standard-size page, so use large sheets of rolled paper or newsprint. For especially large animals one might need to piece paper together.

3. Use the information in this animal book in conjunction with books by Jan Brett, especially *The Mitten*. After reading the information about hedgehogs in Cole's book, discuss how accurate images of the hedgehog are incorporated into the books by Brett. See index for reference to information about hedgehogs in chapter 5.

Cole, Joanna. *The Magic School Bus at the Waterworks*, illustrated by Bruce Degen, Scholastic, 1986; *The Magic School Bus inside the Earth*, illustrated by Bruce Degen, Scholastic, 1987; *The Magic School Bus inside the Human Body*, illustrated by Bruce Degen, Scholastic, 1989; *The Magic School Bus Lost in the Solar System*, illustrated by Bruce Degen, Scholastic, 1990.

The Magic School Bus books contain much information about the fantastic journeys that result from the field trips that the class takes. The books tell readers how water is purified, what goes on inside the earth, how the human body digests food, and where the planets in our solar system are. Ms. Frizzle, a science teacher, lectures to the class as they travel. Her eccentric wardrobes add to the visual fun and foreshadow the action. Each of the books contains scientific reports, information on the topic, jokes, and a humorous story.

1. Before reading any of the titles, brainstorm with the class what they already know about the topic.

    a. Record each bit of volunteered information on a large piece of brown or white wrapping paper.

    b. Do not make any judgments as to the validity of the information submitted.

    c. After the list is made, ask students to get into groups of two or three and discuss the information on the list. Each group should decide if they can accept each item as true or not.

    d. After the groups have had ample time to discuss the list, circle those items on the list that all groups can accept as true—without reservation.

    e. Suggest that the students read books on the featured topic to determine the validity of the uncircled items on the list. To help the students get started, read aloud Joanna Cole and Bruce Degen's book on the topic. Go back to the list and see what statements the information validated; add any additional questions that might have been brought up.

    f. Encourage wide reading on the specific topic. The goal is to verify or disprove as much of the information on the brainstormed list as possible.

    g. Discuss the information garnered from the brainstorming, Cole and Degen's book, and the groups' individual research activity.

2. Read the side panels in each of the books. Perform the experiments and set up the observations suggested. For example, in *The Magic School Bus inside the Human Body*, one side panel suggests a microscope observation of a cell. The panel describes how to obtain cell samples from the inside of one's cheek, make a microscope slide, and use the microscope to see the cells.

3. Read other books about the topics covered in the Magic School Bus series.

The Earth

Gallant, Roy A. *Earth's Changing Climate*. Macmillan, 1979.

Seymour, Simon. *Earth: Our Planet in Space*. Illustrated with photographs. Macmillan, 1984.

Silver, Donald M. *Earth: The Ever-Changing Planet*. Random House Library of Knowledge, No. 9. Random, 1989.

Human Body

Allison, Linda. *Blood and Guts: A Working Guide to Your Own Insides*. Illustrated by Linda Allison. Little, 1976.

Bruun, Ruth D., and Bertel Bruun. *The Human Body*. Random, 1982.

Caselli, Giovanni. *The Human Body*. Illustrated by Giovanni Caselli, et al. Grosset, 1987.

Cole, Joanna. *Cuts, Breaks, Bruises, and Burns*. Illustrated by True Kelley. Crowell, 1985.

Crump, Donald J., editor. *Your Wonderful Body*. Illustrated by photographs. National Geographic, 1982.

Miller, Jonathan. *The Human Body*. Illustrated by David Pelham. Viking, 1983. (A pop-up book)

Silver, Donald M. *Life on Earth: Biology Today*. Illustrations by Patricia J. Wynne. Random, 1983.

Solar System

Blumberg, Rhoda. *First Travel Guide to the Moon: What to Pack, How to Go, and What to See When You Get There*. Illustrated by Roy Doty. Four Winds, 1980.

Branley, Franklyn M. *The Planets in Our Solar System*. Illustrated by Don Madden. Crowell, 1981.

Branley, Franklyn M. *The Sky Is Full of Stars*. Illustrated by Felicia Bond. Crowell, 1981.

Branley, Franklyn M. *The Sun: Our Nearest Star*. Illustrated by Don Madden. Harper, 1988.

Collins, Michael. *Flying to the Moon and Other Strange Places*. Farrar, 1976.

Gallant, Roy A. *The Constellations*. Four Winds, 1979. (Illustrated with black-and-white charts)

Maurer, Richard. *Nova Space Explorer's Guide: Where to Go and What to See*. Clarkson N. Potter, 1985.

Ride, Sally, and Susan Okie. *To Space and Back*. Lothrop, 1986. (Illustrated with photographs)

Simon, Seymour. *Jupiter*. Morrow, 1985. (Illustrated with photographs)

Simon, Seymour. *Look to the Night Sky*. Viking, 1977. (Illustrated with charts)

Simon, Seymour. *Mars*. Morrow, 1987. (Illustrated with photographs)

Simon, Seymour. *The Moon*. Four Winds, 1984. (Illustrated with black-and-white photographs)

Simon, Seymour. *The Sun*. Morrow, 1986. (Illustrated with photographs)

Simon, Seymour. *Uranus*. Morrow, 1987. (Illustrated with photographs)

Stoff, Joshua. *The Voyage of the Ruslan: The First Manned Exploration of Mars*. Illustrated by Joshua Stoff. Atheneum, 1986.

Water

Bennett, David. *Water*. Illustrated by Rosalinda Knightley. Bantam, 1989.

Cochrane, Jennifer. *Water Ecology*. Watts, 1987.

Hammer, Trudy J. *Water Resources*. Watts, 1985.

Johnston, Tom. *Water! Water!* Illustrated by Sarah Pooley. Gareth Stevens, 1987.

Pringle, Laurence. *Water: The Next Great Resource Battle*. Macmillan, 1982.

Seixas, Judith S. *Water: What It Is, What It Does*. Morrow, 1987.

Cole, Joanna. *Monster Manners*. Illustrated by Jared Lee. Scholastic, 1985.
Monsters are supposed to act monstrous, but this young monster does not. Instead she acts sweet and is a great disappointment to her parents. Other books about Rosie and Prunella include *Monster Movie* (Scholastic, 1986) and *Monster Valentines* (Scholastic, 1989).

1. Read Pat Hutchins's *The Very Worst Monster* (Greenwillow, 1985) and Hutchins's *Where's the Baby?* (Greenwillow, 1988).

   a. Compare Hazel and Billy to Rosie and Prunella. In Cole's monster stories Rosie is a friendly monster and Prunella is a mean monster. Characterize Hazel and Billy in relation to Rosie and Prunella.

   b. Using information obtained from Cole's and Hutchins's monster titles, create a comparison chart listing the expectations you believe monster parents have for their children and expectations your parents have for you.

   c. As a class write a list of phrases that would complete the following sentence: I would like to be Prunella for a day because ...

2. After reading about other monsters in the following books, draw a picture of the monster you envision. Write a paragraph describing your monster.

   Alcock, Vivien. *The Monster Garden*. Doubleday, 1988.

   Cole, William, and Mike Thaler. *Monster Knock Knocks*. Illustrated by Mike Thaler. Dell, 1988.

   Crowe, Robert L. *Clyde Monster*. Illustrated by Kay Chorao. Dutton, 1976.

   Flora, James. *The Great Green Turkey Creek Monster*. Illustrated by James Flora. Atheneum, 1976.

   Galdone, Paul. *The Monster and the Tailor*. Illustrated by Paul Galdone. Clarion, 1982.

   Mayer, Mercer. *Liza Lou and the Yeller Belly Swamp*. Illustrated by Mercer Mayer. Four Winds, 1980.

   Moore, Lilian. "The Monster's Birthday." In *Spooky Rhymes and Riddles*. Scholastic, 1972.

   Mueller, Virginia. *Monster and the Baby*. Illustrated by Lynn Munsinger. Viking, 1989.

Prelutsky, Jack. *Nightmares to Trouble Your Sleep.* Illustrated by Arnold Lobel. Greenwillow, 1976.

Ross, Tony. *I'm Coming to Get You.* Illustrated by Tony Ross. Dial, 1984.

Smith, Janice Lee. *The Monster in the Third Dresser Drawer and Other Stories about Adam Joshua.* HarperCollins, 1981.

Stevens, Kathleen. *The Beast in the Bathtub.* Illustrated by Ray Bowler. Gareth Stevens, 1985.

Stevenson, James. *What's under My Bed?* Illustrated by James Stevenson. Greenwillow, 1983.

Ungerer, Tomi. *The Beast of Monsieur Racine.* Illustrated by Tomi Ungerer. Farrar, 1971.

Viorst, Judith. *My Mama Says There Aren't Any Zombies, Ghosts, Vampires, Creatures, Demons, Monsters, Fiends, Goblins, or Things.* Illustrated by Kay Chorao. Atheneum, 1973.

Willis, Jeanne. *The Monster Bed.* Illustrated by Susan Varley. Lothrop, 1987.

Winthrop, Elizabeth. *Maggie and the Monster.* Illustrated by Tomie dePaola. Holiday, 1987.

Zemach, Harve. *The Judge: An Untrue Tale.* Illustrated by Margot Zemach. Farrar, 1969.

Cole, Joanna. *My Puppy Is Born.* Illustrated by Margaret Miller. Morrow, 1991. (Title was originally issued in 1973 by Morrow, with black-and-white photo illustrations by Jerome Wexler.)
The original edition featured Wexler's black-and-white illustrations of the birth, delivery, and early development of a dachshund's litter. This revised edition features crystal-clear color photographs that feature the birth process, growth, and development of Norfolk terrier puppies. Cole expanded the text in the 1991 edition.

1. Encourage students to learn more about dogs and puppies by reading some of the following titles:

Arnold, Caroline. *Pets without Homes.* Illustrated with photographs by Richard Hewett. Clarion, 1983.
Discusses how shelters obtain and care for dogs and how they match their dogs to people who wish to adopt them.

Clutton-Brock, Juliet. *Dogs*. Illustrated by Dave King and Philip Dowell. Knopf, 1991. (Eyewitness book)
Another in the series of books that examine various aspects of a subject's existence. Highly pictorial and full of information.

Cole, Joanna. *A Dog's Body*. Illustrated with photographs by Jim Monteith and Ann Monteith. Morrow, 1986.
Focuses on the development and body language of dogs.

Fischer-Nagel, Heiderose. *A Puppy Is Born*. Illustrated with photographs by Andreas Fischer-Nagel. Putnam, 1985.
Follows the development of a purebred wirehaired dachshund from birth to the age that the puppy is ready to be separated from its mother.

Pinkwater, D. Manus, and Jill Pinkwater. *Superpuppy*. Clarion, 1976.
A 208-page guide in choosing, raising, and training a puppy.

2. Invite a veterinarian to visit your classroom to discuss the care of puppies and dogs. Some localities have active dog clubs, such as The Golden Retriever Club. If a veterinarian is not available to visit your class, perhaps a knowledgeable person from a dog club would visit and discuss the care and training of dogs and the characteristics that make a championship dog.

Cole, Joanna, editor. *A New Treasury of Children's Poetry: Old Favorites and New Discoveries*. Illustrated by Judith G. Brown. Doubleday, 1984.
This collection of over 200 poems, riddles, jump-rope rhymes, and nonsense verse includes poems by Shel Silverstein, N. M. Bodecker, David McCord, and others. Rhymes range from the simple to the complex.

1. Identify a favorite poem that could be shared with others. Hold a Poetry Performance Day. Participants can read their selected poems, recite to a rap beat or musical background, recite from memory, or choral-read their selection.

2. Make an illustrated poster showcasing a selected poem. Be sure to credit the poet on the poster.

Cole, Joanna. *Norma Jean, Jumping Bean*. Illustrated by Lynn Munsinger. Random, 1987. (A Step into Reading book: Step 2)
Norma Jean is the best jumper in school, but she does not know when it is appropriate to jump and when she should not jump. At first her jumping causes many problems, so she decides not to jump anymore. But when she doesn't jump, that causes her problems. Eventually she realizes that jumping at the proper time can help her. She learns that there "is a time and place for jumping."

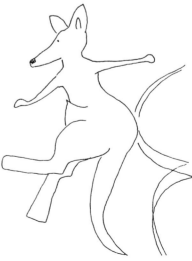

1. Have students classify the behavior of Norma Jean by making a list of

   a. the problems she causes herself when she does jump

   b. the problems she causes herself when she does not jump

  c. the times when she should have jumped but did not

  d. the times she jumped and did not cause a problem

2. Compare the lists generated in activity 1. Discuss the cause-and-effect relationship between the problems and the times Norma Jean jumped and did not jump.

Cole, Joanna, and Stephanie Calmenson, compilers. *Ready ... Set ... Read!* Illustrated by Anne Burgess, et al. Doubleday, 1990.
  Beginning-to-read stories authored by Dr. Seuss, Else Minarik, Arnold Lobel, Joanna Cole, and Bernard Wiseman are included here, in addition to sixteen poems by David McCord, Aileen Fisher, John Ciardi, and several other poets. The selections also include riddles, rebus stories, tongue twisters, and other fun and games selections. All are well chosen for beginning readers but will be enjoyed by students of many ages.

1. Use the selection (or selections) by each author as a read-aloud and as an introduction to the other works of that author.

2. Read "Driving to the Beach," a poem by Joanna Cole, and correlate it to the themes of the following selections:

Aldis, Dorothy. "Picnic." In *All Together* by Dorothy Aldis. Illustrated by Marjorie Flack, Margaret Frieman, and Helen D. Jameson. Putnam, 1925, 1952.

Carrick, Carol. *Sleep-Out*. Illustrated by Donald Carrick. Clarion, 1973.

McCloskey, Robert. *One Morning in Maine*. Illustrated by Robert McCloskey. Viking, 1952.

McCloskey, Robert. *Time of Wonder*. Illustrated by Robert McCloskey. Viking, 1957.

Moore, Lilian. "Encounter." In *Something New Begins* by Lilian Moore. Illustrated by Mary J. Dunton. Atheneum, 1982.

Moore, Lilian. "Until I Saw the Sea." In *By Myself* by Lee Bennett Hopkins. Illustrated by Glo Goalson. HarperCollins, 1980.

Shulevitz, Uri. *Dawn*. Illustrated by Uri Shulevitz. Farrar, 1974.

Thurman, Judith. "Pretending to Sleep." In *By Myself* by Lee Bennett Hopkins. Illustrated by Glo Goalson. HarperCollins, 1980.

3. Read the riddle section of *Ready ... Set ... Read!* and then read other collections of riddles from the list below:

Adler, David A. *A Teacher on Roller Skates: And Other School Riddles*. Illustrated by John Wallner. Holiday, 1989.

Brown, Marc. *Spooky Riddles*. Illustrated by Marc Brown. Random, 1983. (Beginner books)

Cerf, Bennett. *Bennett Cerf's Book of Riddles*. Illustrated by Roy McKie. Random, 1989.

Hall, Katy, and Lisa Eisenberg. *Snakey Riddles*. Illustrated by Simms Taback. Dial, 1990.

Phillips, Louis. *Way Out! Jokes from Outer Space*. Illustrated by Arlene Dubanevich. Viking, 1989.

4. Share the rebus stories "I Like Cake!" "A Whale Tale," and "Come to My House." Discuss with students what a rebus story is and how they would create one. As a group, select a nursery rhyme to write using rebus pictures. Then, depending on the maturity and ability of the students, ask them either to choose their own nursery rhyme to write as a rebus tale or to write an original story in rebus form.

Eric A. Kimmel

From *An Author a Month (for Dimes)* by Sharron L. McElmeel (Libraries Unlimited, 1992)

Eric A. Kimmel

During his growing-up years in Brooklyn, New York, where he was born on October 30, 1946, Eric Kimmel was probably the only child in the neighborhood who bought baseball cards for the gum. Instead of sports heroes, he admired people like Eleanor Roosevelt. His grandmother filled his childhood with eastern European legends, and his father told stories about growing up in a family of seven children in a tenement on Kosciusko Street during the 1920s.

Eric Kimmel graduated from high school in Brooklyn then went to college in the Midwest. He taught school and shared books and stories with children in New York's Harlem and in the Virgin Islands. For the past thirteen years Eric Kimmel and his wife, Doris, have lived in the Pacific Northwest, where he teaches children's literature at Portland State University. Both the Cascade mountains and the Oregon coast are within driving distance. This is a region of rain forests, high deserts, glorious roses, azaleas, and rhododendrons, and lots of rain. Kimmel enjoys being out-of-doors, so he is grateful for the rain or he might never spend time inside writing. Someday he would like to build an adobe oven so that he can bake bread in his backyard. He spins yarn and likes classic knitting patterns. His favorite foods include pizza, baked salmon, ripe tomatoes with basil, and freshly baked bread. The Kimmels live in Portland, Oregon. They have one grown daughter, Bridgett.

Chapter

8

Eric A. Kimmel

ABOUT THE AUTHOR

Eric A. Kimmel was born in Brooklyn, New York, on October 30, 1946. He grew up there with a brother who was two years younger, Jonathan. Kimmel went to P.S. 193 (elementary schools did not have names), where he and his classmates sang, "One Ninety-Three, One Ninety-Three, We hope the H Bomb drops on thee." Later he went to J.H.S. 240, a junior high school that did have a name. The school was named after a notorious pirate, Andries Hudde. Kimmel believes that the school is the only one in the United States named after a pirate. Hudde gained the favor of the English, who ruled America at the time, by attacking Spanish ships in the Caribbean during England's wars with Spain. As a reward, the governor of New York gave Hudde a land grant, where most of the neighborhood (and the school) stand today.

Kimmel went to high school at Midwood, one of the best high schools in Brooklyn, located right across the street from Brooklyn College. When recounting incidents from his growing-up years, Kimmel speaks of the excellent public school system and about using the subway. He said, "For fifteen cents you could ride the subway. It would take you anywhere. My friends and I used the subway system from the time we were in the sixth grade. We went all over town. A typical Saturday might include going to the Museum of Natural History and the Hayden Planetarium, then down to Times Square or Greenwich Village to see what was happening, with a stop at the Prospect Park Zoo and the Botanical Gardens on the way home. Along the way we ate huge delicatessen sandwiches, onion boards, pizza, Chinese food washed down with unique New York concoctions like malteds, frappes, and egg creams."

One summer Kimmel and a friend, Danny Feld, volunteered to work for the Democratic Party during the campaign for mayor. The Democrats sent the two young men over to the Republican headquarters to spy on them. They would work for the Republicans in the morning, go back to Democratic headquarters to report what they had learned, and then work for the Democrats for the rest of the afternoon. The Republicans bought them lunch and so did the Democrats. Kimmel and Feld both gained ten pounds that summer. During the late 1960s young men were being drafted for the Vietnam war. Kimmel hated war, any war, but he couldn't see the point in leaving the country or sitting in some jail. So since teachers were not being drafted, he decided to become a teacher. He taught in Harlem for a year; he was there, in fact, when Martin Luther King, Jr., was assassinated, in 1968, and he saw the riots and strikes that resulted. He later was a librarian in a school in St. Thomas, Virgin Islands, and has been involved in teaching in one way or another ever since.

Kimmel was a storyteller long before he was a writer, but he has been writing stories for children since 1969. Real success did not come until 1986 when Holiday House agreed to publish *Hershel and the Hanukkah Goblins*. He had written that story several years earlier, but it had been rejected so many times that Kimmel had actually given up on it. It was in his files when Marianne Carus of *Cricket* Magazine asked if he had a Hanukkah story for their December 1985 issue. Issac Basheveis Singer had agreed to write one but for some reason could not fulfill the commitment.

Carus needed the story fast, so Kimmel sent her *Hershel and the Hanukkah Goblins*. He thought if she did not like it he would still have time to come up with something else. She did like it, and the magazine's art director, Trina Schart Hyman, illustrated it for the magazine. Meanwhile, an editor at Holiday House, Margery Cuyler, was in the hospital waiting for her baby to arrive. She read the December issue and decided that she wanted Holiday to make it into a picture book. Trina Schart Hyman also wanted a chance to fully illustrate the story as a picture book. The book became a Caldecott honor book in 1990 and garnered success for Kimmel. In addition to Hyman, Kimmel's books have been illustrated by Janet Stevens, Giora Carmi, and Glen Rounds. One of Kimmel's most recent titles, *Aladdin and the Magic Lamp*, is illustrated by Ju-Hong Chen. Chen lives in Portland, also, but the artists who illustrate Kimmel's books and Kimmel have very little contact with one another. Kimmel and his wife did visit Colorado and while there called on Stevens during the time she was creating the illustrations for *Nanny Goat and the Seven Kids*. During their visit Stevens showed him some of the illustrations she was working on.

Kimmel does not necessarily tell stories from his own background nor, he says, is he a folklorist. When he comes across a story he might like to write or tell, he doesn't really care about its appropriateness to the oral tradition. He simply wants a story that will work for him. There has to be something in the story that attracts his attention—something funny, unusual, surprising, or weird. He makes changes in the story to put something of himself in it. That puts the challenge and the joy of writing into the process. Kimmel does not believe that an author or storyteller has to stick to his or her own background in selecting tales. Good tellers can tell good tales regardless of their background. Kimmel does like Jewish stories, however, because he says, "That's my background, and while I am not as fluent in Yiddish or Hebrew as I would like to be, I can read and express myself to a limited extent in both languages." He also likes to travel and meet people, always keeping his ears open for a good story. He has a collection of storybooks from all over the world, including some in languages he cannot read or speak. He recently returned from Stockholm, Sweden, with a set of Swedish folktales in Swedish. He doesn't read Swedish but thinks that someday he might, and there just might be some good stories inside those books.

Eric Kimmel rides a Yamaha 500cc Virago motorcycle and says the best part of riding a motorcycle is that one can always find a place to park. His leisure time is spent baking breads, especially his favorite—heavy, coarse, peasant rye breads. He has a whole library of bread books. Some day he'd like to build an adobe oven in the backyard. He also knits and says that his tastes in knitting are similar to his tastes in bread: he loves the classic folk patterns—Irish Arans and Guernseys. In the fall of 1991, Kimmel learned how to spin his own wool and now has his own spinning wheel. His goal is to some day spin wool and knit his spun wool into a sweater. His wife, Doris, initiated the family's interest in bird watching. She has bird-watched for several years, and now Kimmel can identify a few birds on his own. One day, on Sauvies Island, Doris spotted a great horned owl in a stand of trees. Eric had to use a spotting scope to confirm her find and, sure enough, the owl was there. He says his wife "is amazing when it comes to birds."

For the past thirteen years Eric and Doris and their daughter, Bridgett, have lived in the Pacific Northwest. Kimmel dedicated *I Took My Frog to the Library* to Bridgett, and one can only wonder if the mischievous young girl in the story bears any resemblance to Bridgett during her childhood. Kimmel teaches at Portland State University in Portland, Oregon, where he and Doris live. The Cascade mountains are just an hour away, and the Oregon coast is two hours away in the other direction. Kimmel considers the coastal area to be a "place of spectacular beauty" and the Pacific Northwest to be "the greatest place in the world to live." There are rain forests and high deserts and glorious roses, azaleas, and rhododendrons in the spring. Kimmel enjoys spending time out-of-doors, so much so that he welcomes rainy days, which provide him writing time.

Of all his books, he thinks that children like *Anansi and the Moss-Covered Rock* and *Hershel and the Hanukkah Goblins* best. The Anansi story reminds Kimmel of the wonderful year he spent living on St. Thomas in the Virgin Islands, where he first heard stories about Anansi. The Hershel story came first from his grandmother, who told him stories about Hershel of Ostropol. Kimmel is also fond of the two cowboy stories he's done, *Charlie Drives the Stage* and *Four Dollars and Fifty Cents*, because Wyoming, Montana, and eastern Oregon are among his favorite places. He loves to ride and says that someday he is going to have a horse of his own.

A message he'd like to share with young people who read his books is one from an extremely wise and learned man named Joseph Campbell, "Follow your bliss." Do what you love and the money will come.

SETTING THE STAGE

Kimmel has an extensive collection of storybooks—books that tell folk stories from all over the world. Begin this author study by having a story festival. For two or three weeks encourage students to read many stories from many different countries. Make a list of stories read and star those that a reader especially liked. On a daily basis ask students to share and discuss the stories they have read. Each day, if you can, plan to read one of the ten stories in Adèle Geras's *My Grandmother's Stories: A Collection of Jewish Folk Tales* (Knopf, 1990). At the end of the three weeks, ask students to select a story that they would like to retell. Ask them to reread the story, make note cards for the stories, and then practice telling the story. On a specific day, schedule a storytelling festival at which the students will tell their selected stories. Record the storytelling on audiotape. Put the tapes in a listening area where students may come to listen to the stories. Following the storytelling festival, introduce Eric Kimmel as a storyteller. Besides telling stories he also writes stories. Feature Kimmel in an author center, displaying copies of the poster pages from this book and as many of his books as are available. Plan to read and share his books and then hold another storytelling festival. This time students will tell Kimmel's stories or their own versions of the stories. Record those stories and enjoy them in the listening center.

Gather together as many Anansi stories as possible and display them with Kimmel's *Anansi and the Moss-Covered Rock* and *Anansi Goes Fishing*. Put up a scroll-like piece of paper to generate a list of characteristics about Anansi. At the top of the scroll put the words: "Anansi is...," and then as books about Anansi are read, descriptive words or phrases might be added. As the list becomes longer and longer, attempt to come up with a descriptive paragraph about the character Anansi. Surround the scroll with images of Anansi as depicted by a variety of illustrators.

Display as many books by Eric Kimmel as are available. Encourage children to read as many of the stories as possible. As students read the stories, they might create mini-advertisements for the stories and place them in the author center.

IDEA CUPBOARD

Kimmel, Eric A., *Anansi and the Moss-Covered Rock*. Holiday, 1988. *Anansi Goes Fishing*. Holiday, 1992. Both illustrated by Janet Stevens.

In the first West African tale, often told in the Caribbean culture as well, Anansi the Spider comes upon a stone that puts him to sleep for an hour. When Anansi the trickster awakens, he decides to use the rock to trick food from all the local residents. Each animal is taken to the strange moss-covered rock and promptly falls asleep while Anansi pilfers its food. In the background Little Bush Deer watches all the goings-on. It is the deer who manages to outwit Anansi and return the food to the animals. In *Anansi Goes Fishing*, Anansi is tricked once more. This time Turtle tricks Anansi into weaving a net, setting it in the river, catching the fish, and cooking the fish while Turtle lies back in the lawn chair and "gets tired." But when it is time to eat the fish, Turtle convinces Anansi that it is his turn to lie back in the chair while Anansi's stomach "gets full." Because Turtle eats the fish, it is really Turtle's stomach that gets full. When Anansi appeals to the Warthog under the Justice Tree, he is not believed. But something good comes of Turtle's trick: Spider learns how to spin nets. Wherever you find spiders you will find their nets—spider webs. Stevens portrays the large spider Anansi and the other animals in a realistic, personified manner—they all have facial expressions that have become characteristic of Stevens's illustrative work. The Warthog in *Anansi Goes Fishing* is very similar to the image of Wilburforce Warthog that Stevens created for the character featured in *Wally, the Worry-Warthog* by Barbara Shook Hazen (Clarion, 1990).

1. Read other stories about the trickster Anansi:

    Aardema, Verna. *Behind the Back of the Mountain*. Illustrated by Leo Dillon and Diane Dillon. Dial, 1973.

    Bryan, Ashley. "Ananse the Spider in Search of a Fool." In *The Ox of the Wonderful Horns and Other African Folktales*. Illustrated by Ashley Bryan. Atheneum, 1971.

    Courlander, Harold, and George Herzog. "Anansi and Nothing Go Hunting for Wives." In *The Cow-Tail Switch and Other West African Stories*. Illustrated by Madye Lee Chastain. Holt, 1947.

    Haley, Gail E. *A Story, A Story*. Illustrated by Gail E. Haley. Atheneum, 1970.

    McDermott, Gerald. *Anansi the Spider*. Illustrated by Gerald McDermott. Holt, 1972.

    Sherlock, Philip. *Anansi the Spider Man: Jamaican Folk Tales*. Illustrated by Marcia Brown. Crowell, 1954.

a. In several of the stories cited above, Anansi/Ananse is portrayed as a spider. In other stories Anansi/Ananse is portrayed as a man with spider-like qualities. Use the tales cited to compare and contrast the manner in which illustrators have represented the character Anansi.

b. Use the stories above to prepare a character sketch of the Anansi/Ananse character as he is known in folk literature. What are his common attributes and behaviors? (Correlate with the scroll suggestion in the "Setting the Stage" section.)

2. Compare the manner in which Anansi tricks the villagers out of their food supplies with the way that the soldiers/tramp trick the villagers/woman in the following stories:

Brown, Marcia. *Stone Soup*. Illustrated by Marcia Brown. Scribner, 1947.

Ginsburg, Mirra. "Hatchet Gruel." In *Three Rolls and One Doughnut: Fables from Russia*. Illustrated by Anita Lobel. Dial, 1970.

Greene, Ellin. "Old Woman and the Tramp." In *Clever Cooks: A Concoction of Stories, Charms, Recipes and Riddles*. Illustrated by Trina Schart Hyman. Lothrop, 1973.

Haviland, Virginia. "The Old Woman and the Tramp." In *Favorite Fairy Tales Told in Sweden*. Little, 1966.

Ross, Tony. *Stone Soup*. Illustrated by Tony Ross. Dial, 1987.

Stewig, John Warren. *Stone Soup*. Illustrated by Margot Tomes. Holiday, 1991.

Van Rynbach, Iris. *The Soup Stone*. Illustrated by Iris Van Rynbach. Greenwillow, 1988.

Zemach, Harve. *Nail Soup*. Adapted from the text by Nils Djurklo. Illustrated by Margot Zemach. Follett, 1964.

3. Compare and contrast the video version of this tale, *Anansi and the Moss-Covered Rock* (Live Oak Media, 1990), with the book. The video is close to a verbatim version of the text, with iconographic visuals and minimum background music introducing the narration and providing links to the story phrasing. How does the music affect the presentation of the story, and how does the movement of the camera across the illustrations affect the mood of the story?

4. Compare and contrast the manner in which Turtle tricks Anansi out of food in *Anansi Goes Fishing* to the manner in which Little Bush Deer tricks Anansi out of food for the villagers in *Anansi and the Moss-Covered Rock*.

Kimmel, Eric, reteller. *Baba Yaga: A Russian Folktale*. Illustrated by Megan Lloyd. Holiday, 1991.
Baba Yaga is a Russian witch who lives deep in the forest in a hut that walks about on chicken feet. Baba has teeth made of iron, a pudding face, and bony legs. But the most dreadful thing about Baba is that she likes to eat children. When Marina goes into the forest to ask Baba to remove the horn from her forehead, Baba obliges in return for Marina's promise to put a pot of water on the stove to boil. Baba expects to cook Marina for dinner. When Marina realizes the danger she is in, she manages to escape with the help of those she showed kindness to while on the way to Baba's hut. Kimmel's retelling is based on a story from the Carpathian Mountains that Kimmel heard from his grandmother while he was growing up. The Carpathian region is a borderland where Slavic, Germanic, Magyar, Hebrew, and Turkish cultures mingled.

1. Contrast the image of Baba Yaga (fascinating and harmless, harms only bad children) that Ernest Small portrays in the book cited below with the image portrayed by Kimmel in his story. Contrast the image of Baba Yaga (old hag, and very frightening) that Lent portrays in the illustrations in Small's version with the image portrayed by Lloyd in her illustrations for Kimmel's story.

   Small, Ernest. *Baba Yaga.* Illustrated by Blair Lent. Houghton, 1966.
   Marusia is hunting for turnips in the forest when she sees Baba Yaga. She is too frightened to move. Marusia comes to know Baba Yaga, her house on chicken legs, her magic brews and potions, her irascible temper, and her appetite for BAD Russian children. Marusia and her friend, the hedgehog, match wits with Baba Yaga. This story is drawn from several stories about Baba Yaga in Russian folklore. Lent has used corrugated cardboard block ink prints, with watercolor overlays, to illustrate the story.

2. Other stories that contain the Baba Yaga character include "Vasilisa the Beautiful" tales. Read some of the following stories and then identify the character traits of Baba Yaga that you think the authors and illustrators portray in their stories.

   Silverman, Maida, reteller. *Anna and the Seven Swans.* Illustrated by David Small. Morrow, 1984.

   Vasilisa the Beautiful. Translated by Thomas P. Whitney. Illustrated by Nonny Hogrogian. Macmillan, 1970.

   Winthrop, Elizabeth, adaptor. *Vasilissa the Beautiful: A Russian Folktale.* Illustrated by Alexander Koshkin. HarperCollins, 1991.

3. Correlate with activities suggested in chapter 7 for Joanna Cole's *Bony-Legs* (Macmillan, 1983; Scholastic, 1986). See index.

Kimmel, Eric A., adaptor. *Bearhead: A Russian Folktale.*
Illustrated by Charles Mikolaycak. Holiday, 1991.
   A foundling is adopted by loving parents. But he has the head of a bear and the body of a man. When he is grown he has the strength of ten men. One day Bearhead's father receives a letter from the evil witch, Madame Hexaba, demanding that the father come to her to be her servant. Bearhead implores his father to let him go in his place. Bearhead goes to Madame Hexaba and does everything she bids him to do—literally. When she asks him to quickly clear away the table, Bearhead picks it up and flings it out the window. Bearhead's honesty and cleverness earn Madame Hexaba's respect. But what Bearhead really wants is to outwit Madame Hexaba and go home.

1. Good versus evil seems to be the motif of this tale. Read other folktales and help students compare the theme and motifs in those stories to the motifs in *Bearhead*. Motifs include supernatural adversaries and helpers; extraordinary animals; and magical objects, powers, and transformations. Themes include good overcomes evil; justice triumphs; unselfish love conquers; intelligence wins out over physical strength; kindness, diligence, and hard work bring rewards; jealousy is punished; and greed brings negative results in the final analysis.

In addition to the folktale titles listed below, other appropriate books may be available in the folklore section of your school or public library.

Grimm, Jacob, and Wilhelm Grimm. *The Seven Ravens*. Translated by Elizabeth Crawford. Illustrated by Lisbeth Zwerger. Morrow, 1981.

Grimm, Jacob, and Wilhelm Grimm. *Snow White and the Seven Dwarfs*. Illustrated by Nancy Ekholm Burkert. Farrar, 1972.

Haviland, Virginia. *Favorite Fairy Tales Told in Norway*. Illustrated by Leonard Weisgard. Little, 1961.

Heyer, Marilee. *The Weaver of a Dream: A Chinese Folktale*. Illustrated by Marilee Heyer. Viking, 1986.

Martin, Eva, reteller. *Canadian Fairy Tales*. Illustrated by Laszlo Gal. Douglas & McIntyre, 1984.

Mosel, Arlene. *The Funny Little Woman*. Illustrated by Blair Lent. Dutton, 1972.

Newton, Patricia Montgomery. *The Five Sparrows: A Japanese Folktale*. Illustrated by Patricia Montgomery Newton. Atheneum, 1982.

Wyndham, Robert. *Tales the People Tell in China*. Illustrated by Jay Yang. Messner, 1971.

2. Compare *Bearhead* with other tales that include humans that become animals, or animals that are transformed to human form, such as "Beauty and the Beast," "The Frog Prince," and "Rose Red and Snow White."

3. Bearhead is a foundling. Another story that begins with a foundling being raised by a couple as their own is *The Devil with the Three Golden Hairs: A Tale from the Brothers Grimm*, retold and illustrated by Nonny Hogrogian (Knopf, 1983). After reading both stories, discuss any other similarities that the two stories have. Make a comparison chart.

Kimmel, Eric A. *The Chanukkah Guest*. Illustrated by Giora Carmi. Holiday, 1990.
Bubba Brayna is almost blind and deaf but she still makes the best potato latkes in the village. The rabbi is scheduled to visit her on the first night of Hanukkah, so she prepares a special batch of latkes. When she hears a thumping on the door, she lets in her guest (a guest that says only "RRRughrrr" and "RRRROWRR"). Thinking it's the rabbi, she lets him keep his fur coat on so that he won't get a chill. They eat latkes and play a dreidel game. Bubba's conversation with the bear will bring giggles from readers who realize that the guest is a bear. When it is time to go, the guest gives her a lick on the cheek. Later when the real rabbi and the villagers arrive, they figure out that Bubba's first Hanukkah guest was a bear. Cheerfully they all go back into the kitchen when Bubba begins to cook all over again.

1. If Bubba had not discovered who her guest really was, what might have been her impression of the rabbi? For example, Bubba might have thought that the rabbi was cold-blooded, because he kept his fur coat on during his visit, and that he was a person of few words, since he said only "RRRughrrr" and "RRRROWRR" during his stay.

2. Have students discuss or write about some favorite holiday foods made in their families or communities. Compile a class recipe book of favorite holiday dishes. Be sure to include an explanation of the tradition that is behind each holiday dish or the origin of the recipe.

3. Invite an "expert" from your community to make potato latkes for your class. Ask him or her to show and explain the technique for making latkes.

Kimmel, Eric A. *The Chanukkah Tree*. Illustrated by Giora Carmi. Holiday, 1988.
The people of Chelm are tricked before discovering an unexpected use for their tree.

1. Compare the story with those where other groups of people have been tricked. See the booklist in the entry for *Anansi and the Moss-Covered Rock* in this chapter.

2. Compare and contrast *The Chanukkah Tree* with *Uncle Vova's Tree* by Patricia Polacco (Philomel, 1989).

Kimmel, Eric A. *Charlie Drives the Stage*. Illustrated by Glen Rounds. Holiday, 1989.
Cigar-smoking and dynamite-packing Charlie Drummond drives the stagecoach when no one else will. When the famous Senator Roscoe McCorkle must get to a crucial meeting in Washington, D.C., Charlie is asked to drive the stage and get the senator to the train station. Charlie does not let anything stop the coach and delivers the exhausted and grateful senator to the train. The final surprise is that Charlie is really a daring female, Charlene.

1. The twist ending in this tale spotlights the role of women in United States history. A woman who in real life masqueraded as a man to participate in the American Revolution was Deborah Sampson. Her story is told in *The Secret Soldier: The Story of Deborah Sampson* by Ann McGovern, illustrated by Ann Grifalconi (Four Winds, 1971), and in Bryna Stevens's account *Deborah Sampson Goes to War*, illustrated by Florence Hill (Carolrhoda, 1984). Read either of these stories and have students discuss the role women have played in the history of the United States. Discuss other notable women.

2. A twist at the end of the tale was a typical device of the writer O. Henry. Read aloud some of his stories, especially "The Gift of the Magi." That story is available in many collections of the stories of O. Henry and in collections of tales for holiday reading. A picture book that presents a humorous twist on the story ending is Margaret Mahy's *The Boy Who Was Followed Home*, illustrated by Steven Kellogg (Dial, 1983). Encourage students to do some wide reading to locate stories that have a twist ending. Make a list of those books. Discuss the foreshadowing technique writers use. Reread the books on your list and continue to discuss those authors who use foreshadowing in their stories.

3. Stephen Manes's *Life Is No Fair*, illustrated by Warren Miller (Dutton, 1985), presents a series of one-page situations where the concluding statement is a twist on logical thinking. Use this book to encourage divergent thinking. Read each page and let the class/group brainstorm the next line. Then read Manes's conclusion. As a group try to create some one-page situations and conclusion twists patterned after Manes's text.

Kimmel, Eric A. *Four Dollars and Fifty Cents*. Illustrated by Glen Rounds. Holiday, 1990.
Shorty Long owes everyone in town money, including Big Oscar, the blacksmith, and Widow Macrae. One day Widow Macrae decides that she is going to collect the $4.50 that Shorty owes her, so she drives out to the Circle K Ranch. When Shorty's friends find out that the widow is coming, they decide to have a little fun by putting Shorty in a coffin. When Widow Macrae sees Shorty, she insists on taking him back to town for a proper burial. She sits up all night to watch the body. If he does not move by morning, she'll nail the coffin shut and bury it. If he does move, he pays up. Then along comes a band of outlaws who inadvertently help the Widow Macrae outwit Shorty.

1. Compare the antics in this book with those that take place in Jim Aylesworth's *Shenandoah Noah*, illustrated by Glen Rounds (Holt, 1985). Especially note the similarities and differences between Shenandoah Noah and Shorty.

2. Another book with a wacky sense of humor is *Meanwhile Back at the Ranch* by Trina Hakes Noble, illustrated by Tony Ross (Dial, 1987). Discuss how Noble's story is similar to and different from *Four Dollars and Fifty Cents*.

3. Compare and contrast Rounds's illustrations for the books by Aylesworth and Kimmel with the illustrations by Ross for Noble's book. How do the illustrations in each book contribute to the subtle humor of the story?

Kimmel, Eric A. *The Greatest of All: A Japanese Folktale*. Illustrated by Giora Carmi. Holiday, 1991.

Chuko Mouse wishes to marry a handsome field mouse, Ko Nezumi. But Father Mouse will not have his daughter marrying a common mouse. Chuko must marry someone befitting her own goodness. He insists that Chuko's husband be "The Greatest of All." He sets out to find the perfect match. He visits the emperor, the sun, and the wind before he comes to the conclusion that the field mouse is the best spouse for Chuko after all.

1. Read and discuss the story, focusing on the evolution of power. Compare how Chuko's parents perceived power at the beginning of the story with how they perceived power at the end of the story.

2. Compare and contrast this story with other versions of the mouse wedding tale. Make a comparison chart of the characters and the chain of events that occur.

   Bulatkin, I. F. "The Match-making of a Mouse." In *Eurasian Folk and Fairy Tales*. Clarion, 1985.

   Gackenbach, Dick. *The Perfect Mouse*. Illustrated by Dick Gackenbach. Macmillan, 1984.

   Uchida, Yashiko. "The Wedding of the Mouse." In *The Dancing Kettle, and Other Japanese Folk Tales*. Harcourt, 1949.

3. Continue the theme of power, in this case the seemingly least significant really having the most power, by sharing Gerald McDermott's *The Stonecutter* (Viking, 1957). A filmstrip/cassette version is available from Weston Woods®.

Kimmel, Eric. *Hershel and the Hanukkah Goblins*. Illustrated by Trina Schart Hyman. Holiday, 1989.

Hershel of Ostropol is sure that bright candles, merry songs, and platters of potato latkes will be waiting for him when he arrives in the village on the first night of Hanukkah. But when he arrives in the village, Hershel finds the villagers preoccupied with their fear of the goblins that haunt the old synagogue at the top of the hill. Hershel comes up with a plan to outwit the goblins. The afterword of the book explains the menorah and the "shammes" or "servant" candle; the dreidel, which is a square-shaped top; the instructions for playing the dreidel game; and latkes, delicious potato pancakes eaten hot from the pan with jam, sour cream, or applesauce. Hyman's illustrations show a lesser-known *hanukkiah* as opposed to the more familiar rounded menorah. And although Hanukkah candles are not to be used for any purpose other than a symbolic one, there are several places where Hershel is using the light to see.

1. This is both a Hanukkah tale and a trickster tale. Read other trickster tales and compare Hershel to the tricksters in some of the following tales:

   Kasza, Keiko. *The Wolf's Chicken Stew*. Illustrated by Keiko Kasza. Putnam, 1987.

   McKissack, Patricia. *Monkey-Monkey's Trick: Based on an African Folk Tale*. Illustrated by Paul Meisel. Random, 1988. (A Step into Reading book: Step 2)

   Ross, Tony. *Puss in Boots: The Story of a Sneaky Cat*. Illustrated by Tony Ross. Delacorte, 1981.

   Schatz, Letta. *The Extraordinary Tug-of-War*. Illustrated by John Burningham. Follett, 1968.

2. Read some of the following stories of Hanukkah and investigate traditions associated with the Hanukkah holiday:

   Adler, David. *Malke's Secret Recipe: A Chanukah Story*. Kar Ben, 1989.

   Adler, David A. *A Picture Book of Hanukkah*. Illustrated by Linda Heller. Holiday, 1982.

   Backman, Aidel. *One Night, One Hanukkah Night*. Jewish Publication Society, 1990.

   Birenbaum, Barbara. *Candle Talk*. Peartree, 1991.

   Chaikin, Miriam. *Hanukkah*. Illustrated by Ellen Weiss. Holiday, 1990.

   dePaola, Tomie. *My First Chanukah*. Illustrated by Tomie dePaola. Putnam, 1989.

   Drucker, Malka. *Hanukkah: Eight Nights, Eight Lights*. Illustrated by Brom Hoban. Holiday, 1980.

   Ehrlich, Amy. *The Story of Hanukkah*. Illustrated by Ori Sherman. Dial, 1989.

   Goldin, Barbara. *Just Enough Is Plenty: A Hanukkah Tale*. Puffin, 1990.

   Hanukkah Songs and Games. A cassette recording (24 minutes). Random, 1988.

   Kimmel, Eric A. *The Chanukkah Guest*. Illustrated by Giora Carmi. Holiday, 1990.

   Kimmel, Eric A. *The Chanukkah Tree*. Illustrated by Giora Carmi. Holiday, 1988.

   Koralek, Jerry. *Hanukkah: The Festival of Lights*. Illustrated by Juan Wijngaard. Lothrop, 1990.

   Manushkin, Fran. *Latkes and Applesauce: A Hanukkah Story*. Illustrated by Robin Spowart. Scholastic, 1990.

Schotter, Roni. *Hanukkah!* Joy Street/Little, 1990.

Sussman, Susan. *Hanukkah: Eight Lights around the World*. Illustrated by Judith Friedman. Whitman, 1988.

Kimmel, Eric A. *I Took My Frog to the Library*. Illustrated by Blanche Sims. Viking, 1990.

When a young girl brings a frog, a giraffe, and even a hyena to the library, the antics of the unusual group of readers wreak havoc. The frog frightens the librarian, the hen lays an egg in the card catalog, and the python sheds her skins all over everyone. The hyena laughs at all the wrong times during storytime. But it's not until the big, very big, elephant arrives and wrecks the place that the librarian asks them to leave. Back home the animals enjoy having the elephant read aloud to them. Sims's illustrations portray the literalness of the text and leave room for the reader's imagination to enhance the visualization of the zany story.

1. Compare and contrast the behavior of the animals in this story with the animals in Kay Smith's *Parakeets and Peach Pie*, illustrated by Jose Aruego (Parents, 1970), or with the animals in Trina Hakes Noble's *Jimmy's Boa Bounces Back*, illustrated by Steven Kellogg (Dutton, 1984).

2. Use the animals in this book to write a story about how they might behave in your school classroom. How would their antics change to reflect the new setting?

Kimmel, Eric A., reteller. *Nanny Goat and the Seven Little Kids*. Illustrated by Janet Stevens. Holiday, 1990.

Set in a contemporary household, this story tells of a family of goats that skate, listen to a Walkman, and wear cowboy boots as they play. Toys are everywhere in their "lived-in" house. When Mother (Nanny Goat) leaves, she admonishes her brood to stay inside and not to let the wolf into their house. But the clever wolf tricks them and eats them up. Nanny Goat is resourceful, however, and triumphs over the wolf. Kimmel has trimmed the Grimms' more static narration and has brought a lyrical tone to the text. Stevens's lively illustrations put the story in a rural setting.

1. Compare and contrast Kimmel's text and the tone of Stevens's illustrations with those of Tony Ross's retelling in *Mrs. Goat and Her Seven Little Kids* (Atheneum, 1990). Both are updated approaches to a favorite Grimm tale. Overall, Kimmel's version is somewhat faithful to the original Grimm text, but Ross's version takes great liberties with the story line. Both Ross's and Stevens's illustrations are humorous and zany.

2. After comparing Kimmel's version with Ross's version of "The Wolf and the Seven Kids" story, compare each with some of the following more traditional versions:

Grimm, Jacob, and Wilhelm Grimm. *The Wolf and the Seven Kids*. Illustrated by Kinuko Craft. Troll, 1979.

Grimm, Jacob, and Wilhelm Grimm. *The Wolf and the Seven Kids*. Illustrated by Felix Hoffman. Harcourt, 1957.

Grimm, Jacob, and Wilhelm Grimm. *The Wolf and the Seven Little Kids*. Translated by Anne Rogers; illustrated by Svend Otto S. Larousse, 1977.

Rogers's version has the mother warning her children about the deceitfulness of the wolf; she tells them that they will know him by his gruff voice and his black feet. After the wolf succeeds in tricking the kids into letting him in, he eats them. The nanny goat succeeds in rescuing her kids by using her own wits. She cuts open the wolf, releases her kids, and then fills the wolf's stomach with rocks. When he awakens he feels terrible, stumbles, and falls into the well. In most of the traditional versions, the wolf softens his voice by eating chalk and camouflages his black feet with dough and flour, or only flour. He manages to trick the kids into letting him in the house, where he procedes to eat all the kids except the littlest one, who hides in the cabinet of the grandfather clock. The wolf leaves and falls asleep on his way home. Mother Goat returns home and is told of the tragic events by the lone surviving kid. Together they go to rescue the other kids from the goat. The littlest kid goes to get scissors, a needle, and thread. Mother Goat cuts open the wolf and pulls out her kids. Together they place stones in the stomach of the wolf and sew up the incision. When the wolf awakes he is thirsty, goes for a drink, and stumbles and falls into the well or stream and is drowned.

In Ross's version the wolf changes his voice by going to a voice teacher, camouflages the color of his feet by having an artist paint them white, and adopts a wheat tail after he has a dentist chop off his bushy tail. When the wolf returns to the goats' house, he eats all the kids except the youngest, who has hidden in the coal bucket. When the mother goat returns, she is angry that the wolf has made off with her children. She finds him sitting in her lawn chair drinking a root beer. She butts him in the behind seven times, six to get each of her six children back and once to butt him clear out of the place. Kimmel's story follows the traditional story grammar. The wolf uses chalk to soften his voice and flour to whiten his feet, but when he is let into the house he eats up *all* the kids and waits under the table to eat the mother as well. But Mother Goat is very resourceful; in her apron she has scissors, so she cuts open the wolf's stomach and all the animals escape through the opening. Stones are placed in the wolf's stomach and the wolf drowns.

2. After comparing the story grammar in various versions of "The Wolf and the Seven Kids," compare and contrast the basic story structure with Audrey Wood and Don Wood's *Heckedy Peg* (Harcourt, 1987). Weston Woods® has a filmstrip version of the *Heckedy Peg* title. In the *Heckedy Peg* story the children are changed into a food item. The mother can save them only by naming the specific food item that each child has become.

Janet Stevens

Janet Stevens

From *An Author a Month (for Dimes)* by Sharron L. McElmeel (Libraries Unlimited, 1992)

Janet Stevens

Janet Stevens was born in 1953 in Dallas, Texas. Her father was a naval officer so her family lived in many places, including Italy and Hawaii. She had one brother and one sister. As a child Janet Stevens enjoyed art, and even though she always felt that her brother and sister were smarter than she was, she felt good about being an artist.

Two years after earning a degree in fine arts from the University of Colorado, Janet Stevens became interested in illustrating books. While she tried to get illustrating jobs she continued designing fabric and doing advertising work. In 1978 she went to an illustrator's workshop and met Tomie dePaola. He told her she was a good illustrator and showed some of her work to a book editor. Now she has illustrated books written by Arnold Adoff, Eric A. Kimmel, and Steven Kroll and has illustrated traditional stories that she herself has retold.

She often uses herself and her family, and their belongings, as models for the animals and objects in her books. She draws camels that wear her shoes and rhinoceroses that wear clothes and lie on her rug. She has a lot of animals in pictures just waiting for the right words so they can be in a book. Janet Stevens lives in Boulder, Colorado, with her husband and two children.

Chapter

9

Janet Stevens

ABOUT THE AUTHOR/ILLUSTRATOR

Janet Stevens was born in Dallas, Texas, in 1953. During her growing-up years she and the rest of her family moved with her naval officer father to many different places. The family lived in Hawaii and Italy and many other exciting places. Stevens always felt that her brother and sister were smarter than she was; but she discovered art and felt that art gave her her own niche. She loved animals and often drew animals in her pictures — she still does.

After graduating from high school, she attended the University of Colorado where she earned a bachelor's degree in 1975. She has worked as a fabric designer, as an artist in the advertising industry, and as an architectural illustrator. At the age of twenty-four she decided that she was interested in children's book illustrating, so she attended an illustrator's workshop in New York. She submitted her art portfolio to editors and was asked to illustrate a book of poems collected by Myra Cohn Livingston, *Callooh! Callay! Holiday Poems for Young Readers* (Atheneum, 1978). Although she did not get many other requests to illustrate books, she didn't give up. She continued to work in advertising and design. Then, in 1978, she attended another workshop. This time she met Tomie dePaola. He thought her work showed promise and showed some of her drawings to an editor. Soon she was being asked to illustrate more books. An editor at Holiday contacted her and asked her to illustrate some books for them. She illustrated *The Big Bunny and the Easter Eggs* by Steven Kroll (Holiday, 1982) and her own retelling of Hans Christian Andersen's *The Princess and the Pea* (Holiday, 1982). Since then she has illustrated more than thirty books, in addition to continuing her other artistic work. She has illustrated books by Kroll, Marjorie Sharmat, Sheila Turnage, Eric A. Kimmel, Barbara Shook Hazen, and Polly M. Robertus; she has adapted/illustrated tales from Hans Christian Andersen, Edward Lear, and Aesop.

Janet Stevens has always loved to draw animals, especially the wrinkly rhinoceros. Now she uses the words of stories to provide the stage on which her animals dance and come alive. Often her animals invade her house and don clothing from her family's clothes closets. In *Lucretia the Unbearable* by Marjorie Weinman Sharmat (Holiday, 1981), Lucretia is wearing Janet Stevens's own shoes. In *The Tortoise and the Hare* (Holiday, 1981) the hare is wearing her husband's pink tie, and the tortoise is sitting at Stevens's dining room table eating breakfast cereal and wearing her little girl's pink bunny slippers. The Town Mouse in *The Town Mouse and the Country Mouse* (Holiday, 1987) is depicted wearing some of Stevens's jewelry. When Stevens illustrated *Goldilocks and the Three Bears* (Holiday, 1986), she put them in her living room. When she began to draw the illustrations for Steven Kroll's *The Big Bunny and the Easter Eggs* (Holiday, 1982), she was pregnant so she used herself as a model for the bunny. Later she used her father and mother as the models for Noah and Mrs. Noah in her story *How the Manx Cat Lost Its Tail* (Harcourt, 1990). One of her husband's graduate students became a model for Androcles in *Androcles and the Lion* (Holiday, 1989). Sometimes she has to create her models. When she illustrated Edward Lear's nonsense verse *The Quangle*

Wangle's Hat (Harcourt, 1988), she actually made the Quangle Wangle's hat to see what it would look like.

Stevens enjoys putting details in her books—details that are often lost on readers. For example, in *Wally, the Worry-Warthog* by Barbara Shook Hazen (Clarion, 1990), she has Wally worrying about his encounters with Wilberforce Warthog. Wilberforce's shirt carries the number 7, which is also longtime Denver Broncos quarterback John Elway's jersey number. Football players worry about their encounters with Elway, just as Wally worries about his encounters with number 7, Wilberforce.

Stevens loves to draw rhinoceroses and seeks any opportunity to draw them. Sometimes she sneaks them into books where they are not supposed to be. When her editor doesn't want the rhinoceros in the picture, he red-pencils the illustration and writes, "Get the rhinoceros out of here!" And she does. When she illustrated *Anansi and the Moss-Covered Rock* by Eric A. Kimmel (Holiday, 1988), she had to decide how an animal would look at a rock. In one illustration she had a lion sitting on a porch, fanning himself. She thought that was too corny so did not include the illustration in the book. During the development of the illustrations for *Nanny Goat and the Seven Little Kids* (Holiday, 1990), she had to devise a reasonable way for the wolf to show his flour-white feet to the little kids in the house. She decided to have the wolf lie on the ground and put his feet on the windowsill.

When Stevens prepares the illustrations for a book, she actually makes the sketches as a storyboard showing the thirty-two pages of the picture book. Later she uses the storyboard sketches to help her prepare the dummy. She creates the dummy in the same size that the published book will be. She fleshes out the dummy sketches somewhat, but they are not as finished as the final illustrations will be. The dummy is the first thing her editor sees when Stevens submits her illustration proposals. After Stevens has discussed the illustrations with her editor, she creates the final artwork.

In addition to children's books Janet Stevens has worked on animating children's television specials. In the early 1980s she lived in Atlanta, Georgia, but has returned to live in the Boulder, Colorado, area, where she currently lives with her husband and young children, a son and a daughter. When she is not working on book illustrations, she enjoys outdoor activities: camping, skiing, and biking. And she also worries; she says she is a worrywart like Wally the worry-warthog.

SETTING THE STAGE

Prepare a bulletin board and author's corner to focus on Janet Stevens. Divide the author's corner bulletin board into two sections. The left-hand section should be three times the width of the right-hand section. Cover the left-hand section with characters enlarged from Stevens's books. Include the titles and the author's name on the board. Caption the right-hand section "About the Author." On that section place the poster pages from this book. Across the bottom of the "About the Author" section, place jackets from other books illustrated by Janet Stevens, or use the books themselves.

Several of Stevens's books are illustrated adaptations of stories or poems by Aesop, Edward Lear, or Hans Christian Andersen. Several other illustrators have adapted and illustrated their versions of the same stories. Before beginning the focus on Stevens, read one or two versions by other illustrators of the stories Stevens has illustrated. Refer to the booklists in the entries for Stevens's books in the Idea Cupboard that follows. After reading the other versions, introduce Stevens and her books by focusing on retellings of the same stories that feature her illustrations.

Introduce the rest of Stevens's work by sharing the eleven-minute videocassette of *Anansi and the Moss-Covered Rock* (Live Oak Media, 1990). This is a video version of the West African story retold by Eric A. Kimmel and illustrated by Stevens. The video is close to a verbatim version of the story. Stevens's cartoonish illustrations provide the basis for the iconographic visuals for the video. Use the response activities given for Kimmel's title in the Idea Cupboard in this chapter.

Stevens's illustrations are often anthropomorphic animals, that is, animals that are drawn with human shapes or characteristics. Look at Stevens's illustrations in Steven Kroll's *The Big Bunny and the Easter Eggs* (Holiday, 1982) and *The Big Bunny and the Magic Show* (Holiday, 1986), as well as *The Cabbages Are Chasing the Rabbits* by Arnold Adoff (Harcourt, 1985), *The Dog Who Had Kittens* by Polly M. Robertus (Holiday, 1991), and *Trout the Magnificent* by Sheila Turnage (Harcourt, 1984).

Discuss the common elements in Stevens's illustrations. Discuss the term *anthropomorphic* and discuss how the term relates to her illustrations. Compare and contrast her illustrations of animals with those of other illustrators such as Paul Galdone, Bill Peet, and Eric Carle.

IDEA CUPBOARD

Kimmel, Eric A. *Anansi and the Moss-Covered Rock*. Illustrated by Janet Stevens. Holiday, 1988.

In this West African tale, often told in Caribbean cultures, Anansi the (trickster) Spider comes upon a stone that puts him to sleep for an hour. When he awakens he decides to use the rock to trick food supplies from all the local residents. Each animal is taken to the strange moss-covered rock and promptly falls asleep while Anansi pilfers their food supplies. In the background Little Bush Deer watches all the goings-on. It is the deer who manages to outwit Anansi and return the food to the villagers. Stevens portrays the large spider (Anansi) and the other animals in a realistic manner—although they all have facial expressions that have become characteristic of Stevens's illustrative work.

1. In this story the Little Bush Deer watches all the goings-on and then enters into the story to outwit Anansi. Leo Dillon and Diane Dillon also have used a character in the background in two books they have illustrated:

Aardema, Verna. *Who's in Rabbit's House?* Illustrated by Leo Dillon and Diane Dillon. Dial, 1978.

Aardema, Verna. *Why Mosquitoes Buzz in People's Ears*. Illustrated by Leo Dillon and Diane Dillon. Dial, 1975.

In *Who's in Rabbit's House?* lions are in the background watching all the antics at Rabbit's house. The lions never enter into the story, but if they did, how might the story be changed?

In *Why Mosquitoes Buzz in People's Ears*, the Dillons include a bird in each picture. The bird seems to be assessing the action of the story. What, if anything, would change if the bird entered into the action of the story?

2. Additional activities for this book are suggested in the chapter focusing on the author Eric Kimmel. Refer to chapter 8.

Stevens, Janet, adaptor. *Androcles and the Lion*. Illustrated by Janet Stevens. Holiday, 1989.

Androcles, the slave, escapes from his demanding and cruel master. When he comes upon a lion with a thorn in his paw, he removes it. Later when the lion meets Androcles in the colosseum, the lion returns the favor and saves Androcles from death.

1. Compare the retelling and illustrations of Stevens's version of "Androcles and the Lion" with the following versions:

   Daugherty, James Henry. *Andy and the Lion*. Illustrated by James H. Daugherty. Viking, 1938. (Caldecott honor book, 1939)

   Galdone, Paul. *Androcles and the Lion*. Illustrated by Paul Galdone. McGraw, 1970.

   Grabianski, Janusz. *Androcles and the Lion*. Illustrated by Janusz Grabianski. Watts, 1970.

2. Compare and contrast the Androcles story with the display of kindness returned in the Aesop fable or the La Fontaine version:

   Aesop. *The Lion and the Mouse*. Illustrated by Ed Young. Doubleday, 1980.

   Aesop. "The Lion and the Mouse." In *Aesop's Fables*, retold by Anne Terry White. Illustrated by Helen Siegle. Random, 1964.

   La Fontaine, Jean de. *The Lion and the Rat*. Illustrated by Brian Wildsmith. Watts, 1963.

Andersen, Hans Christian. *The Emperor's New Clothes*. Illustrated by Janet Stevens. Holiday, 1985.

Andersen's tale is retold with vibrant illustrations. The tale is one of Andersen's most familiar—a vain ruler is tricked by two swindlers who weave invisible cloth.

1. Design the clothes the emperor should have had designed for him by the two tailors.

2. Read several versions of this story and compare and contrast them. In addition to Stevens's version, several other illustrators have illustrated Andersen's tale: Erik Blegvad (Harcourt, 1959), Virginia Lee Burton (Houghton, 1949), Jack Kent (Four Winds, 1977), Anne F. Rockwell (Crowell, 1982), and Nadine Bernard Wescott (Little, 1984).

3. Compare and contrast the traditional versions of Andersen's story with Stephanie Calmenson's *The Principal's New Clothes*, illustrated by Denise Brunkus, Scholastic, 1989. In Calmenson's story, the principal, Mr. Bundy, is "the sharpest dresser in town" and is scammed by a pair of con artists in the same fashion that the emperor was flimflammed in Andersen's classic "The Emperor's New Clothes."

Stevens, Janet. *Goldilocks and the Three Bears*. Illustrated by Janet Stevens. Holiday, 1986.
Mama, Papa, and Baby Bear discover they have a visitor in this version of a traditional tale.

1. Correlate activities with suggestions given in chapter 5 for Jan Brett's illustrated version of *Goldilocks and the Three Bears*.

2. After reading Stevens's and other versions of "Goldilocks and the Three Bears," read (and tell) the reverse story depicted in the wordless story by Brinton Turkle in his book *Deep in the Forest* (Dutton, 1976).

3. After becoming totally familiar with the story, write a new version of "The Three Bears." A new character might be introduced into the story. The role of Goldilocks could be played by one of a variety of characters from other stories: Clifford the Big Red Dog (from the books by Norman Bridwell); Jack from "Jack and the Beanstalk"; the wolf from "The Three Little Pigs"; the tramp from *Nail Soup* by Harve Zemach (Follett, 1964); or an invented character such as "Red"—a red-haired boy with a crew cut. Discuss how the new character would change the story. For example, Clifford the Big Red Dog would start by tasting the little bear's porridge and finally settle on the Great Big Bear's bowl, etc. When the bears return home they would find Clifford in the Great Big Bear's bed and Clifford would scare the bears away.

Stevens, Janet, reteller. *How the Manx Cat Lost Its Tail*. Illustrated by Janet Stevens. Harcourt, 1990.
The often-told story of Noah and the flood is the setting for this story, which gives an original explanation of why the Manx cat lost his tail. As Noah and his sons call for the animals to come on board, the cat stays behind. Finally, when Mrs. Noah shows the men the correct way to call a cat, the cat responds, but just in time. Just as the kitty is about to enter the ark, Noah shuts the door and clips its tail off in the process.

1. Two stories are juxtaposed here. Identify the stories and discuss each of the story lines and how they interact.

2. Compare and contrast the images portrayed by Stevens with those created by the illustrators in some of the following versions of the Noah's Ark story:

Bollinger, Max. *Noah and the Rainbow: An Ancient Story*. Translated by Clyde Robert Bulla. Illustrated by Helga Aichinger. Crowell, 1972.

Chase, Catherine. *Noah's Ark*. Illustrated by Elliot Ivenbaum. Dandelion, 1979.

dePaola, Tomie. *Noah and the Ark*. Illustrated by Tomie dePaola. Winston, 1983.

Duvoisin, Roger. *A for the Ark*. Illustrated by Roger Duvoisin. Lothrop, 1952.

Haley, Gail E. *Noah's Ark*. Illustrated by Gail E. Haley. Atheneum, 1971.

Hogrogian, Nonny. *Noah's Ark*. Illustrated by Nonny Hogrogian. Knopf, 1986.

Hutton, Warwick. *Noah and the Great Flood*. Illustrated by Warwick Hutton. Atheneum, 1977.

Ife, Elaine. *Noah and the Ark*. Illustrated by Russell Lee. Rourke, 1983.

Palazzo, Tony. *Noah's Ark*. Illustrated by Tony Palazzo. Doubleday, 1955.

Singer, Isaac Bashevis. *Why Noah Chose the Dove*. Illustrated by Eric Carle. Farrar, 1974.

Spier, Peter. *Noah's Ark*. Illustrated by Peter Spier. Doubleday, 1977.

Wiesner, William. *Noah's Ark*. Illustrated by William Wiesner. Dutton, 1966.

Duvoisin and Singer both use Noah's Ark as the backdrop for another story, as does Stevens. Spier and Hogrogian both use the Bible text as the direct basis for their book. Peter Spier's *Noah's Ark* won the 1978 Caldecott award for "the most distinguished American picture book for children." In his Caldecott acceptance speech at the American Library Association's annual convention in Chicago on June 27, 1978, Spier spoke of having wanted to illustrate Noah's story for years. When he went to the library he found that there were more than twenty "Noahs" in print. He obtained as many of the versions as he could and looked at what the artists had done with the story. He concluded that invariably Noah's voyage was shown as a "joyous, sun-filled Caribbean cruise." The story of the flood did not show any of God's anger. None of them hinted at the unpleasant side of the story. Spier attempted to give that perspective when he prepared the illustrations for his version.

a. List the books you can find that depict life on Noah's Ark during the flood. Then use the copyright dates in the books to categorize the books according to whether they were published before or after Peter Spier made his comments about the "sun-filled" scenes on the ark.

b. Discuss how the illustrator in each book depicts the setting on the ark—is the setting "sun-filled," or is there a focus on the ravages of the flood?

c. React to and discuss Spier's comments in connection with some of the versions of the Noah's Ark story.

3. This is a literary *pourquoi* story. A *pourquoi* (French for "why") story answers a question, or explains how animals, plants, or humans were created and why they have certain characteristics. Read some of the *pourquoi* tales in the following list and discuss what they explain. Then identify an animal's characteristic or an event that occurs in nature and create a story that explains how the animal came to have that characteristic or what caused the event to occur.

Aardema, Verna. *Why Mosquitoes Buzz in People's Ears*. Illustrated by Leo Dillon and Diane Dillon. Dial, 1975.

Bryan, Ashley. *The Cat's Purr*. Illustrated by Ashley Bryan. Atheneum, 1985.

Bryan, Ashley. "How the Animals Got Their Tails." In *Beat the Story-Drum, Pum-Pum*. Illustrated by Ashley Bryan. Atheneum, 1980.

Carew, Jan. *The Third Gift*. Illustrated by Leo Dillon and Diane Dillon. Little, Brown, 1974.

Cole, Judith. *The Moon, the Sun, and the Coyote*. Illustrated by Cecile Schoberle. Simon, 1991.

Courlander, Harold. "The Tiger's Minister of State." In *The Tiger's Whisker and Other Tales and Legends from Asia and the Pacific*. Illustrated by Enrico Arno. Harcourt, 1959.

Dayrell, Elphinstone. *Why the Sun and the Moon Live in the Sky*. Illustrated by Blair Lent. Houghton, 1968; reissued in 1991.

Goble, Paul. *Star Boy*. Illustrated by Paul Goble. Bradbury, 1983.

Haley, Gail E. *A Story—A Story*. Illustrated by Gail E. Haley. Atheneum, 1970.

Haviland, Virginia. "Why the Bear Is Stumpy-Tailed." In *Favorite Fairy Tales Told in Norway*. Illustrated by Leonard Weisgard. Little, 1961.

Kipling, Rudyard. *The Elephant's Child*. Illustrated by Edward Frascino. Simon, 1986.

Lester, Julius. *How Many Spots Does a Leopard Have?... And Other Tales*. Illustrated by David Shannon. Scholastic, 1989.

Robbins, Ruth. *How the First Rainbow Was Made*. Illustrated by Ruth Robbins. Parnassus/Houghton, 1980.

Toye, William. *How Summer Came to Canada*. Illustrated by Elizabeth Cleaver. Walck, 1969.

Van Laan, Nancy. *Rainbow Crow*. Illustrated by Beatriz Vidal. Knopf, 1989.

Andersen, Hans Christian. *It's Perfectly True!* Illustrated by Janet Stevens. Holiday, 1985.

One hen, roosting on a perch in a henhouse, loses a feather. When she comments, "The more I peck out my feathers, the more beautiful I become," she is overheard by a neighboring hen. The hen quickly repeats the story, and in true gossip fashion the comment is repeated over and over again until the story is that "five hens have pecked out all their feathers and have grown skinny and unhappy for the love of a rooster." Stevens's retelling is faithful to Andersen's tale.

1. Andersen's tale is included in some collections. Acquaint students with the procedure for locating books by author and for using the index or the table of contents of books to ascertain if "It's Perfectly True" is included in the available collections of stories. Compare and contrast the versions located with Stevens's picture book version of the story.

2. How statements change as they are repeated is one of the points of this book. Another book with this theme is Barbara Brenner's *Good News*, illustrated by Kate Duke (Bantam, 1991). Brenner's title uses a story line similar to that in Andersen's tale. Canadian Goose announces her "good news"—she is sitting on four eggs. But when Wood Duck retells the good news, the story becomes five eggs, and each time the good news is repeated to another pond animal, the story grows until it is reported that the goose is sitting on eight monster eggs. All the animals scramble to see the monsters as they are hatched. But when the goose steps off the nest, all they see are four tiny geese. And "to think, that four cute baby geese could hatch from eight monster eggs." This story will interest readers because of its cumulative nature and exaggeration. The realistic watercolors add to the interpretation of the text. After reading Stevens's illustrated version of the Andersen tale and Brenner's story, make a list of statements that could evolve if one did not hear clearly. Or play the old game of "telephone." Have all the students line up single file. Whisper a sentence into the ear of the first child. Ask the child to whisper what he or she heard into the ear of the next child. Each child continues to pass the sentence down the line until it reaches the last child, who announces the sentence that has come down the "telephone" line. Compare the final sentence with the original sentence.

Kimmel, Eric A., reteller. *Nanny Goat and the Seven Little Kids*. Illustrated by Janet Stevens. Holiday, 1990.

The house is strewn with children's toys. Kids are skating, a baby is being pushed in a stroller (sucking on a baby bottle), and another, dressed in cowboy boots and hat, is riding a tricycle. When Mother (Nanny Goat) leaves, she admonishes them to stay inside and not to let the wolf into the house. But the clever wolf tricks them and eats them up. Nanny Goat is resourceful and triumphs over the wolf. Kimmel has trimmed Grimm's more static narration and has brought a lyrical tone to the text. Readers will enjoy the twist at the end, which makes a "hero" of the littlest kid. Stevens's lively illustrations put the story in a rural setting.

1. Correlate the following activities with those given for this title in chapter 8.

2. Stevens's illustrations definitely set the story in a contemporary setting. Look at her illustrations and make a list of the details she includes that make the setting contemporary—for example, a Walkman® and an umbrella stroller.

3. Discuss why readers think that Stevens put the wolf in a T-shirt that reads "Big and Bad."

4. Compare and contrast Stevens's version with "The Wolf and the Seven Little Kids." Versions are often included in collections of folktales collected by the Grimm brothers. Compare and contrast Stevens's story and the Grimm versions with *Mrs. Goat and Her Seven Little Kids* by Tony Ross (Atheneum, 1990).

5. Compare the stories about the wolf and her seven little kids with Audrey Wood and Don Wood's *Heckedy Peg* (Harcourt, 1987). A filmstrip of *Heckedy Peg* is available in filmstrip/cassette version from Weston Woods®.

Lear, Edward. *The Owl and the Pussycat*. Illustrated by Janet Stevens. Holiday, 1983.
Stevens's interpretation of Lear's classic poem is imaginative and endearing.

1. Correlate the following activities with those given for Jan Brett's illustrated version of "The Owl and the Pussycat" in chapter 5.

2. Compare the Caribbean island setting of Brett's version with the setting depicted in Stevens's version.

3. In addition to the setting, compare the depiction of such items as the bong tree, the piggy-wig with the ring in his nose, and the wedding of the owl and the pussycat.

4. Print the words to Lear's poem in sections and place them on large sheets of drawing paper (two lines per sheet). Ask students to work individually or in pairs to illustrate their specific phrase or section. When all the illustrations have been completed, compare them with the depictions in the various editions of the poem. Display the pages as a bulletin-board book. Add a title page in the upper left-hand corner of the bulletin board, and later bind the illustrated pages into a big book.

Andersen, Hans Christian. *The Princess and the Pea*. Illustrated by Janet Stevens. Holiday, 1982.

A tiger is found to be the true princess in this retelling of Andersen's classic tale. Stevens's illustrations depict the tale as a story populated by animals, while the text remains relatively faithful to the original Andersen text.

1. It seems reasonable that if a lion is the king of the jungle a tiger might be a princess. Identify other classic fairy tales or literary tales and depict the main character as an animal. For example, what kind of animal would play the part of Cinderella? Snow White? The knight who rescues the princess from the glass hill? Or the giant in "Jack and the Beanstalk"?

2. Andersen's tale has been illustrated by Dick Gackenbach (Macmillan, 1983), Paul Galdone (Clarion, 1978), and Maurice Sendak in *Seven Tales*, translated by Eva Le Gallienne (Harper, 1959). Look for unique elements in these three versions when compared with one another and with Stevens's adaptation. Make a comparison chart comparing both the story grammar used in each retelling and the illustrations used to depict the story.

Stevens, Janet, reteller. *The Three Billy Goats Gruff*. Illustrated by Janet Stevens. Harcourt, 1987.
  The troll is quite fierce in this version, which has "The Big Billy Goats Gruff" wearing the leather jacket that Stevens would like to have owned. The imaginative illustrations give the troll and the Billy Goats Gruff a fresh new look.

1. Read and compare Stevens's version of "The Three Billy Goats Gruff" with those illustrated by Marcia Brown and Paul Galdone, and with the Rockwell retelling.

   Asbjørnsen, P. C., and Jørgen E. Moe. *The Three Billy Goats Gruff*. Illustrated by Marcia Brown. Harcourt, 1957.

   Galdone, Paul. *Three Billy Goats Gruff*. Illustrated by Paul Galdone. Clarion, 1973.

   Rockwell, Anne. "The Three Billy Goats Gruff." In *The Three Bears and 15 Other Stories*. Illustrated by Anne Rockwell, Crowell, 1975; Harper Trophy, 1984.

   a. Compare and contrast the depiction of the troll and the size of the goats in the books.

   b. Recall the story grammar in each of the stories, then focus on the details that flesh out each specific story. For example, ascertain variances in the expressions and statements of the goats or the troll. Note the similarity in the story grammar. The story grammar emphasizes the actual story line, and in most comparison exercises one should emphasize the similarities and common elements in the story line while acknowledging that some details may differ from telling to telling.

2. After readers are familiar with the structure of "The Three Billy Goats Gruff," read "Sody Sallyraytus" from *Grandfather Tales*, a collection of tales edited by Richard Chase (Houghton, 1948). While the structure of "The Three Billy Goats Gruff" tale is based on relating three events with rising action, the "Sody Sallyraytus" tale uses five episodes but details a story line similar to "The Three Billy Goats Gruff" tale.

3. Retell "The Three Billy Goats Gruff" story from the point of view of the troll, or from the viewpoint of a specific goat. How would the tale have changed if the troll had been telling the tale?

Stevens, Janet, adaptor. *The Tortoise and the Hare*. Illustrated by Janet Stevens. Holiday, 1984.

With long lanky legs, the hare dressed in pink running shorts thinks that his flashy style will certainly allow him to outdistance the slow tortoise in the race that he (the hare) challenges the tortoise to enter against him. Stevens takes the challenge from the hare as an opportunity to expand on Aesop's tale. Tortoise has just two and a half weeks to get ready for the race. Illustrations show Tortoise in activities designed to get him in shape. He lifts weights, jogs, and eats healthy meals. Once the race begins, the hare stops three different times. When each time the hare realizes that the tortoise has gone past him, he takes off and overcomes the slow but plodding turtle—each time, that is, except the last. By the time Hare realizes that Tortoise has passed him, it is too late. Tortoise crosses the line just in front of Hare. The tale ends like most other versions of the story: Tortoise wins, proving that "hard work and perseverance bring reward."

1. Compare and contrast the details of Stevens's text and illustrations with other versions of "The Tortoise and the Hare":

Aesop. *The Hare and the Tortoise*. Illustrated by Paul Galdone. Whittlesey House, 1962.

Castle, Caroline, reteller. *The Hare and the Tortoise*. Illustrated by Peter Weevers. Dial, 1985.

Du Bois, William Pène, and Lee Po. *The Hare and the Tortoise and the Tortoise and the Hare: La Liebre y la Tortuga y la Tortuga y la Liebre*. Illustrated by William Pène Du Bois. Doubleday, 1972.

La Fontaine, Jean de. *The Hare and the Tortoise*. Illustrated by Brian Wildsmith. Watts, 1963.

Royds, Caroline, selector. *The Tortoise and the Hare, and Other Stories*. Illustrated by Annabel Spenceley. Putnam, 1986.

2. "The Hare and the Tortoise" is one of Aesop's most familiar fables. A fable, as defined in *Funk & Wagnall's Standard Dictionary of Folklore, Mythology, and Legends* (Funk & Wagnalls, 1949), is "an animal tale with a moral; a short tale in which animals appear as characters, talking and acting like human beings, though usually keeping their animal traits, and having as its purpose the pointing of a moral. The fable consequently has two parts: the narrative which exemplifies the moral, and the statement of the moral often appended in the form of a proverb."

   a. Discuss "The Tortoise and the Hare." Note how the story fits the definition of a fable.

   b. Expand the concept of fables by reading extensively in the genre from the following list:

   Aesop. *Aesop's Fables*. Selected and illustrated by Michael Hague. Henry Holt, 1985.

   Aesop. *Aesop's Fables*. Illustrated by Heidi Holder. Viking, 1981.

   Aesop. *Aesop's Fables*. Retold in verse by Tom Paxton. Illustrated by Robert Rayevsky. Greenwillow, 1988.

   Aesop. *Aesop's Fables*. Selected and adapted by Louis Untermeyer. Illustrated by Alice Provensen and Martin Provensen. Golden, 1966.

   Aesop. *Aesop's Fables*. Illustrated by Lisbeth Zwerger. Picture, 1989.

   Aesop. *The Caldecott Fables*. Illustrated by Randolph Caldecott. Doubleday, 1978.

   Aesop. *Fables from Aesop*. Adapted by James Reeves. Illustrated by Maurice Wilson. Walck, 1962.

   Aesop. *Once in a Wood: Ten Tales from Aesop*. Adapted and illustrated by Eve Rice. Greenwillow, 1979.

   Aesop. *Tales from Aesop*. Retold and illustrated by Harold Jones. Watts, 1982.

   Aesop. *Twelve Tales from Aesop*. Retold and illustrated by Eric Carle. Putnam, 1980.

3. After being immersed in the traditional fables, read "modern" versions. Read *The Exploding Frog and Other Fables from Aesop*, retold by John McFarland and illustrated by James Marshall (Little, 1981), and Tony Ross's *Foxy Fables* (Dial, 1986). In Ross's retelling of "The Hare and the Tortoise," the tortoise passes the hare, but when Hare realizes that he is behind, he jumps up and cracks his head on a low-hanging branch and knocks himself out. The tortoise wins the race. Discuss the details in the illustrations and the text of the Marshall and Ross versions that "modernize" the fables.

Aesop. *The Town Mouse and the Country Mouse*. Adapted and illustrated by Janet Stevens. Holiday, 1987.

The town mouse lives in a lush city apartment and enjoys the "finer" things of life, while her cousin, the country mouse, lives in a barn and works hard every day. When the town mouse visits her cousin, she finds life very boring and very slow. When the town mouse returns to her apartment home, she brings her cousin to see what living a more interesting life is all about. However, there are drawbacks to town living, and the country mouse soon heads home.

1. Evaluate the advantages of life in the city and life in the country. Make a pro and con list based on the positive and negative benefits of living in town and living in the country.

    a. Use the list to help write a persuasive paper on the benefits of living in the city or living in the country.

    b. Hold a debate: city living versus country living.

    c. Draw an illustration of living in the country (or the city). Show as many benefits and drawbacks as possible of the setting in the illustration.

2. Rewrite Stevens's story with the country mouse being female and the city mouse being male. Would their images change any? How would it change the fable, if at all?

3. Examine other illustrated versions of the fable and make a list of the common details that the reteller used or images that the illustrator used to depict the city versus the country setting.

    Aesop. *The Town Mouse and the Country Mouse*. Illustrated by Lorinda Bryan Cauley. Putnam, 1984.

    Aesop. *The Town Mouse and the Country Mouse*. Illustrated by Paul Galdone. McGraw-Hill, 1971.

    Aesop. *The Town Mouse and the Country Mouse*. Illustrated by Tom Garcia. Troll, 1979.

    Aesop. "The Town Mouse and the Country Mouse." In *Aesop's Fables*. Illustrated by Heidi Holder. Viking, 1981.

    Aesop. "The Town Mouse and the Country Mouse." In *Tales from Aesop*. Retold and illustrated by Harold Jones. Watts, 1982.

4. Correlate with the activities focusing on the fable genre suggested in the entry for Stevens's *The Tortoise and the Hare*.

10

Capsule Units

Demi, Keiko Kasza,
Patricia Polacco

Demi

Demi

Charlotte Dumaresq Hunt was born on September 2, 1942, in Cambridge, Massachusetts. During her childhood she was nicknamed "Demi." Demi spent a lot of time in her mother's studio, where she found paints and brushes of all kinds to experiment with and where she watched her mother paint beautiful pictures with watercolors. After graduation from high school, Demi studied art in Mexico, China, and India. After returning from India she settled in New York, where she began to illustrate books.

As time went on, China and its art became very influential in Demi's life. She attempts to bring the magic of Chinese art to her illustrations—to capture life on paper. She uses authentic Chinese materials and paints on fine brilliant silk. For good fortune she adds powdered jade to all of her paints. The black Chinese ink that she uses is ten parts pine soot boiled in Tung River water. The paintings for each book she illustrates are made with four Chinese treasures: the Chinese paintbrush, ink, inkstone, and paper.

Demi is now married to Tze-si Jesse Huang. He has told her traditional folktales and fables that he heard as a child. Demi has retold and illustrated two of them, *The Empty Pot* and *The Magic Boat*. Demi lives in the state of Washington.

Demi

BIBLIOGRAPHY
AND MORE INFORMATION

Selected titles written or illustrated by Demi:

The Adventures of Marco Polo. Written and illustrated by Demi. Holt, 1981.

The Artist and the Architect. Written and illustrated by Demi. Holt, 1991.

Chen Ping and His Magic Axe. Retold and illustrated by Demi. Dodd, 1987.

A Chinese Zoo: Fables and Proverbs. Adapted and illustrated by Demi. Harcourt, 1987.

Chingis Khan. Written and illustrated by Demi. Holt, 1991.

The Classic of Tea. Written by Lu Yu. Translated by Francis Ross Carpenter. Illustrated by Demi Hitz. Little, 1974.

Demi's Count the Animals 1 2 3. Written and illustrated by Demi. Grosset, 1987.

Demi's Find the Animals A B C. Written and illustrated by Demi. Grosset, 1985.

Demi's Opposites. Written and illustrated by Demi. Grosset, 1987.

Demi's Reflective Fables. Retold and illustrated by Demi. Grosset, 1988.

Dragon Kites and Dragonflies. Selected and illustrated by Demi. Harcourt, 1986.

Find Demi's Baby Animals. Written and illustrated by Demi. Grosset, 1990.

Find Demi's Dinosaurs: An Animal Game Book. Written and illustrated by Demi. Grosset, 1989.

Find Demi's Sea Creatures. Written and illustrated by Demi. Grosset, 1991.

The Hallowed Horse: A Folktale from India. Retold and illustrated by Demi. Dodd, 1987.

In the Eyes of the Cat: Japanese Poetry for All Seasons. Selected and illustrated by Demi. Translated by Tse-si Huang. Holt, 1992.

Liang and the Magic Paint Brush. Written and illustrated by Demi. Holt, 1980.

The Nightingale. Written by Hans Christian Andersen. Adapted by Anna Bier. Illustrated by Demi. Harcourt, 1985.

Thumbelina. Written by Hans Christian Andersen. Adapted and illustrated by Demi. Grosset, 1989.

Charlotte Dumaresq Hunt was called Demi during her childhood in Cambridge, Massachusetts, where she was born on September 2, 1942. Now she writes and illustrates books and uses Demi as her pen name. Demi grew up in an artistic household. Her father, William Morris Hunt, was an architect, actor, entrepreneur, producer, and patron of the theater. He was a founder of the Cambridge Drama Festival, and in his own household he encouraged creativity and artistic self-expression. Demi's mother, Rosamond Pier Hunt, was a renowned watercolorist. Demi often visited her mother's painting studio, where she could smell every kind of paint and find every kind of brush and canvas. In the dedication of *A Chinese Zoo*, Demi credits her mother for having taught her "the spirit and love of painting."

Demi attended the Instituto Allende in Guanajuato, Mexico, and the Immaculate Heart College in Los Angeles. Later in 1962, she traveled to India to study on a Fulbright scholarship. After studying in India she returned to New York to live and work. She married James Rawlins Hitz in 1965, and they had one son, James. Using the name Demi Hitz, she created illustrations for a book by Partap Sharma, *The Surangini Tales* (Harcourt, 1973). She illustrated four more books by other writers before writing and illustrating *The Book of Moving Pictures* (Knopf, 1979). Since those first books, Demi has illustrated more than forty books. She has continued to study art and to travel. Through her travels she has become acquainted with tales and art from many cultures. She has retold and illustrated a Japanese tale, *The Leaky Umbrella* (Prentice, 1980), as well as tales from Korea and, more recently, China. Her interest in Chinese painting was stimulated by *The Mustard Seed Garden Manual of Painting*, a book written by Wang Kai in 1679. After reading the book she began to look at all drawings and paintings in a different way. The joy, life, spontaneity, and peace represented in Chinese paintings became her challenge.

She believes that children must be empowered to make choices as they express themselves through the arts. According to Demi, every moment of light and dark is magic—every piece of art is magic. Once she became acquainted with Chinese art she found that empty space was fuller than filled space.

She began to attempt to infuse her illustrations with the magic of Chinese art. Each of her paintings is prepared on fine, brilliant silk. Demi's white paints are made from lead or powdered oyster shell; azurite, indigo, and cinnibar are made from other traditional ingredients. To each paint she adds powdered jade for good luck. The black Chinese ink that she uses is ten parts pine soot boiled in Tung River water. And each of her paintings is made by employing the four Chinese treasures: the Chinese paintbrush, ink, inkstone, and paper.

Chinese techniques of placing outlined landscapes on golden green silk backgrounds were used by Demi for her decorative illustrations illuminating Bier's *The Nightingale*. Demi's illustrations did much to popularize the tale and to highlight the Chinese setting of Andersen's classic story.

Demi has retold and illustrated several Chinese folktales, and recently she has told a story, based on history and legend, of Genghis Khan (spelled "Chingis Khan" in the book's title). Genghis

Khan was a great Chinese leader and military strategist. "By the banks of the Onon River in the year of the Snow Leopard, 1160, a little boy was born." The young boy, Temujin, displays shrewdness and courage, unites the nomadic tribes of Mongolia, and is proclaimed Khan, or king. He leads his people in the conquest of China and Persia to establish the greatest contiguous land empire in history. Temujin becomes the greatest conqueror of all time. Demi's story is illustrated on every page with lavish illustrations filled with many cultural details. On every page gold is the fifth color.

The Empty Pot is a story that was originally told to Demi by her Chinese husband. It is a story he remembered from his childhood. The Chinese emperor is without an heir, so he announces an unusual contest to choose an heir. He invites all the children of the country to come to his palace to receive seeds to plant. The child who raises the best flowers from a seed given by the emperor will become his heir. The seeds do not sprout. Some of the children replace their seeds with new ones that do sprout. Ping, a fine gardener, cannot get his seed to sprout, but he will not replace it. On the day the children are to return to the palace, Ping's flower seed is still not sprouting. Other children arrive with glorious flowers in their pots while Ping must tell the emperor that he has failed to get his seed to sprout. His honesty causes the emperor to declare Ping his heir. The emperor was seeking an honorable heir, and to find such a child he had boiled the seeds before giving them to the children. Since boiled seeds will not germinate, he knew which children had replaced their seeds with others and also knew that Ping was honorable. *The Empty Pot* was selected to be read on "Mrs. Bush's Story Time," an ABC Radio Network program sponsored by the Children's Literacy Initiative.

Liang and the Magic Paint Brush is a retelling of the popular story of Ma Liang and his magic paintbrush. Liang is a poor boy who longs for a paintbrush. When he is given one, it happens that the brush is magic and everything Liang paints comes to life. The greedy emperor wants the brush but Liang refuses to give it up; but he eventually agrees to draw for the emperor. He draws the sea and a boat for the emperor's family. When the emperor commands Liang to paint the wind, he does. The wind is so furious that it capsizes the boat and the emperor and the royal family drown. Liang is thought to be wandering the earth still, "painting for the poor wherever he goes." Demi's husband, Tze-si Huang, created the calligraphy for the jacket of this book, and she dedicated the book to him, "Jesse." Demi's illustrations are detailed watercolors that emulate the Chinese paintings of long ago.

The Magic Boat tells of Chang's adventures with the boat and its unusual crew. Each of Demi's paintings is a fan-shaped illustration accented with gold.

The Artist and the Architect tells the story of a jealous artist who schemes to get rid of the architect by convincing him that the emperor's deceased father wants him to build a palace in heaven. The architect, discovering the jealous artist's plan, manages to escape and plans his revenge.

For her stories, particularly those of Chinese origin, Demi was honored with an invitation to represent the United States at the First International Children's Book Conference in Beijing. There, she and her husband, Tze-si Jesse Huang, received unexpected publicity. They were invited to appear on national television and to meet several influential Chinese, including Chang Wen Jing, the former ambassador to the United States, and Luo Ming, the head of printing for all of China.

Demi's current projects challenge her to bring the magic of life to her paper. She and her husband live in the state of Washington.

1. On each page of *Find Demi's Dinosaurs* is hidden a small prehistoric creature. Sometimes two, three, or four can be found hidden somewhere within the large-scale illustration of a dinosaur. Although Demi's imaginative interpretation brings a unique visual image to each page, all of her dinosaurs are based on fact. Peruse the pages to find the hidden animals. Using the concept of hidden animals Demi uses, create your own dinosaurs within a dinosaur picture. On a large piece of rolled butcher paper create a dinosaur of your own. Inside the dinosaur draw other dinosaurs.

2. *Demi's Opposites* highlights concepts such as black-white, come-go, near-far, rich-poor, beginning-end. After reading the book make a list of opposites you can identify in the book. Brainstorm other opposites: forwards-backwards, up-down, etc. Choose a pair of opposite concepts and illustrate the concepts.

3. Use *Demi's Count the Animals 1 2 3* to count from one to twenty; and Demi has included two ways to count to 100. Using the images in the book to assist, count to 100, and then count to 100 again. Read some of the following counting books and count, count, count:

Aker, Suzanne. *What Comes in Twos, Threes, and Fours?* Illustrated by Bernie Karlin. Simon, 1990.

Anno, Mitsumasa. *Anno's Counting Book*. Illustrated by Mitsumasa Anno. Harper-Collins, 1977.

Aylesworth, Jim. *One Crow: A Counting Rhyme*. Illustrated by Ruth Young. Lippincott, 1988.

Bang, Molly. *Ten, Nine, Eight*. Illustrated by Molly Bang. Greenwillow, 1983.

Calmenson, Stephanie. *Dinner at Panda Place*. Illustrated by Nadine Bernard Westcott. HarperCollins, 1991.

Christelow, Eileen. *Five Little Monkeys Sitting in a Tree*. Illustrated by Eileen Christelow. Clarion, 1991.

Coats, Laura Jane. *Ten Little Animals*. Illustrated by Laura Jane Coats. Macmillan, 1990.

Crews, Donald. *Ten Black Dots*. Illustrated by Donald Crews. Scribner, 1968.

Crossley-Holland, Kevin. *Under the Sun and over the Moon*. Illustrated by Ian Penney. Putnam, 1989.

Dee, Ruby. *Two Ways to Count to Ten: A Liberian Folk Tale*. Illustrated by Susan Maddaugh. Henry Holt, 1988.

Dunbar, Joyce. *Ten Little Mice*. Illustrated by Maria Majewska. Harcourt, 1990.

Ehlert, Lois. *Fish Eyes: A Book You Can Count On*. Illustrated by Lois Ehlert. Harcourt, 1990.

Feelings, Muriel. *Moja Means One: Swahili Counting Book*. Illustrated by Tom Feelings. Dial, 1971.

Gerstein, Mordicai. *Roll Over!* Illustrated by Mordicai Gerstein. Crown, 1984.

Giganti, Paul, Jr. *Each Orange Had 8 Slices: A Counting Book*. Illustrated by Donald Crews. Greenwillow, 1992.

Haskins, Jim. *Count Your Way through Germany*. Illustrated by Helen Byers. Carolrhoda, 1990. *Count Your Way through Italy*. Illustrated by Beth Wright. Carolrhoda, 1990. (Other titles are available in the Count Your Way series.)

Hayes, Sarah. *Nine Ducks Nine*. Illustrated by Sarah Hayes. Lothrop, 1990.

Katz, Michael Jay, selector. *Ten Potatoes in a Pot: And Other Counting Rhymes*. Illustrated by June Otani. Harper, 1990.

MacCarthy, Patricia. *Ocean Parade: A Counting Book*. Illustrated by Patricia MacCarthy. Dial, 1990.

Mack, Stan. *Ten Bears in My Bed: A Goodnight Countdown*. Illustrated by Stan Mack. Pantheon, 1974.

Oliver, Stephen. *My First Look at Numbers*. Illustrated by Stephen Oliver. Random, 1990.

Peek, Merle. *The Balancing Act: A Counting Book*. Illustrated by Merle Peek. Clarion, 1987.

Peek, Merle. *Roll Over! A Counting Song*. Illustrated by Merle Peek. Clarion, 1981.

Rosenberg, Amye. *1 to 100 Busy Counting Book*. Illustrated by Amye Rosenberg. Golden/Western, 1988.

Scott, Ann Herbert. *One Good Horse: A Cowpuncher's Counting Book*. Illustrated by Lynn Sweat. Greenwillow, 1990.

Sendak, Maurice. *One Was Johnny: A Counting Book*. Illustrated by Maurice Sendak. HarperCollins, 1962.

Sheppard, Jeff. *The Right Number of Elephants*. Illustrated by Felicia Bond. HarperCollins, 1990.

Thornhill, Jan. *The Wildlife 1-2-3: A Nature Counting Book*. Illustrated by Jan Thornhill. Simon, 1989.

4. Decide upon a counting theme and then create your own counting book. As a group write a text that counts by ones to any number, or by fives, tens, etc. After the text is written, divide it appropriately and ask individuals or partners to illustrate each section. The counting book might begin: "One little duck sitting in a truck. Two big dogs sitting on logs. Three yellow mittens lost near the kittens. Four gray fish swimming in a dish," etc. Or if the count by five idea is used, the same text might read: "Five little ducks sitting in trucks. Ten big dogs sitting on logs. Fifteen yellow mittens lost near the kittens," etc. Each of the counting pages should be illustrated. The pages could first be used as a bulletin-board book and later bound together into a class big book.

5. Use *Find Demi's Sea Creatures* to find the tiniest sea horse, the giant blue whale, flying fish, and electric eels. Endangered species are noted throughout the book. Expand on the theme of endangered species by reading Alexandra Wright's *Will We Miss Them: Endangered Species* (Charlesbridge, 1991).

6. Locate information about endangered species noted in Demi's book and present information to your class about effots to preserve them. Identify and work on a project to save one of the species; perhaps a bake sale could be held and proceeds sent to an organization involved in preserving that species. Or, if direct involvement is possible, consider contributing time to publicize the plight of a specific species that needs help: make posters, send flyers, or write letters to local news media, etc.

7. Thirteen traditional Chinese fables are retold in *Demi's Reflective Fables*. The illustrations are shaped to represent a Chinese mirror. After reading all the fables, identify the major motifs: good versus evil, long sleep/enchantment, good deeds rewarded, etc. Discuss these fables in terms of fables from Aesop and La Fontaine and the jataka tales from India. Identify the elements/details from Demi's fables that are attributable to the story's origin. Compare and contrast the story grammar, story motifs, and story details with those of fables from other cultures.

8. Compare and contrast Anna Bier's adaptation of *The Nightingale* and Demi's illustrations for that tale with the text and illustrations in other editions of Hans Christian Andersen's classic story.

   Andersen, Hans Christian. *The Nightingale*. Translated by Anthea Bell. Illustrated by Lisbeth Zwerger. Picture Book, 1985.

   Andersen, Hans Christian. *The Nightingale*. Translated by Eva Le Gallienne. Illustrated by Nancy Ekholm Burkert. HarperCollins, 1965.

   Andersen, Hans Christian. *The Nightingale*. Translated by M. R. James. Illustrated by Kaj Beckman. Van Nostrand, 1969.

   Andersen, Hans Christian. *The Nightingale*. Translated by Naomi Lewis. Illustrated by Josef Palecek. North-South, 1990.

9. Compare and contrast the mood and images evoked by Bier's retelling and by Demi's illustrations for *The Nightingale* with the mood and images established in the fifteen-minute 16mm film adaptation of the story *The Nightingale* (Coronet Instructional Films, 1984). The Coronet film uses animated puppets to present the story of the Chinese emperor who finds a true treasure in his own garden.

10. Demi's brilliantly colored flowers, lacy snowflakes, and boldly drawn animals make a visual contrast to her dainty Thumbelina in her adapted and illustrated version of Hans Christian Andersen's *Thumbelina*. Use Demi's colorful volume as a starting point to share the Andersen story. Compare and contrast Demi's adaptation with other interpretations of the same tale. Many adaptations/translations maintain Andersen's leisurely storytelling pace and his characteristic coda. Ehrlich's retelling eliminates the coda entirely and retells the story in a more straight-to-the-point fashion. Illustrations, for some versions, depict the setting as serene and pleasant, whereas others—for example the version retold by Riordan—depict every creature that Thumbelina encounters as horribly grotesque and the setting as dark and threatening, full of sinister roots, thorns, and vines. Some "Thumbelina" titles follow.

Andersen, Hans Christian. "Thumbelina." In *The Random House Book of Fairy Tales* by Amy Ehrlich. Illustrated by Diane Goode. Random, 1985.

Andersen, Hans Christian. *Thumbelina*. Retold by Amy Ehrlich. Illustrated by Susan Jeffers. Dial, 1979.

Andersen, Hans Christian. *Thumbelina*. Translated by M. R. James. Illustrated by Kaj Beckman. Van Nostrand, 1973.

Andersen, Hans Christian. *Thumbelina*. Retold by James Riordan. Illustrated by Wayne Anderson. Putnam, 1991.

Andersen, Hans Christian. *Thumbeline*. Translated by Anthea Bell. Illustrated by Lisbeth Zwerger. Picture Book, 1985.

Andersen, Hans Christian. *Thumbeline*. Translated by Richard Winston and Clara Winston. Illustrated by Lisbeth Zwerger. Morrow, 1980.

11. Compare Demi's *Thumbelina* with Beatrice Schenk deRegniers's *Penny*, illustrated by Betsy Lewin (Lothrop, 1987).

    a. Compare Demi's *Thumbelina* and deRegniers's 1987 *Penny* to an earlier edition by deRegniers, illustrated by Marvin Bilek (Viking, 1966). Of particular significance in this comparison will be the effect or mood evoked by the illustrations.

    b. Compare Demi's *Thumbelina* to the eleven-minute, 16mm film version of the Thumbelina tale, *Thumbelina* (Coronet Instructional Films, 1970).

    c. Make a bedroom for Penny or Thumbelina. Make a bed out of a nutshell, and complete the rest of the bedroom with objects that you adapt for Penny or Thumbelina's use.

12. Compare and contrast Andersen's "Thumbelina" story to some of the following stories from other cultures depicting miniature people.

    Brenner, Barbara. *Little One Inch*. Illustrated by Fred Brenner. Coward, 1977.
    Not bigger than a finger, Issun Boshi floats down the river in a rice-bowl boat to seek his fortune in the city of Kyoto. With a sewing needle for a sword, he manages to trick two Japanese demons; he eventually wins the hand of a human-sized daughter of a merchant and then manages to get the Onis to grant him one wish—that he and the merchant's daughter might become the same size. She becomes one inch tall.

Haviland, Virginia. "Momotaro." In *Favorite Fairy Tales Told in Japan*. Illustrated by George Suyeoka. Little, 1967.
The miniature peach boy comes floating down the river inside a peach. At the age of fifteen, he is a fine young man who decides to go to an island and destroy the demons that live there. He shares his food with three animals who help him with his quest and help him recover the treasure from the demons. He returns home and shares his good fortune with the couple who had been his kindly parents.

Ishii, Momoko. *Issun Boshi, the Inchling: An Old Tale of Japan*. Translated by Yone Mizuta. Illustrated by Fuku Akino. Walker, 1967.
In this version of "Little One Inch," Issun Boshi grows to human size.

13. Demi retells the story of "Liang and the Magic Paint Brush." Compare that retelling and Demi's watercolors with those in the following two titles:

Bang, Molly Garrett. *Tye May and the Magic Brush*. Adapted and illustrated by Molly Garrett Bang. Greenwillow, 1981.

Kimishima, Hisako. *Ma Lien and the Magic Brush*. Translated by Alvin Tresselt. Illustrated by Kei Wakana. Parents, 1968. (Originally published as *Ma Lien To Maho No Fude* by Kaisei Sha, Tokyo, Japan.)

14. The intricate and detailed watercolors in *A Chinese Zoo* are painted on fan-shaped designs. Traditional Chinese fables are told in the solid-color borders that provide the background for the fan-shaped drawings. A fable is defined in *Funk & Wagnall's Standard Dictionary of Folklore, Mythology, and Legends* (Funk & Wagnalls, 1949) as "an animal tale with a moral; a short tale in which animals appear as characters, talking and acting like human beings, though usually keeping their animals traits, and having as its purpose the pointing of a moral. The fable consequently has two parts: the narrative which exemplifies the moral, and the statement of the moral often appended in the form of a proverb." Discuss the characteristics of fables and then compare and contrast selected fables from this book with the fables listed in page 133.

15. After sharing some of the Chinese nursery rhymes in Demi's *Dragon Kites and Dragonflies*, be sure to discuss the rhymes in terms of theme (nature, children at play, and other aspects of Chinese life) and in comparison with the nursery rhymes of Mother Goose. These can be found in the following collections:

Atkinson, Allen, selector. *Mother Goose's Nursery Rhymes*. Illustrated by Allen Atkinson. Ariel/Knopf, 1984 (1987).

Briggs, Raymond, selector. *Mother Goose Treasury*. Illustrated by Raymond Briggs. Coward, 1980. (Weston Woods® has a filmstrip/cassette available for this title.)

De Angeli, Marguerite, selector. *The Book of Nursery and Mother Goose Rhymes*. Illustrated by Marguerite De Angeli. Doubleday, 1954.

dePaola, Tomie, selector. *Tomie dePaola's Mother Goose*. Illustrated by Tomie dePaola. Putnam, 1985.

Gander, Father. *Father Gander Nursery Rhymes: The Equal Rhymes Amendment*. Illustrated by Carolyn. Advocacy Press, 1985. (Father Gander is a pseudonym for Dr. Douglas W. Larche, who rewrites the traditional rhymes to give equal status to male and female. Carolyn's illustrations strive to give an equal image as well.)

Larrick, Nancy, compiler. *Songs from Mother Goose: With the Traditional Melody for Each*. Illustrated by Robin Spowart. HarperCollins, 1989. (Historical information is included.)

Lobel, Arnold. *Gregory Griggs and Other Nursery Rhyme People*. Illustrated by Arnold Lobel. Greenwillow, 1978.

Lobel, Arnold, selector. *Random House Book of Mother Goose*. Illustrated by Arnold Lobel. Random, 1986.

Marshall, James. *James Marshall's Mother Goose*. Illustrated by James Marshall. Farrar, 1979.

Nister, Ernest. *Mother Goose Favorites: A Pop-Up Book*. Illustrated by Ernest Nister. Dutton, 1989.

Opie, Iona, and Peter Opie, editors. *Tail Feathers from Mother Goose: The Opie Rhyme Book*. Little, 1988.

Provensen, Alice, and Martin Provensen, selectors. *The Mother Goose Book*. Illustrated by Alice Provensen and Martin Provensen. Random, 1976.

Rojankovsky, Feodor, selector. *The Tall Book of Mother Goose*. Illustrated by Feodor Rojankovsky. HarperCollins, 1942.

Tripp, Wallace. *Granfa' Grig Had a Pig and Other Nursery Rhyme People*. Illustrated by Wally Tripp. Greenwillow, 1976.

Tudor, Tasha, selector. *Mother Goose*. Illustrated by Tasha Tudor. Walck, 1944.

Watson, Wendy. *Wendy Watson's Mother Goose*. Illustrated by Wendy Watson. Lothrop, 1989.

Wildsmith, Brian, selector. *Brian Wildsmith's Mother Goose*. Illustrated by Brian Wildsmith. Watts, 1963; Oxford, 1982.

Wright, Blanche Fisher, selector. *The Real Mother Goose*. Illustrated by Blanche Fisher Wright. Rand McNally, 1965 (1916).

Wyndham, Robert, editor. *Chinese Mother Goose Rhymes*. Illustrated by Ed Young. World, 1968; Philomel, 1989.

Different illustrators/selectors take different approaches to their collections of traditional verses. Some feel that the Mother Goose rhymes first popularized in England in the eighteenth century were political statements about politicians of the time. Wally Tripp touches on that idea by hiding notable figures from history in some of his illustrations. The observant reader will find Robert Frost, Princess Anne (falling from her horse), Toscanini, Napoleon, and Hitler, among others. Tripp's illustrations provide several examples of puns and literal interpretations of the titles or text. Wendy Watson uses a New England setting for her illustrations, using her own homespun Vermont wedding as the model for the illustration for "Oh, rare Harry Parry,/When will you marry?" Watson's illustrations take the reader through a year, from winter to winter, and span a day's time, from morning to evening. Alice and Martin Provensen use a Victorian setting for their illustrations, and Ernest Nister's are characteristically English. Ed Young's illustrations for Robert Wyndham's collection of Chinese Mother Goose rhymes are shimmering pastels and watercolors that emphasize their Chinese origins.

a. Compare the Mother Goose rhymes from the European tradition with those selected for the Demi and Wyndham collections from China. How do the collections reflect their origins? How do the rhymes compare thematically?

b. Correlate the reading of these rhymes with a social studies or history unit by having students illustrate a favorite verse in a setting during the specific period being studied. Or, have them rewrite or illustrate one of the verses to make a political statement about a specific country or historical situation. Humpty Dumpty could be illustrated to recall the November 1989 fall of the Berlin Wall or the December 1991 toppling of Mikhail Gorbachev from power and the breakup of the Union of Soviet Socialist Republics.

c. Make a big book of selected nursery rhymes from around the world. Choose rhymes that might be illustrated or that bring to mind a particular setting or country. Be sure to include a title page listing the names of the selectors and illustrators of the rhymes.

16. Introduce readers to Japanese poetry by reading haiku from Demi's collection *In the Eyes of the Cat: Japanese Poetry for All Seasons.* Haiku looks simple but is very difficult to write while maintaining the grace of the language. Haiku is unrhymed and is traditionally written about nature. Overemphasis on the structure of haiku (three-line stanzas: the first line having five syllables, the second seven syllables, and the third five syllables) should not be allowed to interfere with creative expression. Before asking children to write haiku, make sure that they have been immersed in the form. Read translations of the Japanese masters—Basho, Issa, and Buson—and modern interpretations of the form.

a. A section on understanding and creating haiku is included in Myra Cohn Livingston's *Poem-making: Ways to Begin Writing Poetry* (HarperCollins/Charlotte Zolotow, 1991). Use this book for a step-by-step approach to the writing of haiku.

b. Other books of haiku:

Atwood, Ann. *My Own Rhythm: An Approach to Haiku.* Scribner, 1973.

Behn, Harry, translator. *Cricket Songs.* Illustrated by Sesshu and others. Harcourt, 1964.

Cassedy, Sylvia, and Kunihiro Suetake, translators. *Birds, Frogs, and Moonlight.* Illustrated by Vo-Dinh. Doubleday, 1967.

Cassedy, Sylvia, and Kunihiro Suetake, translators. *Red Dragonfly on My Shoulder.* Illustrated by Molly Bang. HarperCollins, 1992. (Thirteen selections from *Birds, Frogs, and Moonlight* with new illustrations.)

Higginson, William J. *Wind in the Long Grass: A Collection of Haiku.* Illustrated by Sandra Speidel. Simon, 1991.

Robertson, Joanne. *Sea Witches.* Illustrated by Laszlo Gal. Dial, 1991.

Keiko Kasza

Keiko Kasza

Keiko Kasza was born in Hiroshima-ken, Japan, on December 23, 1951. She grew up and attended school in Japan but came to the United States to study at California State University, Northridge. She earned a degree in graphic design in 1976. For a time she worked as a graphic designer and wrote and illustrated books during evenings and weekends. Shortly after her marriage, her husband's work took them to Ecuador. While she was there she came across a picture book by Leo Lionni, *Frederick*. She decided that she should try to create a book of her own. Her first book was published in Japanese in 1981, *Omu no Itazura* (The Parrot's Trick).

Most of her family is still in Japan, but Keiko Kasza lives in Indiana with her husband and their two young sons. She works every day at her writing and illustrating while her children are at a day-care center.

Her favorite things include tennis, reading, and Japanese food, except raw fish. She says she is a great cook as long as she stays away from baking pastry. Whenever she gets bogged down on a difficult illustration, she dreams of starting her own restaurant.

Keiko Kasza

BIBLIOGRAPHY
AND MORE INFORMATION

Selected titles written or illustrated by Keiko Kasza:

A Mother for Choco. Written and illustrated by Keiko Kasza. Putnam, 1992.

The Pigs' Picnic. Written and illustrated by Keiko Kasza. Putnam, 1988.

When the Elephant Walks. Written and illustrated by Keiko Kasza. Putnam, 1990.

The Wolf's Chicken Stew. Written and illustrated by Keiko Kasza. Putnam, 1987.

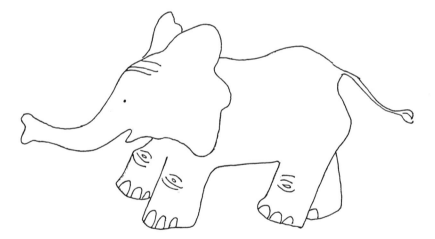

Japan is Keiko Kasza's place of birth and the country where she grew up. In her late teens she came to the United States to attend California State University at Northridge. She graduated magna cum laude with a degree in graphic arts in 1976. She worked as a graphic designer and wrote and painted in her spare time. Soon after her marriage her husband's job took them to Ecuador for a year. While in Ecuador she was unable to work as a graphic designer, so when she came across a picture book by Leo Lionni, *Frederick*, it inspired her to use her time to create a picture book herself. Her art education, combined with this more serious effort at writing and illustrating, produced her first book. It was published in Japan in 1981. Several more books followed. After leaving Ecuador she went back to working as a graphic designer. In 1986 her first son was born, and three years later another son arrived. Because she wanted to spend more time with her children, she felt she had to choose between graphic design and writing books—there was no longer time for both. Writing books won.

In 1987 her first book was published in the United States, when Putnam published *The Wolf's Chicken Stew*. The clever and sly wolf spies a hen who will make a delicious meal—but he reasons that if the hen were fattened up she would make more stew for him. So he sets out to do just that, but the results are not quite what the wolf expected. Kasza's next book, *The Pigs' Picnic*, was published a year later. Mr. Pig, wishing to convince Miss Pig to accompany him on a picnic, picks a flower to give her. Along the way he accepts other gifts for her from his friends—Fox, Lion, and Zebra. They lend Mr. Pig a bushy tail, a shaggy mane, and gray stripes. When Mr. Pig arrives at Miss Pig's house she is scared of the "monster" and threatens to call her friend Mr. Pig if the monster does not go away. Mr. Pig hastens to give back the borrowed items. When he returns to Miss Pig's house, he is warmly welcomed and she accepts his invitation to accompany him on a picnic. Kasza's bright watercolors aptly display the exasperation and humor in each of the episodes.

When the Elephant Walks was published in 1990 by Putnam. This cumulative tale begins with the elephant scaring the bear who runs away and scares the crocodile who swims for his life. When the crocodile swims away he scares the wild hog, and eventually the mouse runs away and scares the elephant who runs away—bringing the story full circle. *A Mother for Choco* tells of a little chick's search for a mother. There is humor in both the search and the resolution of the story. Kasza's next story will be one titled *The Rat and the Tiger*. That book, Kasza says, deals with the frustration she felt, as a six- or seven-year-old, when a friend bossed her around.

Most of Keiko Kasza's family still lives in Japan, so she tries to return there as often as possible. Kasza now lives in Bloomington, Indiana, with her husband and two young sons. Her schedule includes time each weekday for writing and illustrating. Her husband teaches Japanese politics at Indiana University, so after he goes to his office, Keiko takes her two sons to a day-care center. She then returns, energizes herself with some strong coffee, and begins to work on her writing and illustrating. She works from about 10:30 a.m. to 4:30 p.m. and then picks up her children.

Between work and caring for her children, Kasza has little free time. But she does love to play tennis. She feels that she is a pretty good cook if she stays away from baking pastry. Her favorite foods include any Japanese foods except raw fish. She finds cooking therapeutic, especially when she gets bogged down on a particular illustration. Other favorite things include reading and the colors purple and black.

1. Send Ms. Kasza a birthday card for her December 23 birthday. Design the card with drawings of favorite animals from her books.

2. Locate the country and city where Keiko Kasza was born, and discuss its distance and location in relation to where you live.

3. Pat Hutchins's *Rosie's Walk* features a little red hen that struts across her barnyard apparently unaware that a fox is stalking her for his dinner. Compare the opening lines of Hutchins's story with the opening of *The Wolf's Chicken Stew*. Then compare and contrast the rest of the story.

4. After reading *The Wolf's Chicken Stew*, read Tony Ross's *Stone Soup* (Dial, 1987). In Ross's tale a wolf spies a chicken that he approaches with the full intention of making her his dinner. Instead, she offers to make soup for him—with a stone. She then suggests that other ingredients be added. While adding the ingredients she suggests that the wolf do a chore for her. By the end of the story the wolf has taken the clothes off the line, swept her floor, done the dishes, and fixed the television antenna. Finally the soup is finished and the wolf thinks he is outsmarting the chicken when he grabs the stone and makes off down the road as fast as he can. Compare and contrast Ross's story with *The Wolf's Chicken Stew*. Discuss the role each character plays in the story, who actually tricks whom, and the conclusion.

5. *When the Elephant Walks* is a cumulative chain story, as is Verna Aardema's *Why Mosquitoes Buzz in People's Ears*, illustrated by Leo Dillon and Diane Dillon (Dial, 1975). After reading these two stories read other cumulative stories from the following list and discuss the characteristics of a cumulative story.

    Emberley, Barbara. *Drummer Hoff*. Illustrated by Ed Emberley. Prentice, 1967.

    Galdone, Paul. *The Gingerbread Boy*. Illustrated by Paul Galdone. Clarion, 1975.

    Heilbroner, Joan. *This Is the House Where Jack Lives*. Illustrated by Aliki. Harper-Collins, 1962.

    "The House That Jack Built." In *The Three Bears and 15 Other Stories* by Anne Rockwell. Crowell, 1975; Harper Trophy, 1984.

    Lobel, Arnold. *The Rose in My Garden*. Illustrated by Anita Lobel. Greenwillow, 1984.

    "The Old Woman and Her Pig." In *The Old Woman and Her Pig and 10 Other Stories* by Anne Rockwell. Crowell, 1979. (Published in paperback with the title *The Three Sillies and 10 Other Stories to Read Aloud*, Harper Trophy, 1986.)

    Sawyer, Ruth. *Journey Cake, Ho!* Illustrated by Robert McCloskey. Viking, 1953.

    Seuss, Dr. *Thidwick the Big-Hearted Moose*. Illustrated by Dr. Seuss. Random, 1948.

    Wood, Audrey. *The Napping House*. Illustrated by Don Wood. Harcourt, 1984.

    Zemach, Harve. *The Speckled Hen: A Russian Nursery Rhyme*. Illustrated by Margot Zemach. Holt, 1966.

6. View the video version of *The Pigs' Picnic*, available from American School Publishers. Compare and contrast the video with the book.

7. After viewing *The Pigs' Picnic*, as suggested in activity 6, discuss the difference between an iconographic (moving the camera across the page) film and an animated presentation. Weston Woods® has a twenty-five-minute film that describes the animation process, *Gene Deitch: The Picture Book Animated* (Weston Woods®, 1977). This film would be especially appropriate for intermediate students who might be interested in a career in animation, filmmaking, etc.

Patricia Polacco

Patricia Polacco

From *An Author a Month (for Dimes)* by Sharron L. McElmeel (Libraries Unlimited, 1992)

Patricia Polacco

Patricia Polacco's book *The Keeping Quilt* tells the story of her Russian great-grandparents' efforts to remember home and to have "the family in backhome Russia dance around at night." Other of Patricia Polacco's childhood memories are told in *Thunder Cake*, *Uncle Vova's Tree*, *Babushka's Doll*, *Meteor!*, *Chicken Sunday*, and *Rechenka's Eggs*.

Patricia Polacco was born July 11, 1944, in Lansing, Michigan. Her family lived with her grandparents for a while in Michigan. Later the family moved to Florida and in 1954 to Oakland, California. Patricia Polacco has always enjoyed drawing, but reading was very difficult and mathematics was impossible. She did not start writing books until she was forty-one; since then she has written over thirty. She was especially devoted to her babushka (grandmother), and when Patricia Polacco formed a business she named it Babushka, Inc. Her car license plates also read "BABSHKE."

Patricia Polacco and her husband, Enzo-Mario Polacco, live in an old brown-shingle house on a tree-covered lot in the middle of Oakland, just two blocks from her own childhood home. Their daughter, Traci Denise, and son, Steven, are grown. Patricia Polacco enjoys painting Ukrainian eggs (*pisanky*), running, playing with one of her five cats (Tush, Lo Lo, Pitcka, Boris, and Nikita), and rocking in one of her thirteen rocking chairs.

Patricia Polacco

BIBLIOGRAPHY
AND MORE INFORMATION

Selected titles written or illustrated by Patricia Polacco:

Appelemando's Dreams. Written and illustrated by Patricia Polacco. Philomel, 1991.

Babushka's Doll. Written and illustrated by Patricia Polacco. Simon, 1990.

A Boat Ride with Lillian Two Blossom. Written and illustrated by Patricia Polacco. Philomel, 1989.

Casey at the Bat. Written by Ernest Lawrence Thayer. Illustrated by Patricia Polacco. Putnam, 1988.

Chicken Sunday. Written and illustrated by Patricia Polacco. Philomel, 1992.

Just Plain Fancy. Written and illustrated by Patricia Polacco. Bantam, 1990.

The Keeping Quilt. Written and illustrated by Patricia Polacco. Simon, 1988.

Meteor! Written and illustrated by Patricia Polacco. Putnam, 1987.

Mrs. Katz and Tush. Written and illustrated by Patricia Polacco. Bantam, 1992.

Rechenka's Eggs. Written and illustrated by Patricia Polacco. Philomel, 1988.

Thunder Cake. Written and illustrated by Patricia Polacco. Philomel, 1990.

Uncle Vova's Tree. Written and illustrated by Patricia Polacco. Philomel, 1989.

Patricia Polacco was born Patricia Ann Barber in Lansing, Michigan, on July 11, 1944. Her early home was in Williamston, Michigan. In 1947, when Patricia was three, her parents divorced and Patricia and her brother went with their mother to live in Union City, Michigan, with their maternal grandparents. Patricia's mother was a teacher in Battle Creek, Michigan. Just two years later, Patricia's beloved babushka died and her grandfather sold the family farm in Union City. Patricia's family moved to Coral Gables, Florida, where they lived for the next two and a half years. Patricia's mother got a teaching job in Oakland, California, and the family moved there in 1954. From a very young age Patricia enjoyed drawing, and she could draw in perspective when she was four. But during her beginning school years she found reading and mathematics very difficult. Later it was learned that she was learning disabled. When she got help for her dyslexia she excelled, but her memories of failure were very strong. She felt that art was the only thing that she could do well. She says that it was very painful to always feel dumb. So she dreamed a lot; her imagination provided a safe haven. In her imagination she was smart and could do anything. It wasn't until 1985, when she was forty-one, that she started writing.

Many of her memories of family life have become part of the stories she writes. *The Keeping Quilt* tells the story of the quilt that preserved the memories of great-grandparents and their Russian origins through weddings, births, and other family events. Patricia's great-grandmother Anna's babushka (shawl) became part of the quilt, as did pieces of her Uncle Vladimir's shirt, her Aunt Havalah's nightdress, and her Aunt Natasha's apron. Over the years the quilt was used as a tablecloth on the Sabbath, a blanket on the grass where marriage proposals were accepted, a wedding huppa (a canopy for the wedding couple during the ceremony), and a coming-home blanket for a new baby. The quilt welcomed Patricia the day she was born, and while she was growing up the quilt was part of her imaginary play in such places as the "steaming Amazon jungle." When Patricia married Enzo-Mario, the quilt served as her huppa and eventually welcomed their first child, Traci Denise. The pictures in the illustrations give readers a glimpse of Patricia's own family. In the scene depicting Patricia and Enzo-Mario's wedding, family members are shown. Nearby is her best friend, a friend she describes as a Black man who grew up as her neighbor. She says, "He was my neighbor and dearest friend ever since I came to California. His grandmother became my 'Bubby' when mine died." The final picture in the book shows Patricia and Enzo-Mario and their new baby wrapped in the quilt. *The Keeping Quilt* won the 1988 Sydney Taylor Book Award for Younger Children from the Association of Jewish Libraries and was nominated for the National Jewish Book Award in the Children's Picture Book category by the Jewish Book Council.

Patricia Polacco is the descendant of Russian immigrants. When they arrived in Michigan they could not find other Jewish farmers in their area, but they did find other Russians. After a time a section of her family started marrying Russian Orthodox Christians. Patricia was raised to observe both Christian and Jewish traditions. Her respect for other cultures grew when her family moved to Oakland to a "mixed" neighborhood. Upon graduating from high school she entered Laney College and later the California College of Arts and Crafts, both located in Oakland. She studied in Australia for five years and in 1973 earned a master's in fine arts and in 1978 a Ph.D. in art history. Her particular area of interest became Russian and Greek painting and iconographic history. She became a historical consultant to museums in her special art field, Russian and Greek icons. She still enjoys painting and restoring icons, as well as painting Ukrainian eggs (called *pisanky* or *pysanky*).

Polacco did not begin writing until she was forty-one, in 1986, but in five years she created over thirty books. *Meteor!* tells of a meteor crashing into a Michigan farmyard. *Rechenka's Eggs* showcases Babushka's gift for coloring eggs in patterns that come from folklore symbols and images—a gift that Polacco has inherited. *Thunder Cake* tells the story of Polacco's childhood fear of thunder. She says, "I was the little girl and the recipe is the true one that was in my bubby's recipe box." Other tales are original stories and preserve the flavor of a simple culture. *Mrs. Katz and Tush* tells the story of Larnel Moore and Mrs. Katz, who share a concern for an abandoned cat. Larnel, a young African-American child, and Mrs. Katz, a Jewish woman, are brought together by Tush, the cat, and develop a lasting friendship. *Chicken Sunday* features Polacco's rich folk-art style illustrations. A young Russian-American girl is adopted into her neighbors' African-American family in a backyard ritual, which makes Stewart and Winston her brothers and their grandmother, Miss Eula Mae Walker, her adopted grandmother. The three children often go to the Baptist church with Miss Eula Mae and share many special family times. Miss Eula Mae admires a very special hat in Mr. Kodinski's hat store, but the three children do not have enough money to purchase it. Later, the three children are accused of misdeeds by Mr. Kodinski. That incident results in an opportunity for the three children to show Mr. Kodinski that they would not do such a thing and also gives them a chance to earn the money to buy that special hat for Miss Eula Mae.

Babushka's Doll is a story about Natasha and her babushka. Natasha constantly whines and nags Babushka. Natasha wants to be pushed in a swing or pulled in a cart. To teach Natasha to change her ways, Babushka gives Natasha a doll to play with. Babushka had played with the doll just once herself, when she was a child. The doll comes to life and demands so much of Natasha that she comes to realize how demanding her requests of her babushka have been.

Just Plain Fancy is an Amish story—a project that came about over a breakfast attended by Polacco and some Bantam representatives. During breakfast they asked if Polacco had an Amish story. It just happened that she had one "rattling around" in her head. Polacco told them of the story and they bought it on the spot. To write the story she had to do a great deal of reading about the Amish, and she traveled to areas where the Amish live.

Polacco's illustrations for Ernest Lawrence Thayer's poem *Casey at the Bat* gave it a polished new interpretation. Instead of the usual images of adults playing the ill-fated game, Polacco sets the action in a Little League game. Preceding the poem, Polacco inserts an introduction that has an arrogant red-haired boy being prodded by his sister to get to the game on time. When the Mudville Nine's chances in the ballgame are finished with Casey's final strike, he accepts his defeat humbly. He realizes that he was fairly beaten—even if it was his dad, the umpire, who called him out. Polacco's illustrations are large, bold, and brightly colored.

To create the illustrations for her stories, Polacco uses Pentel markers, acrylic paint, numbers 2B and 6B pencils, and oil pastel. Polacco begins with a small rough dummy. The dummy is worked out with drawings that are photocopied and sent off to the publisher for position corrections. When the drawings are returned, they are enlarged 25 percent, with the help of a copy machine. Polacco then completes the color finishes by using a light box. At this point the text is positioned and in place. Sometimes the visual part of the book comes first, but at other times the words come first. Polacco writes and draws every day that she is not at a school or on a publicity tour. She says that she often sees the story first in her mind, while she is rocking. After the story is thought out, she types it on a typewriter.

In addition to her writing and illustrating, Patricia Polacco serves as art director of *Galleys*, a publication serving writers and illustrators in the United States. She is also a consultant on iconographic art and is involved in the Citizens Exchange Council Program for writers and illustrators. Polacco has traveled extensively in the former Soviet Union and supports Russian-American friendships and exchanges of art and artists through Babushka, Inc. This corporation serves as the business vehicle for her writing and illustrating projects as well as a vehicle to promote the exchange of art and artists between the United States and what is now the Confederation of Independent States. In addition to being president of Babushka, Inc., Polacco is a partner in the Avante Garde Children's Art School in Leningrad, where she is also a member of the board of directors. Babushka, Inc. is involved in efforts to establish a children's art school in the United States.

Polacco and her husband, Enzo-Mario, an Italian from Trieste, live in Oakland just two blocks from her childhood home. Their old brown-shingle house is on a lot covered with so many trees that one would think the house was in the middle of the woods. But they are right in the center of Oakland—just three houses from the busiest street in town. Polacco has at least two rocking chairs in almost every room of their house. Their daughter, Traci Denise (born in 1966), and son, Steven (born in 1970), are grown and live in homes of their own. The Polaccos share their house with five cats: Tush, Lo Lo, Pitcka, Boris, and Nikita. Polacco's list of favorites include any type of food; all hues of red, blue, and green; and rocking in one of her thirteen rocking chairs.

1. Leo Lionni has written two books about someone's gift not being valued until a specific event occurs and the gift is recognized as valuable. Compare and contrast Leo Lionni's *Frederick* (Knopf, 1967) and *Matthew's Dream* (Knopf, 1991) with Polacco's *Appelemando's Dreams*.

2. After reading *Appelemando's Dreams*, have students use large sheets of butcher paper to create pictures of their dreams. Display all the dreams around the room, in hallways, and in the school cafeteria.

3. The concept of individual differences is a central theme in *Appelemando's Dreams*. James Stevenson's *Which One Is Whitney?* (Greenwillow, 1990) also celebrates individual differences. Mrs. Dugong and her five children meet Mrs. Grouper who wants to know how to identify each child, particularly Whitney. Whitney turns out to be very clever. Discuss the importance of recognizing individual differences. Over a period of a week or so, make sure that each child in your classroom is recognized for a special talent she or he has.

4. Read *Babushka's Doll*, a story in which Natasha is very demanding of her grandmother.

   a. Discuss why you would or would not like to have Natasha as a friend.

   b. Choose another favorite book character: Ramona (series by Beverly Cleary), Henry Huggins (series by Beverly Cleary), Eddie or Betsy (series by Carolyn Haywood), Julian or Gloria (series by Ann Cameron), or any other identifiable character. Discuss whether or not Natasha would be a good friend to any one of the characters you have chosen. Make a character web for each character and compare the personalities. (See an example of a character web at the end of chapter 6.)

5. In *Casey at the Bat* Polacco's illustrations give the century-old poem a new perspective by showing Casey as a Little League player rather than as the traditional mustachioed old-timer on an adult town team or minor league team. Compare Polacco's version with the humorous version illustrated by Wallace Tripp (*Casey at the Bat: A Ballad of the Republic, Sung in the Year 1888*, Coward, 1980) and with *Casey at the Bat*, illustrated by Paul Frame (Prentice, 1964).

6. *Just Plain Fancy* is a story of people who live a simple life in the Amish tradition. Information books about the Amish can add much interest to this title. For background and information for further discussion read books from the following list:

   Zielinski, John M. *Amish Across America*. 2d ed. Kendall/Hunt, 1983. (Also available from Amish Heritage Publications)

   Zielinski, John M. *Amish: A Pioneer Heritage*. Wallace Homestead Company, 1975. (A pictorial history of the Old Order Amish migration)

   Zielinski, John M. *Amish Barns across America*. Kendall/Hunt, 1986. (Also available from Amish Heritage Publications)

7. *The Keeping Quilt* reinforces the concept that some quilts record family stories and family histories. Extend this idea by sharing Valerie Flournoy's *The Patchwork Quilt*, illustrated by Jerry Pinkney (Dial, 1985), and Ann Jonas's *The Quilt* (Greenwillow, 1984). Sylvia Fair's *The Bedspread* (Morrow, 1982) features an embroidered bedspread, and although it is not a quilt story, it does feature memories and stories. Two sisters embroider their own childhood recollections of the house in which they grew up. The finished bedspread is a surprise to both of them.

a. Students could make a paper quilt to represent some of their own memories. Proceed as follows:

(1) Ask each child to identify a special memory of his or her life.

(2) Give each child a 9"-square piece of drawing paper on which to illustrate a favorite memory. The "quilt square" should have the background completely filled in.

(3) When all the paper squares are completed, check to make sure that the creator has signed his or her block.

(4) Arrange the squares on a backing of brown wrapping paper. Leave a 1" to 3" gap between the squares. Glue the squares in place. If possible include a dedication square in the bottom right-hand corner.

(5) Separate the squares with strips of colored paper. The strips could be a solid color such as black, which would make an attractive border for each square and for the whole "quilt." Or the strips could be a chain of different colors pieced together.

b. A cloth quilt could also be made featuring memories of the children's year in your classroom or each child's favorite book. The quilt squares can be created with fabric paints or transfer pens. The cloth squares would have to be sewn together or, if the quilt will only be displayed, one might consider using a fusible webbing to fuse the cloth squares onto a cloth backing. If the webbing is used, an iron will be needed to iron the cloth squares, fusing, and backing together.

8. Hyperbole is obvious and extravagant exaggeration not meant to be taken literally. After reading *Meteor!* discuss its story line in terms of hyperbole. Other books that might be used in conjunction with this discussion are:

Bauer, Caroline. *Too Many Books!* Illustrated by Diane Paterson. Warne, 1984.

Baylor, Byrd. *The Best Town in the World*. Illustrated by Ronald Himler. Scribner, 1982.

Cole, Babette. *The Trouble with Granddad*. Putnam, 1988.

Hutchins, Pat. *The Very Worst Monster*. Greenwillow, 1985.

Westcott, Nadine Bernard. *The Giant Vegetable Garden*. Little, 1981.

9. In conjunction with reading *Meteor!* individuals or small groups might investigate the topic of meteors and meteorites. Use the index of astronomy books to locate the pages that discuss meteors. "Shooting stars" are really meteors—the light trails of particles burn up as they zoom through the earth's atmosphere at speeds of up to forty-five miles per second. Gather more facts about the sixty-six-ton Hoba West meteorite that fell in southwestern Africa or the thirty-four-ton Ahnighito meteorite that is on display at the American Museum of Natural History in New York City. The Ahnighito meteorite fell to earth in Greenland. Have students prepare a presentation on meteors, being sure to include visuals (charts, posters, etc.).

10. *Rechenka's Eggs* features the art of painting Ukrainian eggs. Instruct students as follows: Make a pinhole in one end of a raw egg and a little larger hole in the other end. If you blow very hard in the pinhole, the egg yolk and white will be blown out of the larger hole. Use tempera paints and small paint brushes (or cotton-tipped swabs) to create your own version of a decorated egg. Display the eggs in a colorful basket or on an egg tree.

11. Correlate the reading of *Thunder Cake* with reading and following directions and mathematical measuring objectives by using the recipe in *Thunder Cake* to create a thunder cake.

12. Compare how fear of a storm is treated in *Thunder Cake* with how the grandfather helps his grandson, Thomas, deal with his fear of a thunderstorm in *Storm in the Night* by Mary Stolz, illustrated by Pat Cummings (HarperCollins, 1988).

13. Compare *Uncle Vova's Tree* with Eric A. Kimmel's *The Chanukkah Tree*, illustrated by Giora Carmi (Holiday, 1988). How are the story lines similar? Compare and contrast the characters in the two stories.

14. To highlight the fact that authors often use incidents and people from their own lives in their writing, identify events and people in Polacco's life that show up in her books. For example, she has a cat named Tush, which is the name of the cat in *Mrs. Katz and Tush*. Use this information to encourage young writers that they, too, have "something" to write about.

Appendix

Addresses of Authors/ Illustrators and Publishers, Photograph Credits

ADDRESSES OF AUTHORS/ILLUSTRATORS

Because addresses often change, it is recommended that correspondence be sent in care of the Children's Book Marketing Division of the author/illustrator's most recent publisher. Address an envelope to the publisher, enclose your letter to the author/illustrator in a stamped envelope, and insert a memo requesting that the publisher forward the letter.

Martha Alexander
c/o Dial Books for Young Readers
2 Park Avenue
New York, NY 10016

Caroline Arnold
c/o Clarion Books
215 Park Avenue South
New York, NY 10003

Graeme Base
c/o Penguin Books
P.O. Box 257
Ringwood 3134, Australia

Byrd Baylor
c/o General Delivery
Arivaca, AZ 85601

Jan Brett
132 Pleasant Street
Norwell, MA 02061

Anthony Browne
c/o Julia MacRae Books
Random Century House
20 Vauxhall Bridge Road
London SW1V 2SA, Great Britain

Joanna Cole
52 Jeremiah Road
Sandy Hook, CT 06482

Demi
c/o Putnam & Grosset Book Group
Attn: Children's Books/Promotion
200 Madison Avenue
New York, NY 10016

Keiko Kasza
2450 N. Browncliff Lane
Bloomington, IN 47408

Eric A. Kimmel
2525 N.E. 35th Avenue
Portland, OR 97212

Patricia Polacco
Babushka, Inc.
6045 Chabot Road
Oakland, CA 94618

Janet Stevens
c/o Harcourt Brace Jovanovich
Books for Children and Young Adults
1250 Sixth Avenue
San Diego, CA 92101

SELECTED PUBLISHERS' ADDRESSES

Note: Publishers' addresses may change. For complete and up-to-date information, see the current edition of *Literary Market Place* or *Children's Books in Print*.

Abrams. *See* Harry N. Abrams, Inc.

Aladdin Books. *See* Macmillan Children's Books.

Albert Whitman & Company
6340 Oakton Street
Morton Grove, IL 60053

Alfred A. Knopf Books for Young Readers
225 Park Avenue South
New York, NY 10003

American School Publishers
P.O. Box 5380
Chicago, IL 60680-5380

Amish Heritage Publications
Box 2660
Iowa City, IA 52244

Arte Publico Press
Division of University of Houston
4800 Calhoun Street
Houston, TX 77204

Atheneum Books for Children
866 Third Avenue
New York, NY 10022

Avon Books
105 Madison Avenue
New York, NY 10022

Ballantine Books
201 E. 50th Street
New York, NY 10016

Bantam Books. *See* Bantam Doubleday Dell Publishing Group, Inc.

Bantam Doubleday Dell Publishing Group, Inc.
Attn: Children's Books Publicity
666 Fifth Avenue
New York, NY 10103

Boyds Mills Press
910 Church Street
Honesdale, PA 18431

Bradbury Press
866 Third Avenue
New York, NY 10022

Carolrhoda Books. *See* Lerner Publications.

Charlesbridge Publishing
85 Main Street
Watertown, MA 02172

Charles Scribner's Sons
866 Third Avenue
New York, NY 10022

Children's Press
5440 N. Cumberland Avenue
Chicago, IL 60656

Clarion Books
215 Park Avenue South
New York, NY 10003

Clarkson Potter. *See* Crown and Clarkson Potter Books for Young Readers.

Collier Books. *See* Aladdin Books.

Creative Arts Book Company
833 Bancraft Way
Berkeley, CA 94710

Crown and Clarkson Potter Books for Young Readers
225 Park Avenue South
New York, NY 10003

Dell Publishing. *See* Bantam Doubleday Dell Publishing Group, Inc.

Dial Books for Young Readers
375 Hudson Street
New York, NY 10014

Doubleday Publishing. *See* Bantam Doubleday Dell Publishing Group, Inc.

Douglas & McIntyre Ltd.
1615 Venables Street
Vancouver, BC V5L 2H1
Canada

Dutton Children's Books
375 Hudson Street
New York, NY 10014

Farrar, Straus & Giroux
19 Union Square West
New York, NY 10003

Four Winds Press
866 Third Avenue
New York, NY 10022

Franklin Watts, Inc.
387 Park Avenue South
New York, NY 10016

Frederick Warne & Company
375 Hudson Street
New York, NY 10014

Gareth Stevens Children's Books
Rivercenter Building, Suite 201
1555 N. Rivercenter Drive
Milwaukee, WI 53212

G. P. Putnam's Sons. *See* Putnam & Grosset Group.

Great Plains National Instructional Television
Library
P.O. Box 80669
Lincoln, NE 68501

Green Tiger Press
1230 Avenue of the Americas
New York, NY 10020

Greenwillow Books
1350 Avenue of the Americas
New York, NY 10019

Harcourt Brace Jovanovich Children's Book
Division
1250 Sixth Avenue
San Diego, CA 92101

Harper & Row, Inc. *See* HarperCollins.

HarperCollins Children's Books
10 E. 53rd Street
New York, NY 10022

Harry N. Abrams, Inc.
100 Fifth Avenue
New York, NY 10011

Henry Holt & Company, Inc.
115 W. 18th Street
New York, NY 10011

Holiday House, Inc.
425 Madison Avenue
New York, NY 10017

Julia MacRae Books
Random Century Children's Books
Random Century House
20 Vauxhall Bridge Road
London SW1V 2SA
Great Britain

Julian Messner, a division of Simon &
Schuster, Inc. *See* Simon & Schuster, Inc.

Kane-Miller Publishing
P.O. Box 529
Brooklyn, NY 11231

Kidstamps
P.O. Box 18699
Cleveland Heights, OH 44118

Knopf Publishers. *See* Alfred A. Knopf Books
for Young Readers.

Larousse & Company, Inc.
572 Fifth Avenue
New York, NY 10036

Lerner Publications
241 First Avenue North
Minneapolis, MN 55401

Little, Brown & Company
34 Beacon Street
Boston, MA 02108

Live Oak Media
P.O. Box 34
Ancramdale, NY 12503

Lodestar Books
375 Hudson Street
New York, NY 10014

Lothrop, Lee & Shepard Books
105 Madison Avenue
New York, NY 10016

Macmillan Children's Books
866 Third Avenue
New York, NY 10022

Margaret K. McElderry Books
866 Third Avenue
New York, NY 10022

McElderry Books. *See* Margaret K. McElderry
    Books.

Merrill Publishing Company
Division of Macmillan Publishing Company
445 Hutchinson Avenue
Columbus, OH 43216

Messner. *See* Simon & Schuster, Inc.

Morrow. *See* William Morrow & Company.

Orchard Books
387 Park Avenue South
New York, NY 10016

Penguin Books Australia
P.O. Box 257
Ringwood 3134
Australia

Penguin USA
375 Hudson Street
New York, NY 10014

Picture Book Studio
10 Central Street
Saxoonville, MA 01701

Pied Piper/Dial Books for Young Readers.
    See Penguin USA.

Puffin Books
375 Hudson Street
New York, NY 10014

Putnam & Grosset Group
200 Madison Avenue
New York, NY 10016

Random House Books for Young Readers
225 Park Avenue South
New York, NY 10003

Scholastic, Inc.
730 Broadway
New York, NY 10003

Scribner. *See* Charles Scribner's Sons.

Silver Burdett Press
190 Sylvan Avenue
Englewood Cliffs, NJ 07632

Simon & Schuster, Inc.
Simon & Schuster Building, Rockefeller
    Center
1230 Avenue of the Americas
New York, NY 10020

SRA School Group
155 N. Wacker Drive
Chicago, IL 60606

Tom Snyder Productions, Inc.
90 Sherman Street
Cambridge, MA 02140

Trumpet Books
666 Fifth Avenue
New York, NY 10103

Viking Children's Books
375 Hudson Street
New York, NY 10014

Walker & Company
720 Fifth Avenue
New York, NY 10019

Wallace Homestead Book Company
580 Waters Edge Road
Lombard, IL 60148

Warne. *See* Frederick Warne & Company

Warner Books
666 Fifth Avenue
New York, NY 10103

Watts. *See* Franklin Watts, Inc.

Weston Woods
Weston, CT 06883

William Morrow & Company, Inc.
1350 Avenue of the Americas
New York, NY 10019

Whitman. *See* Albert Whitman & Company.

PHOTOGRAPH CREDITS

Chapter 1: Photograph of Martha Alexander reprinted by permission of Dial Books for Young Readers.

Book jacket art for *Nobody Asked Me If I Wanted a Baby Sister* by Martha Alexander, © 1971 by Martha Alexander, reproduced courtesy of Dial Books for Young Readers.

Chapter 2: Photograph of Caroline Arnold by Sharron L. McElmeel.

Chapter 3: Photograph of Graeme Base by Robyn Base, reproduced by permission of Penguin Books Australia Ltd.

Chapter 4: Photograph of Byrd Baylor by Sharron L. McElmeel.

Chapter 5: Photograph of Jan Brett by Susan Cushnir, courtesy of Clarion Books; reproduced with permission. Profile photograph of Jan Brett by Sharron L. McElmeel.

Chapter 6: Photograph of Anthony Browne courtesy of Anthony Browne and reproduced with his permission.

Chapter 7: Photograph of Joanna Cole by Sharron L. McElmeel.

Chapter 8: Photograph of Eric A. Kimmel by Sharron L. McElmeel.

Chapter 9: Photograph of Janet Stevens by Sharron L. McElmeel.

Book jacket art for *How the Manx Cat Lost Its Tail* by Janet Stevens. Published by Harcourt Brace Jovanovich. Reproduced with permission of Harcourt Brace Jovanovich.

Book jacket art for *The Three Billy Goats Gruff* by Janet Stevens. Published by Harcourt Brace Jovanovich. Reproduced with permission of Harcourt Brace Jovanovich.

Chapter 10:   Capsule Units

DEMI
> Photograph of Demi by Peter Ziebel, reproduced with permission of G. P. Putnam's Sons.
>
> Book jacket for *Find Demi's Sea Creatures*, illustration by Demi reprinted by permission of Grosset & Dunlap from *Find Demi's Sea Creatures*, © 1991 by Demi.
>
> Book jacket for *Demi's Find the Animal A B C*, illustration by Demi reprinted by permission of Grosset & Dunlap from *Demi's Find the Animal A B C*, © 1985 by Demi.
>
> Book jacket for *The Hallowed Horse*, illustration by Demi reprinted by permission of G. P. Putnam's Sons from *The Hallowed Horse*, © 1987 by Demi.

KEIKO KASZA
> Photograph of Keiko Kasza courtesy of Keiko Kasza and reprinted by permission of G. P. Putnam's Sons and Keiko Kasza.
>
> Book jacket for *The Wolf's Chicken Stew*, illustration by Keiko Kasza reprinted by permission of G. P. Putnam's Sons from *The Wolf's Chicken Stew*, © 1987 by Keiko Kasza.
>
> Book jacket for *When the Elephant Walks*, illustration by Keiko Kasza reprinted by permission of G. P. Putnam's Sons from *When the Elephant Walks*, © 1990 by Keiko Kasza.
>
> Book jacket for *The Pigs' Picnic*, illustration by Keiko Kasza reprinted by permission of G. P. Putnam's Sons from *The Pigs' Picnic*, © 1988 by Keiko Kasza.
>
> Book jacket for *A Mother for Choco*, illustration by Keiko Kasza reprinted by permission of G. P. Putnam's Sons from *A Mother for Choco*, © 1992 by Keiko Kasza.

PATRICIA POLACCO
> Photograph of Patricia Polacco by Bob Guiteras © 1989, courtesy of Patricia Polacco and reproduced with her permission.
>
> Book jacket for *The Keeping Quilt* by Patricia Polacco, book published by Simon & Schuster Children's Books and reproduced with the permission of the publisher.
>
> Book jacket for *Babushka's Doll* by Patricia Polacco, book published by Simon & Schuster Children's Books and reproduced with the permission of the publisher.
>
> Book jacket for *Some Birthday!* by Patricia Polacco, book published by Simon & Schuster Children's Books and reproduced with the permission of the publisher.

Bookpeople/An Author a Month
Cumulative Index

Previous *Author a Month* and *Bookpeople* publications have featured more than 125 authors and illustrators. This book, *An Author a Month (for Dimes)*, showcases an additional twelve authors/illustrators. The cumulative index that follows will direct the user to the publication that includes the unit for each of the authors and illustrators covered in the six publications. The following list provides the code for each publication.

A — *An Author a Month (for Pennies)* (Libraries Unlimited, 1988)

N — *An Author a Month (for Nickels)* (Libraries Unlimited, 1990)

D — *An Author a Month (for Dimes)* (Libraries Unlimited, 1992)

F — *Bookpeople: A First Album* (Libraries Unlimited, 1990)

S — *Bookpeople: A Second Album* (Libraries Unlimited, 1990)

MC — *Bookpeople: A Multicultural Album* (Libraries Unlimited, 1992)

Index

About the Author

In addition to authoring seven reference books for educators, Sharron McElmeel has maintained her role as professional educator, parent, grandparent, book reviewer, and educational consultant. She frequently speaks with educators and parents sharing strategies and tested ideas in the areas of integration, whole language, and, in particular, the infusion of literature-based activities across the curriculum. She earned a B.A. in Education from the University of Northern Iowa; an M.A. in Library Science from the University of Iowa; and has completed post-graduate work in the area of school administration, reading, and library science. Her experience includes classroom and library media center assignments; both elementary and secondary. She currently is a library media specialist in a K-5 school in the Cedar Rapids (Iowa) Community School District.

She is a contributing editor and columnist for *Iowa Reading Journal* and reviews books and nonprint materials for two professional reviewing journals. Her columns on authors and books are regular features in *Mystery Scene Magazine* and the *Iowa Reading Newspaper*. She lectures and conducts inservice sessions and teaches college courses on children's and young adult literature and in reading. In 1987 she was named Iowa Reading Teacher of the Year.

Her previous books include *An Author a Month (for Pennies)*; *An Author a Month (for Nickels)*; *Bookpeople: A First Album*; *Bookpeople: A Second Album*; *My Bag of Book Tricks*; *Bookpeople: A Multicultural Album*; and *Adventures with Social Studies (Through Literature)*. Forthcoming titles include *McElmeel Booknotes: Literature Across the Curriculum* and *The Poet Tree*.

She lives with her husband in a rural area north of Cedar Rapids, Iowa, where, at various times, they have shared their home with six children, grandchildren, a dog, two cats (actually the animals share the garage), and several hundred books.